Succeeding with the Masters® & The Festival Collection®

Y0-BBY-523

Teacher's Handbook

by Helen Marlais with Sue Althouse

About the Teacher's Handbook

The Teacher's Handbook for Succeeding with the Masters® & The Festival Collection® is a guide that organizes the teaching sequence of repertoire by interweaving these two outstanding series together. By combining these two series together (over 450 pieces), teachers and students are provided with a comprehensive, thorough, and pedagogical approach to teaching and learning the repertoire.

This handbook presents the information in a clear and uniform format, using the Practice Strategies from *Succeeding with the Masters®* and applying them to the pieces in *The Festival Collection®*. Teachers can use either *The Festival Collection®* or *Succeeding with the Masters®* as their core curriculum. Since both of these series contain full-performance CD's, historical information, and composer biographies, teachers utilizing this handbook will gain guidance and insight on how to teach this comprehensive literature-based curriculum.

THE FJH MUSIC COMPANY INC.
Frank J. Hackinson

Production: Frank J. Hackinson
Production Coordinators: Nancy Bona-Baker and Joyce Loke
Cover Art Concept: Helen Marlais
Cover Design: Terpstra Design, San Francisco, CA
Text Design and Layout: Andi Whitmer
Printer: Tempo Music Press, Inc.

ISBN-13: 978-1-56939-825-8

The Teacher's Handbook
Succeeding with the Masters® & *The Festival Collection*®

This handbook provides information on how to use *Succeeding with the Masters*® & *The Festival Collection*® together for a thorough and pedagogical approach to learning repertoire.

FJH2050

Part III:

PART I

On Your Way to Succeeding with the Masters®
Correlated with *The Festival Collection*®, *Book 1*

FEATURES OF THIS CORRELATION:

1. *On Your Way to Succeeding with the Masters*® is considered the core curriculum and *The Festival Collection*® is used for supplementary repertoire.

2. The teaching sequence begins with *On Your Way to Succeeding with the Masters*®. *The Festival Collection*®, *Book 1* is introduced in Unit 2. Clear instructions are given so teachers can easily cover both books in the curriculum in an interesting and logical manner.

3. Suggestions are given for introducing students to each era in *On Your Way to Succeeding with the Masters*®.

4. The pieces in both *On Your Way to Succeeding with the Masters*® and *The Festival Collection*®, *Book 1* are carefully correlated according to level of difficulty.

5. The musical eras are evenly distributed throughout each unit, providing constant exposure and review of style characteristics.

6. Practice Strategies are presented in Unit 1, and then suggested for every piece in Units 2 through 5 for a well-rounded curriculum that includes regular review and reinforcement.

7. Much freedom is given for the teachers and students to choose appropriate repertoire once the basic concepts of each era have been presented. The listening CD's provide a valuable resource to aid in the selection process.

FEATURES OF UNITS 2-5:

1. The following abbreviations are used: FC = *The Festival Collection*®; SWTM = *On Your Way to Succeeding with the Masters*®; and Cent. = Centuries.

2. The unit is first organized by musical era, with the pieces in each era listed in order of difficulty.

3. The unit is also organized by Practice Strategy, listed in the order presented in *On Your Way to Succeeding with the Masters*®. The pieces are listed chronologically by musical era.

4. Teachers are encouraged to teach each unit by choosing repertoire with students that includes a balance of style eras and Practice Strategies. Students might not study every piece in the unit.

5. The Practice Strategy assigned to each piece is a suggestion only. Teachers should feel free to change or adapt any Practice Strategy to the needs of the individual student.

6. The Practice Strategy "Getting Ready for a Performance" may be used with any piece at any time students are preparing for an upcoming performance.

SUCCEEDING WITH THE MASTERS® & THE FESTIVAL COLLECTION®
Etudes with Technique

ABOUT THE SERIES

This series is designed to develop healthy, natural, and effective technique so that students can play beautifully as well as with virtuosity. Each book is divided into units and each unit focuses on one technical concept. Technical concepts are introduced using imagery to help the student understand the gesture needed to produce the correct technique. Different imagery is used in each level of this series. Following the text and the imagery, two short technical exercises provide the student's first opportunity to play the technique. These exercises should be memorized so that students can focus on the sound they produce while observing their playing mechanism in action. Several etudes then follow to reinforce each technical concept. In this way, students focus on one technique at a time, and the concept is reinforced through multiple etudes. This method allows the student to master the technique and make it a habit, providing the foundation for effective, natural, relaxed, and enjoyable performances of their repertoire.

The student should concentrate on looking at and being aware of the feeling in their fingers and fingertips, hands, wrists, forearms, elbows, and upper arms in order to produce the correct gestures and sounds. In order to achieve a fluid and solid technique, students must always listen carefully to themselves and the sound that they create.

FJH2050

On Your Way to Succeeding with the Masters®

Pieces in each era arranged in order of difficulty

The Festival Collection®, Book 1

Pieces in each era arranged in order of difficulty

On Your Way to Succeeding with the Masters®

Introducing each historical era and the Practice Strategies:

- Use the information on the activity pages and the pictures on the front cover to discuss the historical era and what the music was like during that era.

- Discuss and demonstrate each Practice Strategy, using the CD. Apply the strategy to the piece from that era.

Begin with these pieces:

Era and Activity Pages	First Piece	Practice Strategy
Medieval p. 4-5	Trouvère p. 6 / CD 1	Learn and Practice p. 5 / CD 38
Renaissance p. 8-9	Hercules' Dance p. 12 / CD 5	Chain Linking p. 9 / CD 39
Baroque p. 14-15	The Statues Are Dancing p. 16 / CD 7	Getting Ready for a Performance p. 15** / CD 40
Classical p. 22-23	Allegro p. 28 / CD 21	Balancing the Melody with the Accompaniment, p. 23 / CD 41
Romantic p. 32-33	In the Garden p. 35 / CD 26	Careful Listening p. 33 / CD 42
20th/21st Centuries p. 40-41	Polka p. 44 / CD 34	3x1 Rule p. 41 / CD 43

** *After "Getting Ready for a Performance" is introduced, it may be used with any piece at any time when the student is preparing for a performance. Therefore, this handbook will include reminders to use this Practice Strategy, but will not include it in the charts for each unit.*

FJH2050

On Your Way to Succeeding with the Masters®

Correlated with *The Festival Collection®, Book I*

Teachers are encouraged to teach each unit by choosing repertoire with the student that includes a balance of styles, eras, and Practice Strategies. The student may not study every piece in the unit. The section "About the Pieces and the Composers" beginning on p. 33 of The Festival Collection®, Book I provides further valuable information.

Reminders:

- The Practice Strategy assigned to each piece is a suggestion only. These strategies can be used interchangeably with practically all of the repertoire pieces. The teacher should feel free to change or adapt any Practice Strategy to the needs of the individual student.

- The Practice Strategy "Getting Ready for a Performance" may be used with any piece at any time the student is preparing for an upcoming performance.

Unit 2 Organized by Era: (pieces in each era arranged in order of difficulty)

Book	Era	Title, Page, and CD Track	Practice Strategy from SWTM
FC	Baroque	Old German Dance, p. 6 / CD 1	Learn and Practice, p. 5 / CD 38
FC	Baroque	Canary, p. 8 / CD 3	Chain-linking, p. 9 / CD 39
SWTM	Classical	The Cobblestone Road, p. 31 / CD 24	Learn and Practice, p. 5 / CD 38
FC	Classical	Allegro, p. 17 / CD 14	Balancing the Melody with the Accompaniment, p. 23/CD 41
SWTM	Classical	Sunset at the Boardwalk, p. 29 / CD 22	Careful Listening, p. 33 / CD 42
SWTM	Classical	Monday March, p. 30 / CD 23	3x1 Rule, p. 41 / CD 43
SWTM	Romantic	The Mighty Hawk, p. 39 / CD 30	3x1 Rule, p. 41 / CD 43
FC	Romantic	The Young Dancer, p. 20 / CD 17	Learn and Practice, p. 5 / CD 38
FC	Romantic	A Song, p. 19 / CD 16	Careful Listening, p. 33 / CD 42
SWTM	Romantic	Soldier's Song, p. 34 / CD 25	Chain-linking, p. 9 / CD 39
FC	20th/21st Cent.	Trumpets, p. 26 / CD 21	Balancing the Melody with the Accompaniment, p. 23/CD 41
SWTM	20th/21st Cent.	Study, p. 43 / CD 32	Careful Listening, p. 33 / CD 42
FC	20th/21st Cent.	Hungarian Song, p. 29 / CD 24	Chain-linking, p. 9 / CD 39
SWTM	20th/21st Cent.	Gradus No. 8, p. 44 / CD 33	Balancing the Melody with the Accompaniment, p. 23/CD 41

Unit 2 Organized by Practice Strategy: (pieces in each box arranged in chronological order)

Practice Strategy	Book	Era	Title and Page
Learn and Practice	FC	Baroque	Old German Dance, p. 6
Learn and Practice	SWTM	Classical	The Cobblestone Road, p. 31
Learn and Practice	FC	Romantic	The Young Dancer, p. 20
Chain-linking	FC	Baroque	Canary, p. 8
Chain-linking	SWTM	Romantic	Soldier's Song, p. 34
Chain-linking	FC	20th/21st Cent.	Hungarian Song, p. 29
Balancing the Melody with the Accompaniment	FC	Classical	Allegro, p. 17
Balancing the Melody with the Accompaniment	FC	20th/21st Cent.	Trumpets, p. 26
Balancing the Melody with the Accompaniment	SWTM	20th/21st Cent.	Gradus No. 8, p. 44
Careful Listening	SWTM	Classical	Sunset at the Boardwalk, p. 29
Careful Listening	FC	Romantic	A Song, p. 19
Careful Listening	SWTM	20th/21st Cent.	Study, p. 43
3x1 Rule	SWTM	Classical	Monday March, p. 30
3x1 Rule	SWTM	Romantic	The Mighty Hawk, p. 39

An Example of a Teaching Sequence for Unit 2 *(not all the pieces in Unit 2 are used)*

Starting the Unit

Book	Era	Title, Page, and CD Track	Practice Strategy from SWTM
FC	Baroque	Old German Dance, p. 6 / CD 1	Learn and Practice, p. 5 / CD 38
FC	Classical	Allegro, p. 17 / CD 14	Balancing the Melody with the Accompaniment, p. 23/CD 41
FC	20th/21st Cent.	Trumpets, p. 26 / CD 21	Balancing the Melody with the Accompaniment, p. 23/CD 41

Advancing Through the Unit

Book	Era	Title, Page, and CD Track	Practice Strategy from SWTM
SWTM	Classical	Sunset at the Boardwalk, p. 29/CD 22	Careful Listening, p. 33 / CD 42
SWTM	Romantic	The Mighty Hawk, p. 39 / CD 30	3x1 Rule, p. 41 / CD 43
SWTM	20th/21st Cent.	Study, p. 43 / CD 32	Careful Listening, p. 33 / CD 42

Wrapping Up the Unit

Book	Era	Title, Page, and CD Track	Practice Strategy from SWTM
FC	Baroque	Canary, p. 8 / CD 3	Chain-linking, p. 9 / CD 39
SWTM	Classical	Monday March, p. 30 / CD 23	3x1 Rule, p. 41 / CD 43
SWTM	Romantic	Soldier's Song, p. 34 / CD 25	Chain-linking, p. 9 / CD 39
SWTM	20th/21st Cent.	Gradus No. 8, p. 44 / CD 33	Balancing the Melody with the Accompaniment, p. 23/CD 41

Fill In Your Own Teaching Sequence for Unit 2

Starting the Unit

Book	Era	Title and Page	Practice Strategy

Advancing Through the Unit

Book	Era	Title and Page	Practice Strategy

Wrapping Up the Unit

Book	Era	Title and Page	Practice Strategy

FJH2050

On Your Way to Succeeding with the Masters®

Correlated with *The Festival Collection*®*, Book I*

Teachers are encouraged to teach each unit by choosing repertoire with the student that includes a balance of styles, eras, and Practice Strategies. The student may not study every piece in the unit. The section "About the Pieces and the Composers" beginning on p. 33 of The Festival Collection®, Book I provides further valuable information.

Reminders:

- *The Practice Strategy assigned to each piece is a suggestion only. These strategies can be used interchangeably with practically all of the repertoire pieces. The teacher should feel free to change or adapt any Practice Strategy to the needs of the individual student.*

- *The Practice Strategy "Getting Ready for a Performance" may be used with any piece at any time the student is preparing for an upcoming performance.*

Unit 3 Organized by Era: *(pieces in each era arranged in order of difficulty)*

Book	Era	Title, Page, and CD Track	Practice Strategy from SWTM
SWTM	Renaissance	Pavanne, p. 10 / CD 3	3x1 Rule, p. 41 / CD 43
SWTM	Renaissance	Skipping Dance, p. 13 / CD 6	Learn and Practice, p. 5 / CD 38
SWTM	Baroque	Two Baroque Musicians, p. 17/CD 8	Chain-linking, p. 9 / CD 39
FC	Baroque	Intrada, p. 10 / CD 5	Learn and Practice, p. 5 / CD 38
FC	Baroque	Allemande, p. 7 / CD 2	Chain-linking, p. 9 / CD 39
FC	Classical	Minuet, p. 13 / CD 9	Balancing the Melody with the Accompaniment, p. 23/CD 41
SWTM	Classical	Allegretto, p. 27 / CD 19	Balancing the Melody with the Accompaniment, p. 23/CD 41
SWTM	Classical	Children's Song, p. 27 / CD 20	Balancing the Melody with the Accompaniment, p. 23/CD 41
FC	Classical	Minuet, p. 12 / CD 7	3x1 Rule, p. 41 / CD 43
FC	Classical	A Carefree Fellow, p. 12 / CD 8	Chain-linking, p. 9 / CD 39
SWTM	Romantic	Happily Exercising, p. 38 / CD 29	Learn and Practice, p. 5 / CD 38
FC	Romantic	Kitten Play, p. 21 / CD 18	Careful Listening, p. 33 / CD 42
FC	20th/21st Cent.	The Shepherd Plays, p. 32 / CD 27	3x1 Rule, p. 41 / CD 43
FC	20th/21st Cent.	Arabian Dance, p. 30 / CD 25	Careful Listening, p. 33 / CD 42
SWTM	20th/21st Cent.	The Sparrow's Song, p. 42 / CD 31	Careful Listening, p. 33 / CD 42
SWTM	20th/21st Cent.	Tiresome Prank, p. 45 / CD 35	3x1 Rule, p. 41 / CD 43

Unit 3 Organized by Practice Strategy: *(pieces in each box arranged in chronological order)*

Practice Strategy	Book	Era	Title and Page
Learn and Practice	SWTM	Renaissance	Skipping Dance, p. 13
Learn and Practice	FC	Baroque	Intrada, p. 10
Learn and Practice	SWTM	Romantic	Happily Exercising, p. 38
Chain-linking	SWTM	Baroque	Two Baroque Musicians, p. 17
Chain-linking	FC	Baroque	Allemande, p. 7
Chain-linking	FC	Classical	A Carefree Fellow, p. 12
Balancing the Melody with the Accompaniment	SWTM	Classical	Allegretto, p. 27
Balancing the Melody with the Accompaniment	SWTM	Classical	Children's Song, p. 27
Balancing the Melody with the Accompaniment	FC	Classical	Minuet, p. 13
Careful Listening	FC	Romantic	Kitten Play, p. 21
Careful Listening	SWTM	20th/21st Cent.	The Sparrow's Song, p. 42
Careful Listening	FC	20th/21st Cent.	Arabian Dance, p. 30
3x1 Rule	SWTM	Renaissance	Pavanne, p. 10
3x1 Rule	FC	Classical	Minuet, p. 12
3x1 Rule	SWTM	20th/21st Cent.	Tiresome Prank, p. 45
3x1 Rule	FC	20th/21st Cent.	The Shepherd Plays, p. 32

An Example of a Teaching Sequence for Unit 3 *(not all the pieces in Unit 3 are used)*

Starting the Unit

Book	Era	Title, Page, and CD Track	Practice Strategy from SWTM
SWTM	Renaissance	Pavanne, p. 10 / CD 3	3x1 Rule, p. 41 / CD 43
FC	Classical	Minuet, p. 13 / CD 9	Balancing the Melody with the Accompaniment, p. 23/CD 41
FC	20th/21st Cent.	Arabian Dance, p. 30 / CD 25	Careful Listening, p. 33 / CD 42

Advancing Through the Unit

Book	Era	Title, Page, and CD Track	Practice Strategy from SWTM
FC	Baroque	Intrada, p. 10 / CD 5	Learn and Practice, p. 5 / CD 38
SWTM	Classical	Allegretto, p. 27 / CD 19	Balancing the Melody with the Accompaniment, p. 23/CD 41
SWTM	Romantic	Happily Exercising, p. 38 / CD 29	Learn and Practice, p. 5 / CD 38

Wrapping Up the Unit

Book	Era	Title, Page, and CD Track	Practice Strategy from SWTM
FC	Baroque	Allemande, p. 7 / CD 2	Chain-linking, p. 9 / CD 39
FC	Classical	A Carefree Fellow, p. 12 / CD 8	Chain-linking, p. 9 / CD 39
SWTM	20th/21st Cent.	Tiresome Prank, p. 45 / CD 35	3x1 Rule, p. 41 / CD 43

Fill In Your Own Teaching Sequence for Unit 3

Starting the Unit

Book	Era	Title and Page	Practice Strategy

Advancing Through the Unit

Book	Era	Title and Page	Practice Strategy

Wrapping Up the Unit

Book	Era	Title and Page	Practice Strategy

FJH2050

On Your Way to Succeeding with the Masters®

Correlated with *The Festival Collection*®, *Book 1*

Teachers are encouraged to teach each unit by choosing repertoire with the student that includes a balance of styles, eras, and Practice Strategies. The student may not study every piece in the unit. The section "About the Pieces and the Composers" beginning on p. 33 of The Festival Collection®, Book 1 provides further valuable information.

Reminders:

- The Practice Strategy assigned to each piece is a suggestion only. These strategies can be used interchangeably with practically all of the repertoire pieces. The teacher should feel free to change or adapt any Practice Strategy to the needs of the individual student.

- The Practice Strategy "Getting Ready for a Performance" may be used with any piece at any time the student is preparing for an upcoming performance.

Unit 4 Organized by Era: (pieces in each era arranged in order of difficulty)

Book	Era	Title, Page, and CD Track	Practice Strategy from SWTM
SWTM	Medieval	Ballade, p. 7 / CD 2	Careful Listening, p. 33 / CD 42
FC	Baroque	Petit Minuet, p. 9 / CD 4	Learn and Practice, p. 5 / CD 38
SWTM	Baroque	Bourrée, p. 19 / CD 10	Chain-linking, p. 9 / CD 39
SWTM	Baroque	Noël, p. 21 / CD 12	Chain-linking, p. 9 / CD 39
SWTM	Classical	Prelude, p. 26 / CD 18	3x1 Rule, p. 41 / CD 43
FC	Classical	Song, p. 16 / CD 13	Careful Listening, p. 33 / CD 42
SWTM	Classical	A Little Waltz, p. 26 / CD 17	3x1 Rule, p. 41 / CD 43
SWTM	Classical	Softly, Like the Wind, p. 25 / CD 16	Balancing the Melody with the Accompaniment, p. 23/CD 41
FC	Classical	Agitato, p. 18 / CD 15	Learn and Practice, p. 5 / CD 38
SWTM	Romantic	Water Sprite, p. 37 / CD 28	Careful Listening, p. 33 / CD 42
FC	Romantic	Spring Waltz, p. 24-25 / CD 20	Balancing the Melody with the Accompaniment, p. 23/CD 41
SWTM	20th/21st Cent.	The Old Gypsy Violin, p. 47 / CD 37	Balancing the Melody with the Accompaniment, p. 23/CD 41
FC	20th/21st Cent.	Snowflakes Gently Falling, p. 27 /CD 22	Learn and Practice, p. 5 / CD 38
SWTM	20th/21st Cent.	Playing, p. 46 / CD 36	Chain-linking, p. 9 / CD 39

Unit 4 Organized by Practice Strategy: (pieces in each box arranged in chronological order)

Practice Strategy	Book	Era	Title and Page
Learn and Practice	FC	Baroque	Petit Minuet, p. 9
Learn and Practice	FC	Classical	Agitato, p. 18
Learn and Practice	FC	20th/21st Cent.	Snowflakes Gently Falling, p. 27
Chain-linking	SWTM	Baroque	Bourrée, p. 19
Chain-linking	SWTM	Baroque	Noël, p. 21
Chain-linking	SWTM	20th/21st Cent.	Playing, p. 46
Balancing the Melody with the Accompaniment	SWTM	Classical	Softly, Like the Wind, Op. 25
Balancing the Melody with the Accompaniment	FC	Romantic	Spring Waltz, p. 24-25
Balancing the Melody with the Accompaniment	SWTM	20th/21st Cent.	The Old Gypsy Violin, p. 47
Careful Listening	SWTM	Medieval	Ballade, p. 7
Careful Listening	FC	Classical	Song, p. 16
Careful Listening	SWTM	Romantic	Water Sprite, p. 37
3x1 Rule	SWTM	Classical	Prelude, p. 26
3x1 Rule	SWTM	Classical	A Little Waltz, p. 26

An Example of a Teaching Sequence for Unit 4 *(not all the pieces in Unit 4 are used)*

Starting the Unit

Book	Era	Title, Page, and CD Track	Practice Strategy from SWTM
SWTM	Medieval	Ballade, p. 7 / CD 2	Careful Listening, p. 33 / CD 42
FC	Baroque	Petit Minuet, p. 9 / CD 4	Learn and Practice, p. 5 / CD 38
SWTM	Classical	Prelude, p. 26 / CD 18	3x1 Rule, p. 41 / CD 43
SWTM	Romantic	Water Sprite, p. 37 / CD 28	Careful Listening, p. 33 / CD 42

Advancing Through the Unit

Book	Era	Title, Page, and CD Track	Practice Strategy from SWTM
SWTM	Baroque	Bourrée, p. 19 / CD 10	Chain-linking, p. 9 / CD 39
SWTM	Classical	A Little Waltz, p. 26 / CD 17	3x1 Rule, p. 41 / CD 43
SWTM	20th/21st Cent.	The Old Gypsy Violin, p. 47 / CD 37	Balancing the Melody with the Accompaniment, p. 23/CD 41

Wrapping Up the Unit

Book	Era	Title, Page, and CD Track	Practice Strategy from SWTM
SWTM	Baroque	Noël, p. 21 / CD 12	Chain-linking, p. 9 / CD 39
FC	Classical	Agitato, p. 18 / CD 15	Learn and Practice, p. 5 / CD 38
FC	Romantic	Spring Waltz, p. 24-25 / CD 20	Balancing the Melody with the Accompaniment, p. 23/CD 41

Fill In Your Own Teaching Sequence for Unit 4

Starting the Unit

Book	Era	Title and Page	Practice Strategy

Advancing Through the Unit

Book	Era	Title and Page	Practice Strategy

Wrapping Up the Unit

Book	Era	Title and Page	Practice Strategy

FJH2050

On Your Way to Succeeding with the Masters®

Correlated with *The Festival Collection®, Book I*

Teachers are encouraged to teach each unit by choosing repertoire with the student that includes a balance of styles, eras, and Practice Strategies. The student may not study every piece in the unit. The section "About the Pieces and the Composers" beginning on p. 33 of The Festival Collection®, Book I provides further valuable information.

Reminders:

- The Practice Strategy assigned to each piece is a suggestion only. These strategies can be used interchangeably with practically all of the repertoire pieces. The teacher should feel free to change or adapt any Practice Strategy to the needs of the individual student.

- The Practice Strategy "Getting Ready for a Performance" may be used with any piece at any time the student is preparing for an upcoming performance.

Unit 5 Organized by Era: *(pieces in each era arranged in order of difficulty)*

Book	Era	Title, Page, and CD Track	Practice Strategy from SWTM
SWTM	Renaissance	A Study in 5/4 Time, p. 11 / CD 4	Learn and Practice, p. 5 / CD 38
SWTM	Baroque	Minuet, p. 18 / CD 9	Learn and Practice, p. 5 / CD 38
SWTM	Baroque	Minuet, p. 20 / CD 11	Careful Listening, p. 33 / CD 42
FC	Baroque	Petit Rondo, p. 11 / CD 6	Chain-linking, p. 9 / CD 39
SWTM	Classical	The Scale Ladder, p. 25 / CD 15	Learn and Practice, p. 5 / CD 38
SWTM	Classical	Scherzo p. 24 / CD 13	3x1 Rule, p. 41 / CD 43
SWTM	Classical	The Bohemian, p. 24 / CD 14	Chain-linking, p. 9 / CD 39
FC	Classical	Sonatina (1st Mvt.), p. 14 / CD 10	Balancing the Melody with the Accompaniment, p. 23/CD 41
FC	Classical	Sonatina (2nd Mvt.), p. 14 / CD 11	Careful Listening, p. 33 / CD 42
FC	Classical	Sonatina (3rd Mvt.), p. 15 / CD 12	3x1 Rule, p. 41 / CD 43
SWTM	Romantic	Going to School, p. 36 / CD 27	Careful Listening, p. 33 / CD 42
FC	Romantic	Valsette, p. 22-23 / CD 19	Balancing the Melody with the Accompaniment, p. 23/CD 41
FC	20th/21st Cent.	The Sparrows, p. 28 / CD 23	3x1 Rule, p. 41 / CD 43
FC	20th/21st Cent.	Air for Southpaw, p. 31 / CD 26	Balancing the Melody with the Accompaniment, p. 23/CD 41

Unit 5 Organized by Practice Strategy: *(pieces in each box arranged in chronological order)*

Practice Strategy	Book	Era	Title and Page
Learn and Practice	SWTM	Renaissance	A Study in 5/4 Time, p. 11
Learn and Practice	SWTM	Baroque	Minuet, p. 18
Learn and Practice	SWTM	Classical	The Scale Ladder, p. 25
Chain-linking	FC	Baroque	Petit Rondo, p. 11
Chain-linking	SWTM	Classical	The Bohemian, p. 24
Balancing the Melody with the Accompaniment	FC	Classical	Sonatina (1st Mvt.), p. 14
Balancing the Melody with the Accompaniment	FC	Romantic	Valsette, p. 22-23
Balancing the Melody with the Accompaniment	FC	20th/21st Cent.	Air for Southpaw, p. 31
Careful Listening	SWTM	Baroque	Minuet, p. 20
Careful Listening	FC	Classical	Sonatina (2nd Mvt.), p. 14
Careful Listening	SWTM	Romantic	Going to School, p. 36
3x1 Rule	SWTM	Classical	Scherzo, p. 24
3x1 Rule	FC	Classical	Sonatina (3rd Mvt.), p. 15
3x1 Rule	FC	20th/21st Cent.	The Sparrows, p. 28

An Example of a Teaching Sequence for Unit 5 (not all the pieces in Unit 5 are used)

Starting the Unit

Book	Era	Title, Page, and CD Track	Practice Strategy from SWTM
SWTM	Baroque	Minuet, p. 18 / CD 9	Learn and Practice, p. 5 / CD 38
SWTM	Classical	The Scale Ladder, p. 25 / CD 15	Learn and Practice, p. 5 / CD 38
SWTM	Romantic	Going to School, p. 36 / CD 27	Careful Listening, p. 33 / CD 42

Advancing Through the Unit

Book	Era	Title, Page, and CD Track	Practice Strategy from SWTM
SWTM	Baroque	Minuet, p. 20 / CD 11	Careful Listening, p. 33 / CD 42
FC	Classical	Sonatina (1st Mvt.), p. 14 / CD 10	Balancing the Melody with the Accompaniment, p. 23/CD 41
FC	Classical	Sonatina (2nd Mvt.), p. 14 / CD 11	Careful Listening, p. 33 / CD 42
FC	20th/21st Cent.	The Sparrows, p. 28 / CD 23	3x1 Rule, p. 41 / CD 43

Wrapping Up the Unit

Book	Era	Title, Page, and CD Track	Practice Strategy from SWTM
SWTM	Renaissance	A Study in 5/4 Time, p. 11 / CD 4	Learn and Practice, p. 5 / CD 38
FC	Baroque	Petit Rondo, p. 11 / CD 6	Chain-linking, p. 9 / CD 39
FC	Classical	Sonatina (3rd Mvt.), p. 15 / CD 12	3x1 Rule, p. 41 / CD 43
FC	20th/21st Cent.	Air for Southpaw, p. 31 / CD 26	Balancing the Melody with the Accompaniment, p. 23/CD 41

Fill In Your Own Teaching Sequence for Unit 5

Starting the Unit

Book	Era	Title and Page	Practice Strategy

Advancing Through the Unit

Book	Era	Title and Page	Practice Strategy

Wrapping Up the Unit

Book	Era	Title and Page	Practice Strategy

You are now ready to begin: **Succeeding with the Masters®, Classical Era, Volume One and The Festival Collection®, Book 2**

Using Succeeding with the Masters®, Volume One
Baroque Era, Classical Era, Romantic Era

Correlated with *The Festival Collection®*, Books 2, 3, and easier selections from Book 4

FEATURES OF THIS CORRELATION:

1. The *Succeeding with the Masters®* series is considered the core curriculum and *The Festival Collection®* is used for supplementary repertoire.

2. This approach is ideal for teachers who believe in the importance of students understanding each of the eras. Students learn about the eras in a social as well as a historical perspective, they learn correct style and interpretation, and they learn the unique musical characteristics of each era. They also learn how to establish excellent practice habits as an important part of their education.

3. The teaching sequence begins with *Succeeding with the Masters®*, *Baroque Era, Volume One* and *The Festival Collection®, Book 2*. Clear instructions are given so teachers can easily cover all books in the curriculum in an interesting and logical manner.

4. Suggestions are given for introducing students to each era and composer in *Succeeding with the Masters®*.

5. The pieces in both *Succeeding with the Masters®* and *The Festival Collection®* are carefully correlated according to level of difficulty.

6. One musical era is studied in detail for each unit. The primary focus era comes from *Succeeding with the Masters®*. Students use pieces in *The Festival Collection®* in order to experience eras that are stylistically different, thus creating a well-rounded curriculum throughout the year. Students study three of the four musical eras at once. The overlapping circles on the front cover of *The Festival Collection®* show how artistic concepts from the different eras overlapped (see the inside front cover of *The Festival Collection®* for more information).

7. The Practice Strategies are presented in *Succeeding with the Masters®* and then applied to pieces in *The Festival Collection®* for regular review and reinforcement.

   The Practice Strategies fall into 3 categories:
   a. Practice Strategies that are specific to a certain feature of a piece.
   b. Practice Strategies that help the student initially learn the piece.
   c. Practice Strategies that help the student put "finishing touches" on a learned piece (while the student is working on interpretation and preparing for a performance).

8. Much freedom is given for teachers and students to choose appropriate repertoire once the initial pieces are learned in each unit. The listening CD's provide a valuable resource to aid in the selection process.

9. The following abbreviations are used: FC = *The Festival Collection®*; SWTM = *Succeeding with the Masters®*; and Cent. = Centuries.

TEACHING SEQUENCE

Succeeding with the Masters®, Volume One*
Classical Era, Baroque Era, Romantic Era

Correlated with **The Festival Collection®, Books 2, 3, and easier selections** *from Book 4*

UNIT 1	Succeeding with the Masters®, Classical Era, Volume One	The Festival Collection®, Book 2 (Choose from) Baroque, Romantic
UNIT 2	Succeeding with the Masters®, Baroque Era, Volume One	The Festival Collection®, Book 2 (Choose from) Classical, 20th/21st Centuries
UNIT 3	Succeeding with the Masters®, Classical Era, Volume One	The Festival Collection®, Book 2 (Choose from) Baroque, Romantic
UNIT 4	Succeeding with the Masters®, Baroque Era, Volume One	The Festival Collection®, Book 2 (Choose from) Classical, 20th/21st Centuries

UNIT 5	Succeeding with the Masters®, Romantic Era, Volume One	The Festival Collection®, Book 3 (Choose from) Classical, 20th/21st Centuries
UNIT 6	Succeeding with the Masters®, Classical Era, Volume One	The Festival Collection®, Book 3 (Choose from) Baroque, Romantic
UNIT 7	Succeeding with the Masters®, Baroque Era, Volume One	The Festival Collection®, Book 3 (Choose from) Classical, Romantic
UNIT 8	Succeeding with the Masters®, Romantic Era, Volume One	The Festival Collection®, Book 3 (Choose from) Baroque, 20th/21st Centuries

UNIT 9	Succeeding with the Masters®, Baroque Era, Volume One	The Festival Collection®, Book 4 (Choose from) Classical, Romantic
UNIT 10	Succeeding with the Masters®, Romantic Era, Volume One	The Festival Collection®, Book 4 (Choose from) Baroque, 20th/21st Centuries

* *Students can use the Succeeding with the Masters® Student Activity Books, Baroque and Classical Eras, Volume One.*
  (See p. 34 for more information.)

FJH2050

Succeeding with the Masters®, Classical Era, Volume One

*Correlated with **The Festival Collection**®, Book 2*

Introducing the Classical Era:

- *Discuss what the music was like during this era, using the information on p. 2-3 and the pictures on p. 19, 29, 31, and 37.*

- *Introduce the 3 master composers using the biographical information on p. 7, 32, and 60.*

- *Listen to pieces by each composer on the CD.*

Begin with these pieces:

Composer	Characteristic	Practice Strategy from SWTM
→Haydn 02/02/11		
German Dance No. 8 in G, p. 9 / CD 1	Binary form, p. 8 Short, repetitive melodic motives, p. 8	Practicing two-note slurs p. 8 / CD 27
→German Dance No. 1 in G, p. 11 / CD 2 3/11	_____	Homophonic texture, p. 10 / CD 28 Marking phrases by breathing, p. 10 / CD 28
→Mozart 03.16.11		
Minuet in F, p. 36 / CD 10	Tuneful classical melodies, p. 34 Contrasting mood within the same piece, p. 35	Straightforward, simple harmonies p. 34 / CD 36
→Minuet in C, K. 6, p. 39 / CD 11	Short and repetitive melodic motives, p. 38 Frequent use of two-note slurs, p. 38	"Chain-linking" practice, p. 38 / CD 37 Shaping phrases, p. 38 / CD 37
Beethoven		
German Dance in C major, p. 63 / CD 19	_____	Playing double-thirds, two-note slurs, p. 62 / CD 45 "Impulse" practicing, p. 62 / CD 45
Ecossaise in G major, p. 65 / CD 20	Four-measure phrases, p. 64 Straightforward, simple harmonies, p. 64 Homophonic texture, p. 64 Varied and repetitive rhythmic motives, p. 64	Shaping phrases, p. 64 / CD 46

*Supplement from these pieces in **The Festival Collection**®, Book 2. Refer to the "About the Pieces and Composers" sections for interesting and insightful information on each piece.*

Page	Era	Title	Suggested Teaching Order
6	Baroque	King William's March	→Etude, p. 33 / CD 22 02/02/11
9	Baroque	Gavotte	→Gavotte, p. 9 / CD 4
12	Baroque	Menuet en Rondeau	→The Hunt, p. 32 / CD 21
31	Romantic	Petite Prelude	→Hunting Horns, p. 37 CD 26
32	Romantic	The Hunt	→King William's March, p. 6 / CD 1
33	Romantic	Etude	Petite Prelude, p. 31 / CD 20
35	Romantic	Song Without Words	Menuet en Rondeau, p. 12 / CD 6
37	Romantic	Hunting Horns	Song Without Words, p. 35 / CD 24

Next: **Succeeding with the Masters®, Baroque Era, Volume One**

Succeeding with the Masters®, Baroque Era, Volume One

Correlated with **The Festival Collection®, Book 2**

Introducing the Baroque Era:

- *Discuss what the music was like during this era, using the information on p. 2-3 and the pictures on p. 46, 49, 55, 58, and 67.*

- *Discuss the keyboard instruments using p. 20 and briefly discuss Baroque Performance Practice using p. 7-9.*

- *Introduce the 3 master composers using the biographical information on p. 10, 40, and 64.*

- *Listen to pieces by each composer on the CD.*

Begin with these pieces:

Composer	Characteristic	Practice Strategy from SWTM
Bach Theme in F major, p. 12 / CD 1	Melodies made up of irregular phrase lengths p. 11	Shaping phrases p. 11 / CD 23
Handel Minuet in G major, p. 42-43 / CD 10	Pieces arranged in suites, p. 41 Popular forms: Binary form, p. 41	Creating a dance feel p. 41 / CD 32
Scarlatti Minuet in G minor, p. 66-67 / CD 18	_____	Bringing a piece to life musically after it is learned, p. 65 / CD 40

Supplement from these pieces in **The Festival Collection®, Book 2**. *Refer to the "About the Pieces and Composers" sections for interesting and insightful information on each piece.*

Page	Era	Title	Suggested Teaching Order
24	Classical	Bagatelle	Little Dance, p. 27 / CD 16
25	Classical	Swabian Tune	The Bear, p. 43 / CD 33
26	Classical	Scotch Dance No. 1	The Hunting Horns and the Echo, p. 29 / CD 18
27	Classical	Little Dance	Una capricciosa nuvola estiva, p. 48 CD 36
28	Classical	Russian Folksong	Russian Folksong, p. 28 / CD 17
29	Classical	The Hunting Horns and the Echo	Mister Czerny in New Orleans, p. 42 / CD 31
42	20th/21st Cent.	Mister Czerny in New Orleans	Bagatelle, p. 24 / CD 13
42	20th/21st Cent.	Waltz Time	Waltz Time, p. 42 / CD 32
43	20th/21st Cent.	The Bear	Swabian Tune, p. 25 / CD 14
48	20th/21st Cent.	Una capricciosa nuvola estiva	Scotch Dance No. 1, p. 26 / CD 15

Incorporate these concepts from **Succeeding with the Masters®, Classical Era:**

Title	Characteristic	Practice Strategy from SWTM
FC - Bagatelle, p. 24 / CD 13	Homophonic texture, p. 64	Shaping phrases, p. 64 / CD 46
FC - Swabian Tune, p. 25 / CD 14	Binary form, p. 8	Marking phrases by breathing, p. 10 / CD 28
FC - Scotch Dance No. 1, p. 26 / CD 15	Contrasting mood within the same piece, p. 35	"Impulse" practicing, p. 62 / CD 45
FC - Little Dance, p. 27 / CD 16	Four-measure phrases, p. 64	Shaping phrases, p. 64 / CD 46
FC - Russian Folksong, p. 28 / CD 17	Frequent use of two-note slurs, p. 38 Varied and repetitive rhythmic motives, p. 64	Practicing two-note slurs, p. 8 / CD 27
FC - The Hunting Horns and the Echo, p. 29 / CD 18	Tuneful classical melodies, p. 34	"Chain-linking" practice, p. 38 / CD 37

Next: **Succeeding with the Masters®, Classical Era, Volume One**

FJH2050

Succeeding with the Masters®, Classical Era, Volume One

Correlated with *The Festival Collection®, Book 2*

Choose from these pieces:

Composer	Characteristic	Practice Strategy from SWTM
Haydn Minuet in C major, p. 13 / CD 3		Practicing ornaments, p. 12 / CD 29
German Dance in F major, p. 15 / CD 4	Rounded binary form, p. 14 Contrast in dynamics, p. 14	Balancing a melody with an accompaniment, p. 14 / CD 30
German Dance in C major, p. 18 / CD 5	Four-measure phrases, p. 17 Contrast in dynamics, p. 17	Playing notes marked by wedges, p. 17 / CD 31
Mozart Minuet in C, p. 41 / CD 12		Practicing contrapuntal phrases, p. 40 / CD 38 Practicing with the metronome, p. 40 / CD 38
Air, p. 44 / CD 13		Breathing at the ends of phrases, p. 42 / CD 39 Playing rolled chords and how to simplify them, p. 42 / CD 39
Minuet in F, K. 2, p. 47 / CD 14	Understanding countermelodies, p. 46	Playing three-note slurs, p. 45 / CD 40
Beethoven Country Dance No. 2 in D major, p. 67 / CD 21	Use of binary form, p. 66	Practicing *sf*, p. 66 / CD 47 Bringing a piece to life by using imagery, p. 66 / CD 47
Ecossaise in E flat major, p. 69 / CD 22	Use of small orchestras, p. 68	Using a "play-prepare" strategy, p. 68 / CD 48
Country Dance No. 1 in D major, p. 71 / CD 23	Homophonic texture, p. 70	"Regrouping," p. 70 / CD 49 Slow vs. fast practicing (3 x 1 rule), p. 70 / CD 49

Supplement from these pieces in **The Festival Collection®, Book 2.** *Refer to the "About the Pieces and Composers" sections for interesting and insightful information on each piece.*

Page	Era	Title	Suggested Teaching Order
7	Baroque	Rigaudon	Theme and Variation, p. 36 / CD 25
8	Baroque	Burleske	Minuet in F major, p. 10-11 / CD 5
10-11	Baroque	Minuet in F major	Mazurka, p. 34 / CD 23
13	Baroque	Sarabande	Sarabande, p. 13 / CD 7
30	Romantic	A Hymn	A Hymn, p. 30 / CD 19
34	Romantic	Mazurka	Rigaudon, p. 7 / CD 2
36	Romantic	Theme and Variation	Night Journey, p. 38 / CD 27
38	Romantic	Night Journey	Burleske, p. 8 / CD 3
39	Romantic	Timid Little Heart	Timid Little Heart, p. 39 / CD 28

Incorporate these concepts from **Succeeding with the Masters®, Baroque Era:**

Title	Characteristic	Practice Strategy with SWTM
FC - Rigaudon, p. 7 / CD 2	Usually sections end with a trill, p. 44 (see Unit 4)	Shaping phrases, p. 11 / CD 23
FC - Burleske, p. 8 / CD 3	*Ostinato* bass, p. 16 (see Unit 4) Repeated melodic and rhythmic patterns p. 44	Shaping phrases, p. 11 / CD 23
FC - Minuet in F major, p. 10-11 / CD 5	Popular forms: Binary form, p. 41	Creating a dance feel, p. 41 / CD 32
FC - Sarabande, p. 13 / CD 7	Pieces arranged in suites, p. 41	Bringing a piece to life musically after it is learned, p. 65 / CD 40

Next: **Succeeding with the Masters®, Baroque Era, Volume One**

Succeeding with the Masters®, Baroque Era, Volume One

*Correlated with **The Festival Collection®, Book 2***

Teach these pieces:

Composer	Characteristic	Practice Strategy from SWTM
Bach		
Minuet in G major, p. 14-15 / CD 2	Popular forms: Binary form, p. 13 One recurring rhythmic pattern, p. 13	Adding ornamentation, p. 13 / CD 24
Musette in D major, p. 18-19 / CD 3	*Ostinato* bass, p. 16 Single mood throughout the piece, p. 16	"Play-prepare" Practice Strategy, p. 16 / CD 25 Practicing the first measure, p. 17 / CD 25
Handel		
Impertinence, p. 45 / CD 11	Repeated melodic and rhythmic patterns, p. 44 Usually sections end with a trill, p. 44 Use of countermelodies, p. 44	Playing baroque articulations, p. 44 / CD 33
Scarlatti		
Minuetto in C major, p. 69 / CD 19	Creation of a piece from short phrase fragments, p. 68	The importance of "hands-alone" work, p. 68 / CD 41 Synchronization between the hands, p. 68 / CD 41

*Supplement from these pieces in **The Festival Collection®, Book 2.** Refer to the "About the Pieces and Composers" sections for interesting and insightful information on each piece.*

Page	Era	Title	Suggested Teaching Order
14-15	Classical	The Village Prophet	Lesson 1, p. 22-23 / CD 12
16-17	Classical	Sonatina in C major	Rippling Waters, p. 41 / CD 30
18-19	Classical	Allegro	The Village Prophet, p. 14-15 / CD 8
20-21	Classical	Sonatina in G	To the Garden, p. 40 / CD 29
22-23	Classical	Lesson 1	Allegro, p. 18-19 / CD 10
40	20th/21st Cent.	To the Garden	Two's Company, p. 46-47 / CD 35
41	20th/21st Cent.	Rippling Waters	Sonatina in C major, p. 16-17 / CD 9
44-45	20th/21st Cent.	Long Gone Blues	Long Gone Blues, p. 44-45 / CD 34
46-47	20th/21st Cent.	Two's Company	Sonatina in G, p. 20-21 / CD 11

*Incorporate these concepts from **Succeeding with the Masters®, Classical Era:***

Title	Characteristic	Practice Strategy from SWTM
FC - The Village Prophet, p. 14-15 / CD 8	Contrast in dynamics, p. 14	Playing three-note slurs, p. 45 / CD 40
FC - Sonatina in C major, p. 16-17 / CD 9	Understanding countermelodies, p. 46	Practicing contrapuntal phrases, p. 40 / CD 38
FC - Allegro, p. 18-19 / CD 10	Frequent use of two-note slurs, p. 38	Practicing two-note slurs, p. 8 / CD 27
FC - Sonatina in G, p. 20-21 / CD 11	Homophonic texture, p. 64	Balancing a melody with an accompaniment, p. 14 / CD 30
FC - Lesson 1, p. 22-23 / CD 12	Rounded binary form, p. 14 Four-measure phrases, p. 17	"Chain-linking" practice, p. 38 / CD 37

Next: **Succeeding with the Masters®, Romantic Era, Volume One**

Succeeding with the Masters®, Romantic Era, Volume One

*Correlated with **The Festival Collection®, Book 3***

Introducing the Romantic Era:

- *Discuss what the music was like during this era, using the information on p. 2-3 and the pictures on p. 19, 23, 33, 37, 39, 67, 71, and 85.*

- *Introduce the 3 master composers using the biographical information on p. 7, 28, and 58.*

- *Listen to pieces by each composer on the CD.*

Begin with these pieces:

Composer	Characteristic	Practice Strategy from SWTM
Schubert		
Ecossaise in C major, p. 9 / CD 1	Binary form, p. 8	The importance of "hands-alone" work, p. 8 / CD 23
German Dance in A major, p. 11 / CD 2	Use of chromatic tones, p. 10	"Play-prepare" Practice Strategy, p. 10 / CD 24
Ecossaise in G major, p. 13 / CD 3	Use of traditional harmonies, p. 12	Practicing scale patterns, p. 12 / CD 25
Schumann		
Soldiers' March, p. 30-31 / CD 9	An example of a programmatic piece, p. 29	How to create a march, p. 29 / CD 31
The Wild Rider, p. 34-35 / CD 10	Drama is an important aspect of the music, p. 32	Playing two-note slurs, p. 32 / CD 32 Practicing with a metronome, p. 32 / CD 32
Tchaikovsky		
The Sick Doll, p. 60-61 / CD 17	Emotion is an important aspect of the music, p. 59 Use of *rubato*, p. 59	Applying *rubato*, p. 59 / CD 39 Adding pedal for an artistic effect, p. 59 / CD 39

FJH2050

*Supplement from these pieces in **The Festival Collection®, Book 3.** Refer to the "About the Pieces and Composers" sections for interesting and insightful information on each piece.*

Page	Era	Title		Suggested Teaching Order
20-21	Classical	Never A Dull Moment		Never A Dull Moment, p. 20-21 / CD 11
22-23	Classical	Adagio		Playing Soldiers, p. 71 / CD 40
24-25	Classical	Sonatina in G (1st Mvt.)		Sonatina in G (1st Mvt.), p. 24-25 / CD 13
26-27	Classical	Sonatina in G (2nd Mvt.)		Highwayman's Tune, p. 58 / CD 33
28-29	Classical	Sonatina in G major		Sonatina in G (2nd Mvt.), p. 26-27 / CD 14
58	20th/21st Cent.	Highwayman's Tune		Little Shepherd, p. 70 / CD 39
62-65	20th/21st Cent.	Five Variations on a Russian Folk Song		Adagio, p. 22-23 / CD 12
70	20th/21st Cent.	Little Shepherd		Five Variations on a Russian Folk Song, p. 62-65 / CD 36
71	20th/21st Cent.	Playing Soldiers		Sonatina in G major, p. 28-29 / CD 15

Incorporate these concepts from **Succeeding with the Masters®, Classical Era:**

Title	Characteristic	Practice Strategy from SWTM
FC - Never A Dull Moment, p. 20-21 / CD 11	Frequent use of two-note slurs, p. 38	Practicing two-note slurs, p. 8 / CD 27 Playing notes marked by wedges, p. 17 / CD 31
FC - Adagio, p. 22-23 / CD 12	Four-measure phrases, p. 17	Breathing at the ends of phrases, p. 42
FC - Sonatina in G (1st Mvt.), p. 24-25 / CD 13	Short, repetitive melodic motives, p. 8	Balancing a melody with an accompaniment, p. 14 / CD 30
FC - Sonatina in G (2nd Mvt.), p. 26-27 / CD 14	Contrast in dynamics, p. 14 Homophonic texture, p. 64	"Regrouping," p. 70 / CD 49 Slow vs. fast practicing (3 x 1 rule), p. 70 / CD 49
FC - Sonatina in G major, p. 28-29 / CD 15	Contrasting moods within the same piece, p. 35	Practicing *sf*, p. 66 / CD 47

Next: **Succeeding with the Masters®, Classical Era, Volume One**

Succeeding with the Masters®, Classical Era, Volume One

Correlated with *The Festival Collection®, Book 3*

Choose from these pieces:

Composer	Characteristic	Practice Strategy from SWTM
Haydn		
German Dance in B flat major, p. 21 / CD 6	_____	"Blocking" Practice Strategy, p. 20 / CD 32
Minuet in B flat major, p. 24 / CD 7	Simple harmonies throughout, p. 22 Contrast in dynamics, p. 22	Straightforward, simple harmonies, p. 22 Practicing with the metronome, p. 23 / CD 33
Minuet and Trio in F major, p. 26-27 / CD 8	Contrast of mood, dynamics, and melodies, p. 25 Popular forms: Use of Minuet and Trio, p. 25	Bringing a piece to life musically after it is learned, p. 25 / CD 34
Dance in B flat major, p. 30 / CD 9	_____	Voicing *legato* double notes within one hand, p. 28 / CD 35
Mozart		
Andante and Maestoso, p. 50 / CD 15	_____	Balancing a melody with an accompaniment, p. 48 Voicing a melody, p. 49 / CD 41
Minuet and Trio, K. 1, p. 52-53 / CD 16	Popular forms: Minuet and Trio, p. 51	"Impulse" practicing, p. 51 / CD 42
Allegro Moderato, p. 55 / CD 17	_____	Bringing a piece to life musically after it is learned, p. 54 / CD 43
Allegro, K. 3, p. 58 / CD 18	_____	"Blocking" Practice Strategy, p. 56 / CD 44
Beethoven		
Minuet and Trio in G major, p. 74-75 / CD 24	Popular forms: Minuet and Trio, p. 73 Four-measure phrases, p. 73 Homophonic texture, p. 73	Shaping phrases, p. 73 / CD 50
German Dance in G major, p. 78-79 / CD 25	Contrasting melodies within one piece, p. 77	Practicing *Alberti* basses, p. 77 / CD 51
Country Dance in D minor, p. 81 / CD 26	Use of straightforward, simple harmonies, p. 80	"Impulse" practicing, p. 80

*Supplement from these pieces in **The Festival Collection®, Book 3**. Refer to the "About the Pieces and Composers" sections for interesting and insightful information on each piece.*

Page	Era	Title	Suggested Teaching Order
6	Baroque	Minuet in A minor	Through Forest and Field, p. 40-41 / CD 23
7	Baroque	Minuet in G major	Fantasie, p. 8-9 / CD 3
8-9	Baroque	Fantasie	Hunting Music, p. 48-49 / CD 27
10	Baroque	Minuet in E minor	Minuet in C major, p. 11 / CD 5
11	Baroque	Minuet in C major	Arabesque, p. 46-47 / CD 26
40-41	Romantic	Through Forest and Field	Minuet in A minor, p. 6 / CD 1
46-47	Romantic	Arabesque	Romantic Study, Op. 139, No. 49, p. 52 / CD 29
48-49	Romantic	Hunting Music	Minuet in E minor, p. 10 / CD 4
50-51	Romantic	Praeludium	Romantic Study, Op. 261, No. 54, p. 53 / CD 30
52	Romantic	Romantic Study, Op. 139, No. 49	Minuet in G major, p. 7 / CD 2
53	Romantic	Romantic Study, Op. 261, No. 54	Praeludium, p. 50-51 / CD 28

FJH2050

Incorporate these concepts from **Succeeding with the Masters®, Baroque Era:**

Title	Characteristic	Practice Strategy from SWTM
FC - Minuet in A minor, p. 6 / CD 1	Use of countermelodies, p. 44	Adding ornamentation, p. 13 / CD 24
FC - Minuet in G major, p. 7 / CD 2	One recurring rhythmic pattern, p. 13	Adding ornamentation, p. 13 / CD 24
FC - Fantasie, p. 8-9 / CD 3	Creation of a piece from short phrase fragments, p. 68	Practicing the first measure, p. 17
FC - Minuet in E minor, p. 10 / CD 4	Popular forms: Binary form, p. 41	Playing baroque articulations, p. 44 / CD 33
FC - Minuet in C major, p. 11 / CD 5	Single mood throughout the piece, p. 16	The importance of "hands-alone" work, p. 68

Incorporate these concepts from **Succeeding with the Masters®, Romantic Era:**

Title	Characteristic	Practice Strategy from SWTM
FC - Through Forest and Field, p. 40-41 / CD 23	An example of a programmatic piece, p. 29	Practicing with a metronome, p. 32 / CD 32
FC - Arabesque, p. 46-47 / CD 26	Drama is an important aspect of the music, p. 32	Practicing with a metronome, p. 32 / CD 32
FC - Hunting Music, p. 48-49 / CD 27	An example of a programmatic piece, p. 29	Playing two-note slurs, p. 32 / CD 32 Practicing with a metronome, p. 32 / CD 32
FC - Praeludium, p. 50-51 / CD 28	Use of *rubato*, p. 59	Applying *rubato*, p. 59 / CD 39 Adding pedal for an artistic effect, p. 59 / CD 39
FC - Romantic Study, Op. 139, No. 49, p. 52 / CD 29	Use of traditional harmonies, p. 12	The importance of "hands-alone" work, p. 8 / CD 23
FC - Romantic Study, Op. 261, No. 54, p. 53 / CD 30	Use of traditional harmonies, p. 12	The importance of "hands-alone" work, p. 8 / CD 23

Next: **Succeeding with the Masters®, Baroque Era, Volume One**

Succeeding with the Masters®, Baroque Era, Volume One

Correlated with *The Festival Collection*®, *Book 3*

Choose from these pieces:

Composer	Characteristic	Practice Strategy from SWTM
Bach		
Minuet in G minor, p. 22-23 / CD 4	The importance of the minuet, p. 21 Popular forms: Rounded binary form, p. 21	Practicing with the metronome, p. 21 / CD 26
Minuet in D minor, p. 26-27 / CD 5	Polyphonic texture, p. 24	Creating clear sixteenth-note patterns, p. 24 / CD 27 Shaping the left-hand phrases, p. 25 / CD 27
Minuet in G major, p. 30-31 / CD 6	Rhythm as a distinctive element of the era, p. 28	"Activating" rhythmic patterns, p. 28 / CD 28
Minuet in G major, p. 33-34 / CD 7	Imitation, p. 32	Shaping phrases, p. 32 / CD 29
Handel		
Minuet in F major, p. 48-49 / CD 12	Rhythm as a distinctive element of the era, p. 47 Popular forms: Rounded binary form, p. 47 Usually sections end with a trill, p. 47	Creating a tasteful baroque *ritardando*, p. 47 / CD 34
Aria, p. 51 / CD 13	Pieces written without many articulations, p. 50	Balancing the melody with an equally important bass line, p. 50 / CD 35
Gavotte in G major, p. 53 / CD 14	The use of dance pieces, p. 52	Slow vs. fast practicing (3 x 1 rule), p. 52 / CD 36
Scarlatti		
Larghetto in D minor, p. 72-73 / CD 20	_____	Adding embellishments, p. 70 / CD 42 Learning to "Follow the leader," p. 71 / CD 42

Supplement from these pieces in **The Festival Collection**®, **Book 3.** *Refer to the "About the Pieces and Composers" sections for interesting and insightful information on each piece.*

Page	Era	Title	Suggested Teaching Order
30-31	Classical	Sonata in F major, Hob. XVI: 9	Innocence, p. 38 / CD 21
32-33	Classical	Sonatina in C major (1st Mvt.)	Dance, p. 37 / CD 20
34	Classical	Sonatina in C major (2nd Mvt.)	In the Garden, p. 42-43 / CD 24
35-36	Classical	Sonatina in C major (3rd Mvt.)	Sonata in F major, Hob. XVI: 9, p. 30-31 / CD 16
37	Classical	Dance	Progress, p. 39 / CD 22
38	Romantic	Innocence	Sonatina in C major (1st Mvt.), p. 32-33 / CD 17
39	Romantic	Progress	Song, p. 44-45 / CD 25
42-43	Romantic	In the Garden	Sonatina in C major (2nd Mvt.), p. 34 / CD 18
44-45	Romantic	Song	Kamarinskaya, p. 55-57 / CD 32
54	Romantic	Andantino	Sonatina in C major (3rd Mvt.), p. 35-36 / CD 19
55-57	Romantic	Kamarinskaya	Andantino, p. 54 / CD 31

FJH2050

Incorporate these concepts from **Succeeding with the Masters®, Classical Era:**

Title	*Characteristic*	*Practice Strategy from SWTM*
FC - Sonata in F major, Hob. XVI: 9, p. 30-31 / CD 16	Rounded binary form, p. 14 Use of straightforward, simple harmonies, p. 80	Shaping phrases, p. 73 / CD 50
FC - Sonatina in C major (1st Mvt.), p. 32-33 / CD 17	Contrast in dynamics, p. 14 Short, repetitive melodic motives, p. 8	Bringing a piece to life musically, p. 25 / CD 34 Practicing *Alberti* basses, p. 77
FC - Sonatina in C major (2nd Mvt.), p. 34 / CD 18	Homophonic texture, p. 64	Breathing at the ends of phrases, p. 42
FC - Sonatina in C major (3rd Mvt.), p. 35-36 / CD 19	Contrast in dynamics, p. 14 Tuneful classical melodies, p. 34	Balancing a melody with accompaniment, p. 48
FC - Dance, p. 37 / CD 20	Rounded binary form, p. 14 Varied and repetitive rhythmic motives, p. 64	Playing three-note slurs, p. 45 / CD 40

Incorporate these concepts from **Succeeding with the Masters®, Romantic Era:**

Title	*Characteristic*	*Practice Strategy from SWTM*
FC - Innocence, p. 38 / CD 21	Binary form, p. 8	Practicing scale patterns, p. 12 / CD 25
FC - Progress, p. 39 / CD 22	Use of symmetrical phrases, p. 14 (see Unit 8)	Playing two-note slurs, p. 14 / CD 32 Practicing with a metronome, p. 14 / CD 32
FC - In the Garden, p. 42-43 / CD 24	An example of a programmatic piece, p. 29	Using half and quarter pedal, p. 16 / CD 27 (see Unit 8)
FC - Song, p. 44-45 / CD 25	Homophonic texture, p. 16	Keen listening, p. 37 / CD 33 (see Unit 8)
FC - Andantino, p. 54 / CD 31	Emotion is an important aspect of the music, p. 59	Applying *rubato*, p. 59 / CD 39 Adding pedal for an artistic effect, p. 59 / CD 39
FC - Kamarinskaya, p. 55-57 / CD 32	Strong sense of rhythm helping to define a piece, p. 66 (see Unit 8)	"Chain-linking" Practice Strategy, p. 66 / CD 41 (see Unit 8)

Next: **Succeeding with the Masters®, Romantic Era, Volume One**

Succeeding with the Masters®, Romantic Era, Volume One

Correlated with *The Festival Collection*®, *Book 3*

Choose from these pieces:

Composer	Characteristic	Practice Strategy from SWTM
Schubert		
Ländler in G, p. 15 / CD 4	Use of symmetrical phrases, p. 14	Practicing two-note slurs, p. 14 / CD 26
Ländler in B flat, p. 17 / CD 5	Homophonic texture, p. 16	Using half and quarter pedal, p. 16 / CD 27 Playing a measure written for a large hand, p. 16 / CD 27
Schumann		
Melody, p. 38 / CD 11	*Espressivo* dynamic markings, p. 36	How to play notes with an *espressivo* marking, p. 36 Keen listening, p. 37 / CD 33
A Hymn, p. 41 / CD 12	_____	Practicing chordal pieces, p. 40 / CD 34 Adding your own dynamics, p. 40 / CD 34
Humming Song, p. 44-45 / CD 13	Use of a melody and a countermelody, p. 42	How to practice a melody with an accompaniment and a countermelody, p. 42 / CD 35
Tchaikovsky		
The New Doll, p. 63-65 / CD 18	Phrases of varying lengths, p. 62 An example of a programmatic piece, p. 62	Shaping phrases, p. 62 / CD 40 How to play repeated notes quickly and lightly, p. 62 / CD 40
Russian Song, p. 68-69 / CD 19	Strong sense of rhythm helping to define a piece, p. 66	"Chain-linking" Practice Strategy, p. 66 / CD 41
Old French Song, p. 72-73 / CD 20	Use of traditional forms (ternary), p. 70 Emotion and tenderness as important aspects of the music, p. 70	Balancing melody with accompaniment, p. 70 / CD 42

FJH2050

*Supplement from these pieces in **The Festival Collection®, Book 3**. Refer to the "About the Pieces and Composers" sections for interesting and insightful information on each piece.*

Page	Era	Title
12	Baroque	Minuet in A minor
13	Baroque	Gigue
14-15	Baroque	Minuet in G minor, BWV 115
16-17	Baroque	Minuet in D minor
18-19	Baroque	The Fifers
59	20th/21st Cent.	Play It Again
60-61	20th/21st Cent.	Machines on the Loose
66-67	20th/21st Cent.	The Elegant Toreador
68-69	20th/21st Cent.	Waltz
72	20th/21st Cent.	Waves

Suggested Teaching Order

Waves, p. 72 / CD 41
Gigue, p. 13 / CD 7
Waltz, p. 68-69 / CD 38
Minuet in A minor, p. 12 / CD 6
The Elegant Toreador, p. 66-67 / CD 37
The Fifers, p. 18-19 / CD 10
Play It Again, p. 59 / CD 34
Minuet in D minor, p. 16-17 / CD 9
Machines on the Loose, p. 60-61 / CD 35
Minuet in G minor, BWV 115, p. 14-15 / CD 8

*Incorporate these concepts from **Succeeding with the Masters®, Baroque Era:***

Title	Characteristic	Practice Strategy from SWTM
FC - Minuet in A minor, p. 12 / CD 6	The importance of the minuet, p. 21	Practicing with the metronome, p. 21 / CD 26
FC - Gigue, p. 13 / CD 7	Rhythm as a distinctive element of the era, p. 28 Pieces arranged in suites, p. 41	Slow vs. fast practicing (3 x 1 rule), p. 52 / CD 36
FC - Minuet in G minor, BWV 115, p. 14-15 / CD 8	Rhythm as a distinctive element of the era, p. 28	"Activating" rhythmic patterns, p. 28 / CD 28
FC - Minuet in D minor, p. 16-17 / CD 9	Popular forms: Rounded binary form, p. 21 Polyphonic texture, p. 24	Creating a tasteful baroque *ritardando*, p. 47 / CD 34
FC - The Fifers, p. 18-19 / CD 10	One recurring rhythmic pattern, p. 13	Creating a dance feel, p. 41 / CD 32

Next: **Succeeding with the Masters®, Baroque Era, Volume One**

Succeeding with the Masters®, Baroque Era, Volume One

Correlated with **easier selections from** *The Festival Collection*®, *Book 4*

Choose from these pieces:

Composer	Characteristic	Practice Strategy from SWTM
Bach		
Minuet in C minor, p. 36-37 / CD 8	Perpetual motion, p. 35	Focus on forward motion, p. 35 / CD 30 "8 times to perfection" Practice Strategy, p. 35 / CD 30
Prelude in C major, p. 39 / CD 9	Enduring energy, p. 38 Use of ornamentation, p. 38	"Impulse" practicing, p. 38 / CD 31
Handel		
Sarabande, p. 56-57 / CD 15	Repeated use of small details, changed slightly, p. 54	Practicing two-note slurs, p. 54 / CD 37 "First beat" practice, p. 55 / CD 37
Air in B flat major, p. 60-61 / CD 16	_____	Creating clear passagework, p. 59 / CD 38 Creating the mood of the piece, p. 59 / CD 38
Sonatina in G major, p. 63 / CD 17	Enduring energy, p. 62	"Smart" fingering, p. 62 / CD 39
Scarlatti		
Minuetto in B flat major, p. 76-77 / CD 21	Use of repeated melodic and rhythmic patterns, p. 74 Perpetual motion without predictable cadences, p. 74	Balancing the melody with an equally important bass line, p. 74 / CD 43 Playing with a *cantabile* sound, p. 75 / CD 43
Minuetto in C minor, p. 80-81 / CD 22	Most sections end with a trill, p. 78 Use of phrases that are not symmetrical, p. 78 Two melodic lines within the same hand, p. 78 Pieces written without fingering, dynamics, and articulations, p. 79	Practicing different voices within the same hand, p. 78 / CD 44

Supplement from these pieces in The Festival Collection®, *Book 4. Refer to the "About the Pieces and Composers" sections for interesting and insightful information on each piece.*

Page	Era	Title	Suggested Teaching Order
26-28	Classical	Sonatina in G, Op. 36, No. 2 (1st Mvt.)	Spinning Song, p. 54-57 / CD 23
29-31	Classical	La Caroline	Rondo in B flat major, p. 32-33 / CD 13
32-33	Classical	Rondo in B flat major	The Shepherdess, Op. 100, No. 11, p. 58-59 / CD 24
36-37	Classical	Sonatina in G	Sonatina in G, p. 36-37 / CD 15
38-39	Classical	Rondo in F major	Polka, p. 60-61 / CD 25
54-57	Romantic	Spinning Song	Rondo in F major, p. 38-39 / CD 16
58-59	Romantic	The Shepherdess, Op. 100, No. 11	Allemande in E flat, p. 62-63 / CD 26
60-61	Romantic	Polka	Sonatina in G, Op. 36, No. 2 (1st Mvt.), p. 26-28 / CD 11
62-63	Romantic	Allemande in E flat	Sicilienne, Op. 68, No. 11, p. 64-65 / CD 27
64-65	Romantic	Sicilienne, Op. 68, No. 11	La Caroline, p. 29-31 / CD 12
68-69	Romantic	Little Flower	Little Flower, p. 68-69 / CD 29

FJH2050

Incorporate these concepts from **Succeeding with the Masters®, Classical Era:**

Title	*Characteristic*	*Practice Strategy from SWTM*
FC - Sonatina in G, Op. 36, No. 2, (1st Mvt.), p. 26-28 / CD 11	Contrast in dynamics, p. 14 Short, repetitive melodic motives, p. 8	"Regrouping," p. 70 / CD 49 Slow vs. fast practicing (3 x 1 rule), p. 70 / CD 49 Shaping phrases, p. 73 / CD 50
FC - La Caroline, p. 29-31 / CD 12	Contrasting mood within the same piece, p. 35	Bringing a piece to life musically, p. 25 / CD 34 Voicing a melody, p. 49 / CD 41
FC - Rondo in B flat major, p. 32-33 / CD 13	Short, repetitive melodic motives, p. 8 Simple harmonies throughout, p. 22	Straightforward, simple harmonies, p. 22 / CD 33 "Impulse" practicing, p. 51 / CD 42
FC - Sonatina in G, p. 36-37 / CD 15	Homophonic texture, p. 64 Varied and repetitive rhythmic motives, p. 64	"Blocking" Practice Strategy, p. 20, 56 / CD 32, 44
FC - Rondo in F major, p. 38-39 / CD 16	Four-measure phrases, p. 73 Contrasting melodies within one piece, p. 77	"Impulse" practicing, p. 51 / CD 42

Incorporate these concepts from **Succeeding with the Masters®, Romantic Era:**

Title	*Characteristic*	*Practice Strategy from SWTM*
FC - Spinning Song, p. 54-57 / CD 23	Use of traditional forms (ternary), p. 22 (see Unit 10) Strong sense of rhythm helping to define a piece, p. 66	How to play repeated notes quickly and lightly, p. 62 Bringing a piece to life musically, p. 26 / CD 30 (see Unit 10)
FC - The Shepherdess, Op. 100, No. 11, p. 58-59 / CD 24	A piece designed to teach some aspect of technique, p. 54 (see Unit 10) Expansion of the harmonic language for added color, p. 80 (see Unit 10)	Energizing the melody, p. 50 / CD 37 Using imagery, p. 51 "Chain-linking" Practice Strategy, p. 66 / CD 41
FC - Polka, p. 60-61/ CD 25	More dynamic markings, p. 46 (see Unit 10) Use of traditional forms (ternary), p. 26 (see Unit 10)	"8 times to perfection" Practice Strategy, p. 22 / CD 29 (see Unit 10) "Blocking" Practice Strategy, p. 54
FC - Allemande in E flat, p. 62-63 / CD 26	A piece designed to teach some aspect of technique, p. 54 (see Unit 10) Different dynamics creating drama, p. 26 (see Unit 10)	Practicing scale patterns, p. 12 / CD 25
FC - Sicilienne, Op. 68, No. 11, p. 64-65 / CD 27	Use of major and minor tonalities, p. 18 More dynamic markings, p. 46 (see Unit 10)	Bringing a piece to life musically, p. 26 / CD 30 (see Unit 10)
FC - Little Flower, p. 68-69 / CD 29	Use of a melody and a countermelody, p. 42 Use of *rubato*, p. 74	Keen listening, p. 37 / CD 33 How to practice a melody with an accompaniment and a countermelody, p. 42 / CD 35

Next: **Succeeding with the Masters®, Romantic Era, Volume One**

Succeeding with the Masters®, Romantic Era, Volume One

Correlated with **easier selections from** *The Festival Collection*®, *Book 4*

Choose from these pieces:

Composer	Characteristic	Practice Strategy from SWTM
Schubert		
Waltz in B minor, p. 20-21 / CD 6	Use of major and minor tonalities, p. 18	Perfect rhythm, p. 18 / CD 28 Creating the mood of the piece, p. 19 / CD 28
Ländler in G major, p. 24-25 / CD 7	Use of traditional forms (ternary), p. 22	"8 times to perfection" Practice Strategy, p. 22 / CD 29
Waltz in A major, p. 27 / CD 8	Different dynamics creating drama, p. 26	Bringing a piece to life musically after it is learned, p. 26 / CD 30
Schumann		
First Loss, p. 48-49 / CD 14	Emotion is an important aspect of a piece, p. 46 More dynamic markings, p. 46	Shaping phrases, p. 46 / CD 36 Using half and quarter pedal, p. 47 / CD 36
The Merry Farmer, p. 52-53 / CD 15	Melody and accompaniment in the same hand, p. 50	Energizing the melody, p. 50 / CD 37 Using imagery, p. 51 / CD 37
Little Study, p. 55-57 / CD 16	A piece designed to teach some aspect of technique, p. 54	"Blocking" Practice Strategy, p. 54 / CD 38 Practicing to perform with the utmost evenness, p. 54 / CD 38
Tchaikovsky		
Waltz, p. 76-79 / CD 21	Use of *rubato*, p. 74	Practicing a waltz bass, p. 74 / CD 43 Practicing with the metronome, p. 75 / CD 43
March of the Wooden Soldiers, p. 82-84 / CD 22	Expansion of the harmonic language for added color, p. 80	Playing dotted rhythms, p. 80 Getting ready for a performance, p. 81 / CD 44

FJH2050

Supplement from these pieces in **The Festival Collection**®, **Book 4.** Refer to the "About the Pieces and Composers" sections for interesting and insightful information on each piece.

Page	Era	Title	Suggested Teaching Order
6-7	Baroque	The Little Trifle	The Little Trifle, p. 6-7 / CD 1
8	Baroque	Fantasia in G major	Elephant Tune, p. 76 / CD 33
9	Baroque	Polonaise	Fantasia in G major, p. 8 / CD 2
10-11	Baroque	Minuet in G minor	Tango in C minor, p. 77 / CD 34
16-17	Baroque	Loure	Polonaise, p. 9 / CD 3
76	20th/21st Cent.	Elephant Tune	Song of the Range Rider, p. 78 / CD 35
77	20th/21st Cent.	Tango in C minor	Minuet in G minor, p. 10-11 / CD 4
78	20th/21st Cent.	Song of the Range Rider	Rustic Dance, Op. 24, No. 1, p. 84-85 / CD 39
84-85	20th/21st Cent.	Rustic Dance, Op. 24, No. 1	Loure, p. 16-17 / CD 6
86-87	20th/21st Cent.	Ivan's Song	Ivan's Song, p. 86-87 / CD 40

Incorporate these concepts from **Succeeding with the Masters**®, **Baroque Era:**

Title	Characteristic	Practice Strategy from SWTM
FC - The Little Trifle, p. 6-7/ CD 1	Polyphonic texture, p. 24 Perpetual motion, p. 35 Enduring energy, p. 38 Single mood throughout a piece, p. 16	Focus on forward motion, p. 35 / CD 30 "8 times to perfection" Practice Strategy, p. 35 / CD 30
FC - Fantasia in G major, p. 8 / CD 2	Polyphonic texture, p. 24 Popular forms: Binary form, p. 41	Creating the mood of the piece, p. 59 "Smart" fingering, p. 62 / CD 39 Balancing the melody with an important bass line, p. 74 / CD 43
FC - Polonaise, p. 9 / CD 3	Popular forms: Binary form, p. 41 Repeated melodic and rhythmic patterns, p. 44	Creating clear sixteenth-note patterns, p. 24 / CD 27 "Activating" rhythmic patterns, p. 28 / CD 28
FC - Minuet in G minor, p. 10-11 / CD 4	Rhythm as a distinctive element of the era, p. 28 Use of ornamentation, p. 38	Creating a tasteful baroque *ritardando*, p. 47 / CD 34 Adding embellishments, p. 70 / CD 42 Learning to "Follow the leader," p. 71 / CD 42
FC - Loure, p. 16-17 / CD 6	Use of ornamentation, p. 38 Two melodic lines within the same hand, p. 78	Practicing different voices within the same hand, p. 78 / CD 44

Next: **Succeeding with the Masters**®, **Volume Two**

BAROQUE ERA • Volume One
CLASSICAL ERA • Volumes One & Two

SUCCEEDING
WITH THE MASTERS®
Student Activity Book and *Teacher's Handbook*

by Helen Marlais
with Kristen Avila

Note to Teachers

This *Student Activity Books* are full of enjoyable activities that will help your students learn about the master composers of the Baroque and Classical Era. The stories, games, puzzles, and activities for listening, drawing, and writing are an easy way to engage students in an understanding not only of important information about the composers' lives, but also of their music.

Students will be able to complete the activities in these books by reading the composer biographies, looking at the music, listening to the CD, and using the glossary in the *Succeeding with the Masters®* Performance Books. The activities are designed for you to help your students in imaginative ways.

Supplementary *Teacher's Handbooks* provide the answers to the student activities as well as some additional ideas for group activities. We hope you enjoy these books with your students!

Helen Marlais and Kristen Avila

A special thanks to Susan Hellard, whose outstanding illustrations have brought the pages of this publication to life.

Student Activity Book - Baroque Era,
Volume One   **FF1660 / $6.95**

Teacher's Handbook - Baroque Era,
Volume One   **FF1661 / $6.95**

Student Activity Book - Classical Era,
Volume One   **FF1656 / $6.95**

Teacher's Handbook - Classical Era,
Volume One   **FF1657 / $6.95**

Student Activity Book - Classical Era,
Volume Two   **FF1658 / $6.95**

Teacher's Handbook - Classical Era,
Volume Two   **FF1659 / $6.95**

FJH2050

Using Succeeding with the Masters®, Volume Two
Baroque Era, Classical Era, Romantic Era

*Correlated with **The Festival Collection®, Books 4** (more difficult selections), 5, and 6*

FEATURES OF THIS CORRELATION:

1. The *Succeeding with the Masters®* series is considered the core curriculum and *The Festival Collection®* is used for supplementary repertoire.

2. This approach is ideal for teachers who believe in the importance of students understanding each of the eras. Students learn about the eras in a social as well as a historical perspective, they learn correct style and interpretation, and they learn the unique musical characteristics of each era. They also learn how to establish excellent practice habits as an important part of their education.

3. The teaching sequence begins with *Succeeding with the Masters®, Baroque Era, Volume Two* and *The Festival Collection®, Book 4*. Clear instructions are given so teachers can easily cover all six books in the curriculum in an interesting and logical manner.

4. Suggestions are given for introducing students to each era and composer in *Succeeding with the Masters®*.

5. The pieces in both *Succeeding with the Masters®*, and *The Festival Collection®* are carefully correlated according to level of difficulty.

6. One musical era is studied in detail for each unit. The primary focus era comes from *Succeeding with the Masters®*. Students use pieces in *The Festival Collection®* in order to experience eras that are stylistically different, thus creating a well-rounded curriculum throughout the year. Students study three of the four musical eras at once. The overlapping circles on the front cover of *The Festival Collection®* show how artistic concepts from the different eras overlapped (see the inside front cover of *The Festival Collection®* for more information).

7. The Practice Strategies are presented in *Succeeding with the Masters®*, and then applied to pieces in *The Festival Collection®* for regular review and reinforcement. They can be used in multiple situations at this level of literature by taking into consideration the student's age, maturity level and prior exposure to *Succeeding with the Masters®, Volume One*.

   The Practice Strategies fall into 3 categories:
   a. Practice Strategies that are very specific to a certain feature of a piece.
   b. Practice Strategies that help the student initially learn the piece.
   c. Practice Strategies that help the student put "finishing touches" on a learned piece (while the student is working on interpretation and preparing for a performance).

8. Much freedom is given for teachers and students to choose appropriate repertoire once the initial pieces are learned in each unit. The listening CD's provide a valuable resource to aid in the selection process.

9. The following abbreviations are used: FC = *The Festival Collection®*; SWTM = *Succeeding with the Masters®*; and Cent. = Centuries.

TEACHING SEQUENCE

Succeeding with the Masters®, Volume Two*
Baroque Era, Classical Era, Romantic Era

*Correlated with **The Festival Collection®, Books 4 (more difficult selections), 5, and 6***

Each of the following units gradually increases in difficulty level. It is most advantageous when students study pieces from at least three different eras at the same time. In each of the following units, students focus on one or two eras with Succeeding with the Masters®, while using pieces from The Festival Collection® (from different eras) to create a well-rounded repertoire curriculum. The length of time spent on each unit is at the teacher's discretion.

Intermediate Repertoire

UNIT 1	*Succeeding with the Masters®, Baroque Era, Volume Two*	*The Festival Collection®, Book 4 (Choose from) Classical, Romantic, 20th/21st Centuries*
UNIT 2	*Succeeding with the Masters®, Romantic Era, Volume Two*	*The Festival Collection®, Book 4 (Choose from) Baroque, Classical, 20th/21st Centuries*
UNIT 3	*Succeeding with the Masters®, Classical Era, Volume Two*	*The Festival Collection®, Book 4 (Choose from) Baroque, Romantic, 20th/21st Centuries*
UNIT 4	*Succeeding with the Masters®, Romantic Era, Volume Two*	*The Festival Collection®, Book 4 (Choose from) Baroque, Classical, 20th/21st Centuries*
UNIT 5	*Succeeding with the Masters®, Classical Era, Volume Two*	*The Festival Collection®, Book 5 (Choose from) Baroque, Romantic, 20th/21st Centuries*
UNIT 6	*Succeeding with the Masters®, Baroque Era, Volume Two*	*The Festival Collection®, Book 5 (Choose from) Classical, Romantic, 20th/21st Centuries*

Late Intermediate Repertoire

UNIT 7	*Succeeding with the Masters®, Classical Era, Volume Two* *Succeeding with the Masters®, Romantic Era, Volume Two*	*The Festival Collection®, Book 5 (Choose from) Baroque, 20th/21st Centuries*
UNIT 8	*Succeeding with the Masters®, Baroque Era, Volume Two* *Succeeding with the Masters®, Romantic Era, Volume Two*	*The Festival Collection®, Book 5 (Choose from) Classical, 20th/21st Centuries*
UNIT 9	*Succeeding with the Masters®, Baroque Era, Volume Two* *Succeeding with the Masters®, Classical Era, Volume Two*	*The Festival Collection®, Book 5 (Choose from) Romantic, 20th/21st Centuries*
UNIT 10	*Succeeding with the Masters®, Baroque Era, Volume Two*	*The Festival Collection®, Book 5 (Choose from) Classical, Romantic, 20th/21st Centuries*
UNIT 11	*Succeeding with the Masters®, Classical Era, Volume Two* *Succeeding with the Masters®, Romantic Era, Volume Two*	*The Festival Collection®, Book 5 (Choose from) Baroque, 20th/21st Centuries*
UNIT 12	*Succeeding with the Masters®, Classical Era, Volume Two* *Succeeding with the Masters®, Romantic Era, Volume Two*	*The Festival Collection®, Book 5 (Choose from) Baroque, 20th/21st Centuries*

* Students can use the Succeeding with the Masters® Student Activity Book, Classical Era, Volume Two.

FJH2050

Late Intermediate to Early Advanced Repertoire

UNIT 13	*Succeeding with the Masters®, Romantic Era, Volume Two*	*The Festival Collection®, Book 5* *(Choose from)* *Baroque, Classical, 20th/21st Centuries*
UNIT 14	*Succeeding with the Masters®, Baroque Era, Volume Two* *Succeeding with the Masters®, Classical Era, Volume Two*	*The Festival Collection®, Book 5* *(Choose from)* *Romantic*
UNIT 15	*Succeeding with the Masters®, Classical Era, Volume Two*	*The Festival Collection®, Book 6* *(Choose from)* *Baroque, Romantic, 20th/21st Centuries*
UNIT 16	*Succeeding with the Masters®, Baroque Era, Volume Two* *Succeeding with the Masters®, Romantic Era, Volume Two*	*The Festival Collection®, Book 6* *(Choose from)* *Classical, Romantic, 20th/21st Centuries*
UNIT 17	*Succeeding with the Masters®, Classical Era, Volume Two* *Succeeding with the Masters®, Romantic Era, Volume Two*	*The Festival Collection®, Book 6* *(Choose from)* *Baroque, 20th/21st Centuries*
UNIT 18	*Succeeding with the Masters®, Baroque Era, Volume Two* *Succeeding with the Masters®, Romantic Era, Volume Two*	*The Festival Collection®, Book 6* *(Choose from)* *Classical, 20th/21st Centuries*

Early Advanced Repertoire

UNIT 19	*Succeeding with the Masters®, Baroque Era, Volume Two*	*The Festival Collection®, Book 6* *(Choose from)* *Classical, Romantic, 20th/21st Centuries*
UNIT 20	*Succeeding with the Masters®, Classical Era, Volume Two*	*The Festival Collection®, Book 6* *(Choose from)* *Baroque, Classical, Romantic,* *20th/21st Centuries*
UNIT 21	*Succeeding with the Masters®, Romantic Era, Volume Two*	*The Festival Collection®, Book 6* *(Choose from)* *Baroque, Classical, Romantic,* *20th/21st Centuries*
UNIT 22	————————————————	*The Festival Collection®, Book 6* *(Choose from)* *Baroque, Classical, Romantic,* *20th/21st Centuries*
UNIT 23	*Succeeding with the Masters®, Romantic Era, Volume Two*	*The Festival Collection®, Book 6* *(Choose from)* *Baroque, Classical, Romantic,* *20th/21st Centuries*
UNIT 24	*Succeeding with the Masters®, Romantic Era, Volume Two*	*The Festival Collection®, Book 6* *(Choose from)* *Baroque, Classical, 20th/21st Centuries*

Succeeding with the Masters®, Baroque Era, Volume Two

*Correlated with **more difficult selections from The Festival Collection®, Book 4***

Introducing the Baroque Era, Volume Two:

- *Discuss the Preface on p. 2-3 and the Baroque Performance Practices on p. 7-9.*
- *Review Bach's biographical information on p. 10-11.*
- *Use the pictures on p. 12 and 15 for further discussion of Bach and the Baroque era.*
- *Review Handel's biographical information on p. 44.*
- *Review Scarlatti's biographical information on p. 74-75.*
- *Use the picture on p. 77 for further discussion of Scarlatti and the Baroque era.*
- *Listen to the pieces in this unit on the CD's.*

Succeeding with the Masters®, Repertoire:

Composer	Characteristic	Practice Strategy from SWTM
Bach Minuet in E major, p. 14-15 / CD 1	Importance of the minuet, p. 13	"Smart" fingering, p. 13 / CD 26
Handel Minuet in A minor, p. 46 / CD 10	Polyphonic texture, p. 45	Learning to "Follow the leader," p. 45 / CD 35
Scarlatti Aria, p. 78-79 / CD 18	_____	Slow vs. fast practicing (3x1 rule), p. 76 / CD 43

*Supplement from these pieces in **The Festival Collection®, Book 4**. Refer to the "About the Pieces and Composers" sections for interesting and insightful information on each piece.*

Page	Era	Title
40-42	Classical	Sonatina in C major, Op. 168, No. 3 (3rd Mvt.)
43	Classical	Strong, Sturdy Character
72-73	Romantic	Turkish March, Op. 101, No. 9
74-75	Romantic	Etude in A minor, Op. 47, No. 3
79	20th/21st Cent.	Prelude (Op. 138)

Suggested Teaching Order (both books)

Group 1: Sonatina in C major, Op. 168, No. 3 (3rd Mvt.)
     FC, p. 40-42 / CD 17
   Etude in A minor, Op. 47, No. 3
     FC, p. 74-75 / CD 32
   Minuet in A minor
     SWTM, p. 46 / CD 10

Group 2: Strong, Sturdy Character
     FC, p. 43 / CD 18
   Aria
     SWTM, p. 78-79 / CD 18

Group 3: Turkish March, Op. 101, No. 9
     FC, p. 72-73 / CD 31
   Minuet in E major
     SWTM, p. 14-15 / CD 1
   Prelude (Op. 138)
     FC, p. 79 / CD 36

Incorporate these concepts from **Succeeding with the Masters®, Classical Era, Volume Two:**

<u>Title</u>	<u>Characteristic</u>	<u>Practice Strategy from SWTM</u>
FC - Sonatina in C major, Op. 168, No. 3 (3rd Mvt.), p. 40-42 / CD 17	Well-balanced and symmetrical phrases, p. 12 Melodies that are elegant, graceful, and easy to sing, p. 36	Balancing the melody with the accompaniment, p. 9 Tonic and dominant chords, p. 17 / CD 26
FC - Strong, Sturdy Character, p. 43 / CD 18	Varied rhythmic motives	Using the *una corda* pedal, p. 87 / CD 44

<u>*"Learning the Piece" Practice Strategies: (choose any)*</u>

Improving muscle memory, p. 47 / CD 34	"Smart" fingering, p. 70 / CD 40

<u>*"Once the Piece Is Learned" Practice Strategies: (choose any)*</u>

Communicating a piece to an audience, p. 44	Practicing in different rhythms, p. 71

Incorporate these concepts from **Succeeding with the Masters®, Romantic Era, Volume Two:**

<u>Title</u>	<u>Characteristic</u>	<u>Practice Strategy from SWTM</u>
FC - Turkish March, Op. 101, No. 9, p. 72-73 / CD 31	Use of traditional forms, p. 10 Programmatic piece, p. 41	Playing dotted rhythms, p. 57 / CD 43 Contrast in music to create drama, p. 34 / CD 38 Strong sense of rhythm defining a piece, p. 41 / CD 39
FC - Etude in A minor, Op. 47, No. 3, p. 74-75 / CD 32	Phrases of varying length, p. 77	Strong sense of rhythm defining a piece, p. 41 / CD 39

<u>*"Learning the Piece" Practice Strategies: (choose any)*</u>

Improving muscle memory, p. 24 / CD 36	Unit, section and performance practice, p. 24-25 / CD 36	The importance of hands-alone practice, p. 77	How to play a piece faster, p. 68

<u>*"Once the Piece Is Learned" Practice Strategies: (choose any)*</u>

"Follow the leader," p. 60 / CD 44	Shaping phrases p. 14 / CD 34 p. 52 / CD 42	Practicing with forward direction, p. 20 / CD 35	Finding places to relax for better facility, p. 44 / CD 40

Next: **Succeeding with the Masters®, Romantic Era, Volume Two**

Succeeding with the Masters®, Romantic Era, Volume Two

*Correlated with more difficult selections from **The Festival Collection**®, **Book 4***

Introducing the Romantic Era, Volume Two:

- *Discuss the Preface on p. 2-3.*
- *Review Schubert's biographical information on p. 8.*
- *Use the picture on p. 9 for further discussion of Schubert and the Romantic era.*
- *Review Schumann's biographical information on p. 23.*
- *Review Tchaikovsky's biographical information on p. 56*
- *Listen to the pieces in this unit on the CD's.*

Succeeding with the Masters®, Repertoire:

Composer	Characteristic	Practice Strategy from SWTM
Schubert Melancholy Waltz in A flat major, Op. 9, No. 2, p. 11 / CD 1	Use of traditional forms (binary), p. 10	Voicing the melody, p. 10 / CD 33
Schumann Little Romance, p. 26-27 / CD 9	Character piece, p. 24	*Cantabile* playing, p. 24 Improving muscle memory, p. 24 / CD 36 Unit, section, and performance practice, p. 24 / CD 36
Tchaikovsky Mazurka, p. 58-59 / CD 17	Expansion of the harmonic language, p. 57	Playing dotted rhythms, p. 57 / CD 43

*Supplement from these pieces in **The Festival Collection**®, **Book 4**. Refer to the "About the Pieces and Composers" sections for interesting and insightful information on each piece.*

Page	Era	Title
20-21	Baroque	Verso in E minor
22-24	Baroque	Intrada
44-45	Classical	Minuet in F major, K. 5
46-47	Classical	Capriccio
80-81	20th/21st Cent.	Two Roosters

Suggested Teaching Order

Group 1: Minuet in F major, K. 5
FC, p. 44-45 / CD 19
Little Romance
SWTM, p. 26-27 / CD 9
Intrada
FC, p. 22-24 / CD 9
Two Roosters
FC, p. 80-81 / CD 37

Group 2: Capriccio
FC, p. 46-47 / CD 20
Mazurka
SWTM, p. 58-59 / CD 17
Verso in E minor
FC, p. 20-21 / CD 8
Melancholy Waltz in A flat major, Op. 9, No. 2
SWTM, p. 11 / CD 1

FJH2050

Incorporate these concepts from **Succeeding with the Masters®, Baroque Era, Volume Two:**

<u>Title</u>	<u>Characteristic</u>	<u>Practice Strategy from SWTM</u>
FC - Verso in E minor, p. 20-21	Polyphonic texture, p. 45 Compelling energy, p. 22 and p. 54	"Smart" fingering, p. 13 / CD 26
FC - Intrada, p. 22-24	Recurring rhythmic or melodic patterns, p. 22 Popular dance forms: Rounded binary p. 47	Slow vs. fast practicing (3x1 rule), p. 76 / CD 43

<u>**"Once the Piece Is Learned" Practice Strategies:**</u> *(choose any)*

Learning to "Follow the leader," p. 45 / CD 35	Practicing back to front, p. 22 / CD 29	"Inner listening," p. 54 / CD 38

Incorporate these concepts from **Succeeding with the Masters®, Classical Era, Volume Two:**

<u>Title</u>	<u>Characteristic</u>	<u>Practice Strategy from SWTM</u>
FC - Minuet in F major, K. 5 p. 44-45 / CD 19	Binary form, p. 60 Many dynamic changes, p. 42 Varied rhythmic motives, p. 60	_____
FC - Capriccio, p. 46-47 / CD 20	Contrast of mood, p. 28 and 74	Playing sixteenth notes evenly, p. 83 / CD 43

<u>**"Learning the Piece" Practice Strategies:**</u> *(choose any)*

Improving muscle memory, p. 47 / CD 34	"Smart" fingering, p. 70 / CD 40

<u>**"Once the Piece Is Learned" Practice Strategies:**</u> *(choose any)*

Communicating a piece to an audience, p. 44	Practicing in different rhythms, p. 71

Next: **Succeeding with the Masters®, Classical Era, Volume Two**

Succeeding with the Masters®, Classical Era, Volume Two

Correlated with more difficult selections from **The Festival Collection®, Book 4**

Introducing the Classical Era, Volume Two:

- *Discuss the Preface on p. 2-3.*
- *Review Haydn's biographical information on p. 7.*
- *Review Mozart's biographical information on p. 40-41.*
- *Listen to the pieces in this unit on the CD's.*

Succeeding with the Masters®, Repertoire:

Composer	Characteristic	Practice Strategy from SWTM
Haydn Minuet in D major, p. 10-11 / CD 1	The form of a minuet and trio, p. 8	Practicing ornaments, p. 8 / CD 24 Balancing the melody with the accompaniment, p. 9 / CD 24
Mozart Klavierstück in F, p. 43 / CD 9	Homophonic texture, p. 42 Many dynamic changes, p. 42 Straightforward, simply harmonies, p. 42	Creating a dance-like accompaniment pattern, p. 42 / CD 32

Supplement from these pieces in **The Festival Collection®, Book 4.** *Refer to the "About the Pieces and Composers" sections for interesting and insightful information on each piece.*

Page	Era	Title
18-19	Baroque	Bourrée in A minor
25	Baroque	Dedicated Most Humbly to the Right-Hand Little Finger
51-53	Romantic	Boys Round Dance, Op. 36, No. 3B
66-67	Romantic	Miniature Waltz, Op. 10, No. 10
70-71	Romantic	Mazurka
88	20th/21st Cent.	Oriental Flower

<u>Suggested Teaching Order</u>

Group 1: Minuet in D major
   SWTM, p. 10-11 / CD 1
   Miniature Waltz, Op. 10, No. 10
      FC, p. 66-67 / CD 28
   Dedicated Most Humbly to the Right-Hand
   Little Finger
      FC, p. 25 / CD 10

Group 2: Mazurka
      FC, p. 70-71 / CD 30
   Bourrée in A minor
      FC, p. 18-19 / CD 7
   Boys Round Dance, Op. 36, No. 3B
      FC, p. 51-53 / CD 22

Group 3: Klavierstück in F
   SWTM, p. 43 / CD 9
   Oriental Flower
      FC, p. 88 / CD 41

Incorporate these concepts from **Succeeding with the Masters®, Baroque Era, Volume Two:**

Title	Characteristic	Practice Strategy from SWTM
FC - Bourrée in A minor, p. 18-19 / CD 7	Popular dances, Melodies made up of short phrase fragments of irregular lengths, p. 86	"Unit" practicing, p. 80 / CD 44
FC - Dedicated Most Humbly to the Right-Hand Little Finger, p. 25 / CD 10	Compelling energy, p. 22 and 54 Single mood or affect, p. 30 and 86	"Smart" fingering, p. 13 / CD 26

"Once the Piece Is Learned" Practice Strategies: (choose any)

Learning to "Follow the leader," p. 45 / CD 35	Practicing back to front, p. 22 / CD 29	"Inner listening," p. 54 / CD 38

Incorporate these concepts from **Succeeding with the Masters®, Romantic Era, Volume Two:**

Title	Characteristic	Practice Strategy from SWTM
FC - Boys Round Dance, Op. 36, No. 3B, p. 51-53 / CD 22	Drama as an important Romantic element	Contrast in music to create drama, p. 34 / CD 38 Strong sense of rhythm defining a piece, p. 41 / CD 39
FC - Miniature Waltz, Op. 10, No. 10, p. 66-67 / CD 28	Phrases of varying length, p. 77 Use of *rubato*, p. 29	Applying *rubato*, p. 29 Applying *rubato*, p. 77 / CD 48
FC - Mazurka, p. 70-71 / CD 30	The mazurka, p. 90	Applying *rubato*, p. 29 Applying *rubato*, p. 77 / CD 48

"Learning the Piece" Practice Strategies: (choose any)

Improving muscle memory, p. 24 / CD 36	Unit, section and performance practice, p. 24-25 / CD 36	The importance of hands-alone practice, p. 77	How to play a piece faster, p. 68

"Once the Piece Is Learned" Practice Strategies: (choose any)

"Follow the leader," p. 60 / CD 44	Shaping phrases p. 14 / CD 34 p. 52 / CD 42	Practicing with forward direction, p. 20 / CD 35	Finding places to relax for better facility, p. 44 / CD 40

Next: **Succeeding with the Masters®, Romantic Era, Volume Two**

Succeeding with the Masters®, Romantic Era, Volume Two

*Correlated with more difficult selections from **The Festival Collection**®, **Book 4***

- *Listen to the pieces in this unit on the CD's.*

Succeeding with the Masters®, Repertoire:

Composer	Characteristic	Practice Strategy from SWTM
Schubert		
Waltz in A flat major, Op. 9, No. 3, p. 12 / CD 2	Use of traditional forms (binary), p. 10	Voicing the melody, p. 10 / CD 33
Waltz in A flat major, Op. 9, No. 6, p. 13 / CD 3	Use of traditional forms (binary), p. 10	Voicing the melody, p. 10 / CD 33
Tchaikovsky		
Neapolitan Song, p. 61-63 / CD 18	An example of exoticism, p. 60	Playing rapid *staccato* notes in the left hand, p. 60 "Follow the leader," p. 60 / CD 44

*Supplement from these pieces in **The Festival Collection**®, **Book 4**. Refer to the "About the Pieces and Composers" sections for interesting and insightful information on each piece.*

Page	Era	Title	Suggested Teaching Order (both books)
12-15	Baroque	Ciaccona with Five Variations	**Group 1:** Ciaccona with Five Variations FC, p. 12-15 / CD 5
34-35	Classical	Angloise in D major	Angloise in D major FC, p. 34-35 / CD 14
48-50	Classical	Sonatina in G major, Op, 55, No. 2 (1st Mvt.)	Daydreaming FC, p. 82-83 / CD 38
82-83	20th/21st Cent.	Daydreaming	**Group 2:** Sonatina in G major, Op. 55, No. 2 (1st Mvt.) FC, p. 48-50 / CD 21
			Neapolitan Song SWTM, p. 61-63 / CD 18
			Waltz in A flat major, Op. 9 , No. 3 SWTM, p. 12 / CD 2
			Waltz in A flat major, Op. 9, No. 6 SWTM, p. 13 / CD 3

Incorporate these concepts from **Succeeding with the Masters®, Baroque Era, Volume Two:**

<u>Title</u>	<u>Characteristic</u>	<u>Practice Strategy from SWTM</u>
FC - Ciaccona with Five Variations, p. 12-15 / CD 15	Recurring rhythmic or melodic patterns, p. 22	"Unit" practicing, p. 80 / CD 44

"Once the Piece Is Learned" Practice Strategies: (choose any)

Learning to "Follow the leader," p. 45 / CD 35	Practicing back to front, p. 22 / CD 29	"Inner listening," p. 54 / CD 38

Incorporate these concepts from **Succeeding with the Masters®, Classical Era, Volume Two:**

<u>Title</u>	<u>Characteristic</u>	<u>Practice Strategy from SWTM</u>
FC - Angloise in D major, p. 34-35 / CD 14	Well-balanced and symmetrical phrases, p. 12 Straightforward, simple harmonies, p. 82	Practicing ornaments, p. 20 / CD 27
FC - Sonatina in G major, Op. 55, No. 2 (1st Mvt.), p. 48-50 / CD 21	Sonata form, p. 32 Homophonic texture, p. 70	Balancing the melody with the accompaniment, p. 9 Practicing *Alberti* basses, p. 66 / CD 39 Tonic and dominant chords, p. 17 / CD 26

"Learning the Piece" Practice Strategies: (choose any)

Improving muscle memory, p. 47 / CD 34	"Smart" fingering, p. 70 / CD 40

"Once the Piece Is Learned" Practice Strategies: (choose any)

Communicating a piece to an audience, p. 44	Practicing in different rhythms, p. 71	"Regrouping," p. 75 / CD 41

Next: **Succeeding with the Masters®, Classical Era, Volume Two**

Succeeding with the Masters®, Classical Era, Volume Two

*Correlated with **The Festival Collection®, Book 5***

Reviewing the Classical Era, Volume Two:

- Review Beethoven's biographical information on p. 64-65.
- Use the pictures on p. 65 and p. 67 for further discussion of Beethoven and the Classical era.
- Listen to the pieces in this unit on the CD's.

Succeeding with the Masters®, Repertoire:

Composer	Characteristic	Practice Strategy from SWTM
Haydn Minuet in B flat major, p. 14-15 / CD 2	Well-balanced, symmetrical phrases, p. 12	"Blocking," p. 12 Practicing forwards as well as backwards, p. 13 / CD 25
Mozart Andante in F, p. 45-46 / CD 10	_____	Communicating a piece to an audience, p. 44 "Finger pedaling," p. 44 / CD 33
Beethoven German Dance in E flat major, p. 68-69 / CD 16	Minuet and trio form, p. 66 Well-balanced, symmetrical phrases, p. 66 Use of *sf*, p. 66	Practicing *Alberti* basses, p. 66 / CD 39

*Supplement from these pieces in **The Festival Collection®, Book 5**. Refer to the "About the Pieces and Composers" sections for interesting and insightful information on each piece.*

Page	Era	Title
12-13	Baroque	The Prince of Denmark's March
14-15	Baroque	Marche
58-59	Romantic	The Avalanche, Op. 45, No. 2
94-96	20th/21st Cent.	Toccatina No. 1

Suggested Teaching Order (both books)

Group 1: Minuet in B flat major
     SWTM, p. 14-15 / CD 2
Andante in F
     SWTM, p. 45-46 / CD 10
Toccatina No. 1
     FC, p. 94-96 / CD 35

Group 2: The Prince of Denmark's March
     FC, p. 12-13 / CD 3
German Dance in E flat major
     SWTM, p. 68-69 / CD 16
Marche
     FC, p. 14-15 / CD 4
The Avalanche, Op. 45, No. 2
     FC, p. 58-59 / CD 20

FJH2050

Incorporate these concepts from **Succeeding with the Masters®, Baroque Era, Volume Two:**

Title	Characteristic	Practice Strategy from SWTM
FC - The Prince of Denmark's March, p. 12-13 / CD 3	Recurring rhythmic or melodic patterns, p. 47 Single mood or affect, p. 30 and 86	"Finger *legato*," p. 20 / CD 28
FC - Marche, p. 14-15 / CD 4	Compelling energy, p. 22 and 54 Popular forms: Binary form, p. 80	Slow vs. fast practicing (3x1), CD 43

"Once the Piece Is Learned" Practice Strategies: (choose any)

Learning to "Follow the leader," p. 45 / CD 35	Practicing back to front, p. 22 / CD 29	"Inner listening," p. 54 / CD 38

Incorporate these concepts from **Succeeding with the Masters®, Romantic Era, Volume Two:**

Title	Characteristic	Practice Strategy from SWTM
FC - The Avalanche, Op. 45, No. 2, p. 58-59 / CD 20	Character piece, p. 24	_____

"Learning the Piece" Practice Strategies: (choose any)

Improving muscle memory, p. 24 / CD 36	Unit, section, and performance practice, p. 24-25 / CD 36	The importance of hands-alone practice, p. 77	How to play a piece faster, p. 68

"Once the Piece Is Learned" Practice Strategies: (choose any)

"Follow the leader," p. 60 / CD 44	Shaping phrases, p. 14 / CD 34 p. 52 / CD 42	Practicing with forward direction, p. 20 / CD 35	Finding places to relax for better facility, p. 44 / CD 40

Next: **Succeeding with the Masters®, Baroque Era, Volume Two**

Succeeding with the Masters®, Baroque Era, Volume Two

Correlated with **The Festival Collection®, Book 5**

Reviewing the Baroque Era, Volume Two:

- *Use the picture on p. 81 for further discussion of Scarlatti and the Baroque era.*
- *Listen to the pieces in this unit on the CD's.*

Succeeding with the Masters®, Repertoire:

Composer	Characteristic	Practice Strategy from SWTM
Bach		
Prelude in C major, p. 18-19 / CD 2	Perpetual motion, p. 16 Pedal point, p. 16	"Blocking," p. 16 / CD 27
Handel		
Minuet in G minor, p. 48-49 / CD 11	Rounded binary form, p. 47 Recurring rhythmic and melodic patterns, p. 47	Finger independence, p. 47 / CD 36
Scarlatti		
Minuet in A major, p. 82-83 / CD 19	Binary form, p. 80	"Unit" practicing, p. 80 / CD 44

Supplement from these pieces in **The Festival Collection®, Book 5.** *Refer to the "About the Pieces and Composers" sections for interesting and insightful information on each piece.*

Page	Era	Title
30-33	Classical	Allegro, Op. 52, No. 2
38-40	Classical	Sonata in G major, Hob. XVI:8 (1st Mvt.)
55-57	Romantic	Pantalon
66-67	Romantic	Waltz, Op. 12, No. 2
86-87	20th/21st Cent.	Russian Dance

Suggested Teaching Order (both books)

Group 1: Russian Dance
    FC, p. 86-87 / CD 31
  Prelude in C major
    SWTM, p. 18-19 / CD 2
  Allegro, Op. 52, No. 2
    FC, p. 30-33 / CD 11
  Pantalon
    FC, p. 55-57 / CD 19

Group 2: Minuet in A major
    SWTM, p. 82-83 / CD 19
  Sonata in G major, Hob. XVI:8 (1st Mvt.)
    FC, p. 38-40 / CD 13
  Minuet in G minor
    SWTM, p. 48-49 / CD 11
  Waltz, Op. 12, No. 2
    FC, p. 66-67 / CD 23

Incorporate these concepts from **Succeeding with the Masters®, Classical Era, Volume Two:**

<u>Title</u>	<u>Characteristic</u>	<u>Practice Strategy from SWTM</u>
FC - Allegro, Op. 52, No. 2, p. 30-33 / CD 11	Varied rhythmic motives	Playing sixteenth notes evenly, p. 83 / CD 43
FC - Sonata in G major, Hob. XVI:8 (1st Mvt.), p. 38-40 / CD 13	Sonata form, p. 32 Varied rhythmic motives	Practicing ornaments, p. 20 / CD 27

<u>"Learning the Piece" Practice Strategies: (choose any)</u>

Improving muscle memory, p. 47 / CD 34	"Smart" fingering, p. 70 / CD 40	Creating clear passagework, p. 52 / CD 36

<u>"Once the Piece Is Learned" Practice Strategies: (choose any)</u>

Communicating a piece to an audience, p. 44	Practicing in different rhythms, p. 71	"Regrouping," p. 75 / CD 41

Incorporate these concepts from **Succeeding with the Masters®, Romantic Era, Volume Two:**

<u>Title</u>	<u>Characteristic</u>	<u>Practice Strategy from SWTM</u>
FC - Pantalon, p. 55-57 / CD 19	Character piece, p. 24	Playing with a supple wrist, p. 68 / CD 46
FC - Waltz, Op. 12, No. 2, p. 66-67 / CD 23	Use of traditional forms, p. 10 Phrases of varying length, p. 77	Contrast in music to create drama, p. 34 / CD 38

<u>"Learning the Piece" Practice Strategies: (choose any)</u>

Improving muscle memory, p. 24 / CD 36	Unit, section, and performance practice, p. 24-25 / CD 36	The importance of hands-alone practice, p. 77	How to play a piece faster, p. 68

<u>"Once the Piece Is Learned" Practice Strategies: (choose any)</u>

"Follow the leader," p. 60 / CD 44	Shaping phrases, p. 14 / CD 34 p. 52 / CD 42	Practicing with forward direction, p. 20 / CD 35	Finding places to relax for better facility, p. 44 / CD 40

Next: **Succeeding with the Masters®, Classical Era and Romantic Era, Volume Two**

Succeeding with the Masters®, Classical Era, Volume Two and Succeeding with the Masters®, Romantic Era, Volume Two

*Correlated with **The Festival Collection®, Book 5***

Reviewing the Classical Era, Volume Two:

- *Review "More About Haydn" on p. 16.*
- *Use the picture on p. 16 for further discussion of Haydn and the Classical era.*
- *Use the picture on p. 73 for further discussion of Beethoven and the Classical era.*
- *Listen to the pieces in this unit on the CD's.*

Succeeding with the Masters®, Classical Repertoire:

Composer	Characteristic	Practice Strategy from SWTM
Haydn Gypsy Dance in C major, p. 18-19 / CD 3	Tonic and dominant chords, p. 17	Tonic and dominant chords, p. 17 / CD 26
Mozart Minuet in F, p. 49 / CD 11	_____	Improving muscle memory, p. 47 / CD 34 "Impulse" practicing, p. 47-48 / CD 34
Beethoven Bagatelle in A minor, p. 72 / CD 17	Homophonic texture, p. 70	"Smart" fingering, p. 70 / CD 40 Practicing in different rhythms, p. 71

Succeeding with the Masters®, Romantic Repertoire:

Composer	Characteristic	Practice Strategy from SWTM
Schubert Ländler in A minor, p. 15 / CD 4	Use of longer romantic phrases, p. 14	Shaping phrases, p. 14 / CD 34
Schumann Mignon, p. 30-31 / CD 10	Melody and accompaniment in the same hand, p. 28 Use of *rubato*, p. 28	Keeping a continuous flow, p. 28 Unit, section, and performance practice, p. 28 Applying *rubato*, p. 29 / CD 37
Little Cradle Song, p. 32-33 / CD 11	Melody and accompaniment in the same hand, p. 28 Use of *rubato*, p. 28	Keeping a continuous flow, p. 28 Unit, section, and performance practice, p. 28 Applying *rubato*, p. 29 / CD 37

Supplement from these pieces in **The Festival Collection®, Book 5.** *Refer to the "About the Pieces and Composers" sections for interesting and insightful information on each piece.*

Page	Era	Title
16-17	Baroque	Hornpipe
80-81	20th/21st Cent.	The Banjo Player

<u>Suggested Teaching Order (both books)</u>

Group 1: Gypsy Dance in C major
     SWTM Classical, p. 18-19 / CD 3
Mignon
     SWTM Romantic, p. 30-31 / CD 10
Ländler in A minor
     SWTM Romantic, p. 15 / CD 4
The Banjo Player
     FC, p. 80-81 / CD 29

Group 2: Minuet in F
     SWTM Classical, p. 49 / CD 11
Hornpipe
     FC, p. 16-17 / CD 5
Little Cradle Song
     SWTM Romantic, p. 32-33 / CD 11
Bagatelle in A minor
     SWTM Classical, p. 72 / CD 17

Incorporate these concepts from **Succeeding with the Masters®, Baroque Era, Volume Two:**

<u>Title</u>	<u>Characteristic</u>	<u>Practice Strategy from SWTM</u>
FC - Hornpipe, p. 16-17	Recurring rhythmic or melodic patterns, p. 22 Melodies made up of short phrase fragments of irregular lengths, p. 86	"Smart" fingering, p. 13 / CD 26

"Once the Piece Is Learned" Practice Strategies: (choose any)

Learning to "Follow the leader," p. 45 / CD 35	Practicing back to front, p. 22 / CD 29	"Inner listening," p. 54 / CD 38

Next: **Succeeding with the Masters®, Baroque Era and Romantic Era, Volume Two**

Succeeding with the Masters®, Baroque Era, Volume Two and Succeeding with the Masters®, Romantic Era, Volume Two

Correlated with **The Festival Collection®, Book 5**

- *Listen to the pieces in this unit on the CD's.*

Succeeding with the Masters®, Baroque Repertoire:

Composer	Characteristic	Practice Strategy from SWTM
Bach Minuet in G minor, p. 21 / CD 3	One recurring rhythmic pattern, p. 20 Polyphonic texture, p. 20	"Finger *legato*," p. 20 / CD 28
Handel Sarabande, p. 51-53 / CD 12	Popular dances, p. 50	Understanding variations, p. 50 / CD 37
Scarlatti Sonata in D minor, p. 85 / CD 20	What the musical score looked like, p. 84	Bringing a piece to life, p. 84 / CD 45

Succeeding with the Masters®, Romantic Repertoire:

Composer	Characteristic	Practice Strategy from SWTM
Schubert Valse sentimentale in A major, p. 16-17 / CD 5	Use of longer romantic phrases, p. 14	Shaping phrases, p. 14 / CD 34
Tchaikovsky Sweet Dream, p. 65-67 / CD 19	Use of traditional forms, p. 64 Emotion as an important aspect of the era, p. 64	Balancing melody with accompaniment, p. 64 / CD 45

Supplement from these pieces in **The Festival Collection®, Book 5.** *Refer to the "About the Pieces and Composers" sections for interesting and insightful information on each piece.*

Page	Era	Title
24-26	Classical	Sonatina in G major, Op. 20, No. 1 (1st Mvt.)
41-45	Classical	Sonatina in C major, Op. 36, No. 3 (1st Mvt.)
45	Classical	Sonatina in C major, Op. 36, No. 3 (2nd Mvt.)
92-93	20th/21st Cent.	Moonlit Meadows, Op. 65, No. 12

Suggested Teaching Order (both books)

Group 1: Sonatina in G major, Op. 20, No. 1 (1st Mvt.)
FC, p. 24-26 / CD 9
Sarabande
SWTM Baroque, p. 51-53 / CD 12
Moonlit Meadows, Op. 65, No. 12
FC, p. 92-93 / CD 34

Group 2: Minuet in G minor
SWTM Baroque, p. 21 / CD 3
Sonata in D minor
SWTM Baroque, p. 85 / CD 20
Sweet Dream
SWTM Romantic, p. 65-67 / CD 19

Group 3: Sonatina in C major, Op. 36, No. 3 (1st Mvt.)
FC, p. 41-45 / CD 14
Sonatina in C major, Op. 36, No. 3 (2nd Mvt.)
FC, p. 45 / CD 15
Valse sentimentale in A major
SWTM Romantic, p. 16-17 / CD 5

FJH2050

Incorporate these concepts from **Succeeding with the Masters®, Classical Era, Volume Two:**

Title	Characteristic	Practice Strategy from SWTM
FC - Sonatina in G major, Op. 20, No. 1 (1st Mvt.) p. 24-26 / CD 9	Homophonic texture, p. 70￼ Many dynamic changes	Voicing the melody, p. 28-29 / CD 29￼ Balancing melody with the accompaniment, p. 9￼ Using the *una corda* pedal, p. 87 / CD 44
FC - Sonatina in C major, Op. 36, No. 3 (1st Mvt.) p. 41-45 / CD 14	Sonata form, p. 32	
FC - Sonatina in C major, Op. 36, No. 3 (2nd Mvt.) P. 45 / CD 15	Binary form￼ Melodies that are elegant, graceful, and easy to sing, p. 36	"Finger pedaling," p. 44 / CD 33￼ Incorporating the pedal, p. 57 / CD 37￼ Creating long phrases, p. 57

"Learning the Piece" Practice Strategies: (choose any)

Improving muscle memory, p. 47 / CD 34	"Smart" fingering, p. 70 / CD 40	Creating clear passagework, p. 52 / CD 36

"Once the Piece Is Learned" Practice Strategies: (choose any)

Communicating a piece to an audience, p. 44	Practicing in different rhythms, p. 71
"Regrouping," p. 75 / CD 41	Bringing the piece to life, p. 25

Next: **Succeeding with the Masters®, Baroque Era and Classical Era, Volume Two**

Succeeding with the Masters®, Baroque Era, Volume Two and Succeeding with the Masters®, Classical Era, Volume Two

*Correlated with **The Festival Collection®, Book 5***

Reviewing the Baroque Era, Volume Two:

- *Use the musical score on p. 23 for further discussion of Bach and the Baroque era.*
- *Use the pictures on p. 55 and 59 for further discussion of Handel and the Baroque era.*

Reviewing the Classical Era, Volume Two:

- *Use the pictures on p. 21 for further discussion of Haydn and the Classical era.*
- *Listen to the pieces in this unit on the CD's.*

Succeeding with the Masters®, Baroque Repertoire:

Composer	Characteristic	Practice Strategy from SWTM
Bach Prelude in F major, p. 24-25 / CD 4	Compelling energy, p. 22 Recurring rhythmic and melodic patterns, p. 22 What the musical score looked like, p. 23	Practicing back to front, p. 22 / CD 29
Handel Sonatina, p. 56-57 / CD 13	Enduring energy, p. 54	"Inner listening," p. 54 / CD 38
Prelude in F major, p. 60-61 / CD 14	Single mood, p. 58 Recurring rhythmic or melodic patterns, p. 58	"Unit" practicing, p. 58 / CD 39

Succeeding with the Masters®, Classical Repertoire:

Composer	Characteristic	Practice Strategy from SWTM
Haydn Minuet in D major, p. 22-23 / CD 4	Melodies that are elegant, graceful, and easy, to sing, p. 20 Melodies that move to predictable cadences, p. 20	Practicing ornaments, p. 20 / CD 27
Beethoven Allemande in A, p. 76-77 / CD 18	Contrast of mood, p. 74	Practicing arpeggios, p. 74 Regrouping, p. 75 / CD 41

FJH2050

Supplement from these pieces in **The Festival Collection**®, **Book 5.** Refer to the "About the Pieces and Composers" sections for interesting and insightful information on each piece.

Page	Era	Title
52-54	Romantic	L'adieu, Op. 100, No. 12
68-69	Romantic	Elves' Dance, Op. 12, No. 4
90-91	20th/21st Cent.	Caravan

<u>Suggested Teaching Order (both books)</u>

Group 1: Minuet in D major
SWTM Classical, p. 22-23 / CD 4
Sonatina
SWTM Baroque, p. 56-57 / CD 13
Caravan
FC, p. 90-91 / CD 33
Elves' Dance, Op. 12, No. 4
FC, p. 68-69 / CD 24

Group 2: Prelude in F major (Handel)
SWTM Baroque, p. 60-61 / CD 14
L'adieu, Op. 100, No. 12
FC, p. 52-54 / CD 18
Allemande in A
SWTM Classical, p. 76-77 / CD 18
Prelude in F major (Bach)
SWTM Baroque, p. 24-25 / CD 4

Incorporate these concepts from **Succeeding with the Masters**®, **Romantic Era, Volume Two:**

Title	Characteristic	Practice Strategy from SWTM
FC - L'adieu, Op. 100, No. 12, p. 52-54 / CD 18	Use of traditional forms Drama as an important romantic element	Contrast in music to create drama, p. 34 / CD 38
FC - Elves' Dance, Op. 12, No. 4, p. 68-69 / CD 24	Programmatic piece, p. 41	_____

"Learning the Piece" Practice Strategies: (choose any)

Improving muscle memory, p. 24 / CD 36	Unit, section and performance practice, p. 24-25 / CD 36	The importance of hands-alone practice, p. 77	How to play a piece faster, p. 68

"Once the Piece Is Learned" Practice Strategies: (choose any)

"Follow the leader," p. 60 / CD 44	Shaping phrases, p. 14 / CD 34 p. 52 / CD 42	Practicing with forward direction, p. 20 / CD 35
Finding places to relax for better facility, p. 44 / CD 40	Keen listening, p. 48 / CD 41	The importance of a singing *legato*, p. 86-87 / CD 50

Next: **Succeeding with the Masters**®, **Baroque Era, Volume Two**

Succeeding with the Masters®, Baroque Era, Volume Two

*Correlated with **The Festival Collection®, Book 5***

Reviewing the Baroque Era, Volume Two:

- *Use the picture on p. 62 for further discussion of Handel and the Baroque era.*
- *Listen to the pieces in this unit on the CD's.*

Succeeding with the Masters®, Baroque Repertoire:

Composer	Characteristic	Practice Strategy from SWTM
Bach		
Prelude in C minor, p. 27-29 / CD 5	Perpetual motion without predictable cadences, p. 26	Attention to articulations, p. 26 Making every note count, p. 26 / CD 30
Handel		
Prelude in C minor, p. 63 / CD 15	Music that is highly decorative and grand, p. 62	Focus on interpretation, p. 62 / CD 40

*Supplement from these pieces in **The Festival Collection®, Book 5**. Refer to the "About the Pieces and Composers" sections for interesting and insightful information on each piece.*

Page	Era	Title
27-29	Classical	Sonatina in F major, Op. 168, No. 1 (3rd Mvt.)
46-48	Classical	Arietta with Variations, Hob, XVII:2
60-63	Romantic	Minuet, Op. 23, No. 1
72-73	Romantic	Prelude in C minor, Op. 8, No. 1
88-89	20th/21st Cent.	Play: for Piano

Suggested Teaching Order (both books)

Group 1: Prelude in C minor (Handel)
SWTM, p. 63 / CD 15
Prelude in C minor, Op. 8, No. 1
FC, p. 72-73 / CD 26
Sonatina in F major, Op. 168, No. 1 (3rd Mvt.)
FC, p. 27-29 / CD 10
Play: for Piano
FC, p. 88-89 / CD 32

Group 2: Arietta with Variations, Hob, XVII:2
FC, p. 46-48 / CD 16
Minuet, Op. 23, No. 1
FC, p. 60-63 / CD 21
Prelude in C minor (Bach)
SWTM, p. 27-29 / CD 5

FJH2050

Incorporate these concepts from **Succeeding with the Masters®, Classical Era, Volume Two:**

Title	Characteristic	Practice Strategy from SWTM
FC - Sonatina in F major, Op. 168, No. 1, (3rd Mvt.), p. 27-29 / CD 10	Straightforward, simple harmonies, p. 42 Homophonic texture, p. 70	Balancing the melody with the accompaniment, p. 9
FC - Arietta with Variations, Hob. XVII:2, p. 46-48 / CD 16	Theme and Variations	

"Learning the Piece" Practice Strategies: (choose any)

Improving muscle memory, p. 47 / CD 34	"Smart" fingering, p. 70 / CD 40	Creating clear passagework, p. 52 / CD 36

"Once the Piece Is Learned" Practice Strategies: (choose any)

Communicating a piece to an audience, p. 44	Practicing in different rhythms, p. 71
"Regrouping," p. 75 / CD 41	Bringing the piece to life, p. 25

Incorporate these concepts from **Succeeding with the Masters®, Romantic Era, Volume Two:**

Title	Characteristic	Practice Strategy from SWTM
FC - Minuet, Op. 23, No. 1, p. 60-63 / CD 21	Use of longer phrases, p. 14 The romantic interest in emotional expression, p. 52	Voicing the melody, p. 10 / CD 33
FC - Prelude in C minor, Op. 8, No. 1, p. 72-73 / CD 26	Expansion of the harmonic language, Use of *rubato*, p. 29	Playing dotted rhythms, p. 57 / CD 43 Applying *rubato*, p. 29 Applying *rubato*, p. 77 / CD 48

"Learning the Piece" Practice Strategies: (choose any)

Improving muscle memory, p. 24 / CD 36	Unit, section, and performance practice, p. 24-25 / CD 36	The importance of hands-alone practice, p. 77	How to play a piece faster, p. 68

"Once the Piece Is Learned" Practice Strategies: (choose any)

"Follow the leader," p. 60 / CD 44	Shaping phrases, p. 14 / CD 34 p. 52 / CD 42	Practicing with forward direction, p. 20 / CD 35
Finding places to relax for better facility, p. 44 / CD 40	Keep listening, p. 48 / CD 41	The importance of a singing *legato*, p. 86-87 / CD 50

Next: **Succeeding with the Masters®, Classical Era and Romantic Era, Volume Two**

Succeeding with the Masters®, Classical Era, Volume Two and Succeeding with the Masters®, Romantic Era, Volume Two

Correlated with *The Festival Collection*®, *Book 5*

Reviewing the Classical Era, Volume Two:

• *Use the pictures on p. 25 for further discussion of Haydn and the Classical era.*

Reviewing the Romantic Era, Volume Two:

• *Discuss Chopin's biographical information on p. 76.*

• *Listen to the pieces in this unit on the CD's.*

Succeeding with the Masters®, Classical Repertoire:

Composer	Characteristic	Practice Strategy from SWTM
Haydn Minuet in C major, p. 26-27 / CD 5	_____	Playing "2 against 3," p. 24 Bringing a piece to life after it is learned, p. 25 / CD 28
Mozart Little Funeral March, p. 51 / CD 12	Use of varied rhythms, p. 50	Bringing the piece to life musically, p. 50 / CD 35

Succeeding with the Masters®, Romantic Repertoire:

Composer	Characteristic	Practice Strategy from SWTM
Schubert Valse noble in A minor, p. 18-19 / CD 6	Use of longer romantic phrases, p. 14	Shaping phrases, p. 14 / CD 34
Chopin Sostenuto in E flat major, p. 78-79 / CD 22	Phrases of varying length, p. 77	Applying *rubato*, p. 77 / CD 48 The importance of hands-alone practice, p. 77 / CD 48

Supplement from these pieces in **The Festival Collection**®, **Book 5**. *Refer to the "About the Pieces and Composers" sections for interesting and insightful information on each piece.*

Page	Era	Title
18-19	Baroque	Passepied
22-23	Baroque	Bourrée in G minor
74-76	20th/21st Cent.	Evening at the Village

<u>Suggested Teaching Order (both books)</u>

Group 1: Passepied
    FC, p. 18-19 / CD 6
Evening at the Village
    FC, p. 74-76 / CD 27
Valse noble in A minor
    SWTM Romantic, p. 18-19 / CD 6

Group 2: Minuet in C major
    SWTM Classical, p. 26-27 / CD 5
Little Funeral March
    SWTM Classical, p. 51 / CD 12
Bourrée in G minor
    FC, p. 22-23 / CD 8
Sostenuto in E flat major
    SWTM Romantic, p. 78-79 / CD 22

Incorporate these concepts from **Succeeding with the Masters®, Baroque Era, Volume Two:**

<u>Title</u>	<u>Characteristic</u>	<u>Practice Strategy from SWTM</u>
FC - Passepied, p. 18-19 / CD 6	Polyphonic texture, p. 45 Compelling energy, p. 22, 54	"Unit" practicing, p. 58 / CD 39, p. 80 / CD 44
FC - Bourrée in G minor, p. 22-23 / CD 8	Popular dances	Establishing an "inner pulse," p. 38 / CD 33 Finger independence, p. 47 / CD 36

<u>"Once the Piece Is Learned" Practice Strategies:</u> (choose any)

Learning to "Follow the leader," p. 45 / CD 35	Practicing back to front, p. 22 / CD 29	"Inner listening," p. 54 / CD 38	Practicing cadence points, p. 64 / CD 41	Shaping irregular phrases, p. 86-87 / CD 46

Next: **Succeeding with the Masters®, Classical Era and Romantic Era, Volume Two**

Succeeding with the Masters®, Classical Era, Volume Two and Succeeding with the Masters®, Romantic Era, Volume Two

*Correlated with **The Festival Collection®, Book 5***

Reviewing the Classical Era, Volume Two:

- *Use the pictures on p. 53 for further discussion of Mozart and the Classical era.*
- *Use the picture on p. 79 for further discussion of Beethoven and the Classical era.*
- *Listen to the pieces in this unit on the CD's.*

Succeeding with the Masters®, Classical Repertoire:

<u>Composer</u>	<u>Characteristic</u>	<u>Practice Strategy from SWTM</u>
Haydn Scherzo in F major, p. 30-31 / CD 6	Contrast of mood, p. 28	Voicing the melody, p. 28 / CD 29 Playing repeated notes quickly, p. 29 / CD 29
Mozart Moderato in F major, p. 54-55 / CD 13	_____	Creating clear passagework, p. 52 / CD 36 Articulating wedges and *staccatos*, p. 53 / CD36
Beethoven Waltz in E flat major, p. 80-81 / CD 19	The emergence of the waltz, p. 78	Practicing a waltz bass, p. 78 / CD 42 Practicing with the metronome, p. 78 Using imagery, p. 79 / CD 42

Succeeding with the Masters®, Romantic Repertoire:

<u>Composer</u>	<u>Characteristic</u>	<u>Practice Strategy from SWTM</u>
Schubert Ecossaise in D flat major, p. 21 / CD 7	_____	Practicing with forward direction, p. 20 / CD 35
German Dance in B flat major, p. 22 / CD 8	_____	Practicing with forward direction, p. 20 / CD 35
Chopin Prelude in A major, Op. 28, No. 7, p. 82 / CD 23	Emotion is a strong aspect of the music, p. 80	Conveying the mood and using the pedal, p. 80 / CD 49 Creating your own interpretation through listening, p. 81 / CD 49

FJH2050

Supplement from these pieces in **The Festival Collection®, Book 5.** Refer to the "About the Pieces and Composers" sections for interesting and insightful information on each piece.

Page	Era	Title
20-21	Baroque	Rigaudon
82-85	20th/21st Cent.	First Gymnopédie

<u>Suggested Teaching Order (both books)</u>

Group 1: Rigaudon
  FC, p. 20-21 / CD 7
Scherzo in F major
  SWTM Classical, p. 30-31 / CD 6
Ecossaise in D flat major
  SWTM Romantic, p. 21 / CD 7
First Gymnopédie
  FC, p. 82-85 / CD 30

Group 2: Moderato in F major
  SWTM Classical, p. 54-55 / CD 13
German Dance in B flat major
  SWTM Romantic, p. 22 / CD 8
Waltz in E flat major
  SWTM Classical, p. 80-81 / CD 19
Prelude in A major, Op. 28, No. 7
  SWTM Romantic, p. 82 / CD 23

Incorporate these concepts from **Succeeding with the Masters®, Baroque Era, Volume Two:**

<u>Title</u>	<u>Characteristic</u>	<u>Practice Strategy from SWTM</u>
FC - Rigaudon, p. 20-21 / CD 7	Polyphonic texture, p. 45	Slow vs. fast practicing (3x1 rule), p. 76 / CD 43

<u>**"Once the Piece Is Learned" Practice Strategies:** (choose any)</u>

Learning to "Follow the leader," p. 45 / CD 35	Practicing back to front, p. 22 / CD 29	"Inner listening," p. 54 / CD 38	Practicing cadence points, p. 64 / CD 41	Shaping irregular phrases, p. 86-87 / CD 46

Next: **Succeeding with the Masters®, Romantic Era, Volume Two**

Succeeding with the Masters®, Romantic Era, Volume Two

Correlated with *The Festival Collection*®, *Book 5*

- *Listen to the pieces in this unit on the CD's.*

Succeeding with the Masters®, *Romantic Repertoire:*

Composer	Characteristic	Practice Strategy from SWTM
Schumann St. Nicholas (Knecht Ruprecht), p. 36-39 / CD 12	Drama as an essential element, p. 34	Contrast in music to create drama, p. 34 / CD 38
Tchaikovsky The Lark's Song, p. 70-71 / CD 20	The importance of nature, p. 68	Playing with a supple wrist, p. 68 / CD 46 How to play a piece faster, p. 68 / CD 46

Supplement from these pieces in **The Festival Collection**®, **Book 5**. *Refer to the "About the Pieces and Composers" sections for interesting and insightful information on each piece.*

Page	Era	Title
6-8	Baroque	Bourrée in F major
9-11	Baroque	Aire
34-37	Classical	Sonatina in E flat major, Op. 37, No. 1 (1st Mvt.)
77-79	20th/21st Cent.	Le petit nègre

Suggested Teaching Order (both books)

Group 1: Bourrée in F major
    FC, p. 6-8 / CD 1
Le petit nègre
    FC, p. 77-79 / CD 28
St. Nicholas (Knecht Ruprecht)
    SWTM, p. 36-39 / CD 12

Group 2: Aire
    FC, p. 9-11 / CD 2
Sonatina in E flat major, Op. 37, No. 1 (1st Mvt.)
    FC, p. 34-37 / CD 12
The Lark's Song
    SWTM, p. 70-71 / CD 20

FJH2050

Incorporate these concepts from **Succeeding with the Masters®, Baroque Era, Volume Two:**

<u>Title</u>	<u>Characteristic</u>	<u>Practice Strategy from SWTM</u>
FC - Bourrée in F major, p. 6-8 / CD 1	Perpetual motion, p. 16, 26, and 69 Popular dances	"Blocking," p. 16-17 / CD 27
FC - Aire p. 9-11 / CD 2	Recurring rhythmic or melodic patterns, p. 22 Polyphonic texture, p. 45 Binary form, p. 80	Establishing an "inner pulse," p. 38 / CD 33

"Once the Piece Is Learned" Practice Strategies: (choose any)

Learning to "Follow the leader," p. 45 / CD 35	Practicing back to front, p. 22 / CD 29	"Inner listening," p. 54 / CD 38	Practicing cadence points, p. 64 / CD 41	Shaping irregular phrases, p. 86-87 / CD 46

Incorporate these concepts from **Succeeding with the Masters®, Classical Era, Volume Two:**

<u>Title</u>	<u>Characteristic</u>	<u>Practice Strategy from SWTM</u>
FC - Sonatina in E flat major, Op. 37, No. 1 (1st Mvt.), p. 34-37 / CD 12	Well-balanced and symmetrical phrases, p. 12	Practicing ornaments, p. 20 / CD 27 "Finger pedaling," p. 44 / CD 33 Incorporating the pedal, p. 57 / CD 37 Creating long phrases, p. 57

"Learning the Piece" Practice Strategies: (choose any)

Improving muscle memory, p. 47 / CD 34	"Smart" fingering, p. 70 / CD 40	Creating clear passagework, p. 52 / CD 36	Practicing with the metronome, p. 78-79

"Once the Piece Is Learned" Practice Strategies: (choose any)

Communicating a piece to an audience, p. 44	Practicing in different rhythms, p. 71	"Regrouping," p. 75 / CD 41
Bringing the piece to life, p. 25	Finding places to relax for better facility, p. 83	

Next: **Succeeding with the Masters®, Baroque Era and Classical Era, Volume Two**

Succeeding with the Masters®, Baroque Era, Volume Two and Succeeding with the Masters®, Classical Era, Volume Two

*Correlated with **The Festival Collection®, Book 5***

Reviewing the Baroque Era, Volume Two:

- *Use the pictures on p. 65 and 68 for further discussion of Handel and the Baroque era.*

Reviewing the Classical Era, Volume Two:

- *Discuss "The Pianoforte" on p. 56.*
- *Listen to the pieces in this unit on the CD's.*

Succeeding with the Masters®, Baroque Repertoire:

Composer	Characteristic	Practice Strategy from SWTM
Bach Prelude in E minor, p. 32-33 / CD 6	Single mood, p. 30	Improving muscle memory, p. 30 / CD 31
Handel Allemande, p. 66-67 / CD 16	_____	"8 times to perfection," p. 64 Practicing cadence points, p. 64 / CD 41 Playing contrapuntal pieces with success, p. 65
Scarlatti Sonata in E minor, p. 88-89 / CD 21	Single mood, p. 86 Melodies of short phrases fragments / irregular lengths, p. 86	Shaping irregular phrases, p. 87 / CD 46

Succeeding with the Masters®, Classical Repertoire:

Composer	Characteristic	Practice Strategy from SWTM
Mozart Adagio in C for Glass Harmonica, p. 58-59 / CD 14	_____	Creating long phrases, p. 57 Incorporating the pedal, p. 57 / CD 37
Beethoven Minuet in C major, p. 84-85 / CD 20	Straightforward harmonies, p. 82	Playing sixteenth notes evenly, p. 83 / CD 43 Finding places to relax for better facility, p. 83 / CD 43

FJH2050

Supplement from these pieces in The Festival Collection®, Book 5. *Refer to the "About the Pieces and Composers" sections for interesting and insightful information on each piece.*

Page	Era	Title
49-51	Romantic	Romance, Op. 31, No. 7
64-65	Romantic	Vals sentimental
70-71	Romantic	Improvisation, Op. 18

<u>Suggested Teaching Order (both books)</u>

Group 1: Allemande
SWTM Baroque, p. 66-67 / CD 16
Minuet in C major
SWTM Classical, p. 84-85 / CD 20
Adagio in C for Glass Harmonica
SWTM Classical, p. 58-59 / CD 14

Group 2: Prelude in E minor
SWTM Baroque, p. 32-33 / CD 6
Romance, Op. 31, No. 7
FC, p. 49-51 / CD 17

Group 3: Sonata in E minor
SWTM Baroque, p. 88-89 / CD 21
Improvisation, Op. 18
FC, p. 70-71 / CD 25
Vals sentimental
FC, p. 64-65 / CD 22

Incorporate these concepts from Succeeding with the Masters®, Romantic Era, Volume Two:

Title	Characteristic	Practice Strategy from SWTM
FC - Romance, Op. 31, No. 7, p. 49-51 / CD 17	The romantic interest in emotional expression, p. 52 Use of *rubato*, p. 29	Voicing the melody, p. 10 / CD 33 Applying *rubato*, p. 29 and p. 77 / CD 48
FC - Vals sentimental, p. 64-65 / CD 22	Use of longer phrases, p. 14 Trills as part of the melodic line, p. 90	Voicing the melody, p. 10 / CD 33 Applying *rubato*, p. 29 and p. 77 / CD 48 Trills as part of the melodic line, p. 90-91 / CD 51
FC - Improvisation, Op. 18, p. 70-71 / CD 25	Melody and accompaniment in the same hand, p. 28	Voicing the melody, p. 10 / CD 33 Applying *rubato*, p. 29 and p. 77 / CD 48

"Learning the Piece" Practice Strategies: (choose any)

Improving muscle memory, p. 24 / CD 36	Unit, section, and performance practice, p. 24-25 / CD 36	The importance of hands-alone practice, p. 77	How to play a piece faster, p. 68

"Once the Piece Is Learned" Practice Strategies: (choose any)

"Follow the leader," p. 60 / CD 44	Shaping phrases, p. 14 / CD 34 p. 52 / CD 42	Practicing with forward direction, p. 20 / CD 35
Finding places to relax for better facility, p. 44 / CD 40	Keen listening, p. 48 / CD 41	The importance of a singing *legato*, p. 86-87 / CD 50

Next: Succeeding with the Masters®, Classical Era, Volume Two

Succeeding with the Masters®, Classical Era, Volume Two

Correlated with *The Festival Collection®, Book 6*

- *Listen to the pieces in this unit on the CD's.*

Succeeding with the Masters®, Classical Repertoire:

Composer	Characteristic	Practice Strategy from SWTM
Haydn Andante in G minor, p. 33-35 / CD 7	Sonata form, p. 32	Brining the piece to life, p. 32 / CD 30
Mozart Presto in B flat major, p. 62-63 / CD 15	Dynamic changes, p. 60 Use of binary form, p. 60 Varied rhythmic motives, p. 60	"Blocking," p. 60 Shaping phrases, p. 61 / CD 38

Supplement from these pieces in **The Festival Collection®, Book 6.** *Refer to the "About the Pieces and Composers" sections for interesting and insightful information on each piece.*

Page	Era	Title
8-11	Baroque	Sonata in D minor, K. 89c, L. 211
18-19	Baroque	Toccata in G minor
68	Romantic	Prelude in E minor, Op. 28, No. 4
72-73	Romantic	Morning Bell, Op. 109, No. 9
82-83	Romantic	The Storm, Op. 109, No.13
90-93	20th/21st Cent.	Rondo Toccata, Op. 60, No. 4

Suggested Teaching Order (both books)

Group 1: Sonata in D minor, K. 89c, L. 211
FC, p. 8-11 / CD 2
The Storm, Op. 109, No. 13
FC, p. 82-83 / CD 31
Andante in G minor
SWTM, p. 33-35 / CD 7
Prelude in E minor, Op. 28, No. 4
FC, p. 68 / CD 23

Group 2: Presto in B flat major
SWTM, p. 62-64 / CD 15
Toccata in G minor
FC, p. 18-19 / CD 6
Morning Bell, Op. 109, No. 9
FC, p. 72-73 / CD 26
Rondo Toccata, Op. 60, No. 4
FC, p. 90-93 / CD 34

FJH2050

Incorporate these concepts from **Succeeding with the Masters®, Baroque Era, Volume Two:**

<u>Title</u>	<u>Characteristic</u>	<u>Practice Strategy from SWTM</u>
FC - Sonata in D minor, K. 89c, L. 211, p. 8-11 / CD 2	Perpetual motion, p. 16, 26, and 69 Compelling or enduring energy, p. 22 and 54	_____
FC - Toccata in G minor, p. 18-19 / CD 6	Perpetual motion, p. 16, 26, and 69 Compelling energy, p. 22 and 54 Piece created from broken chords and scale passages, p. 34	Detached-note practicing, p. 41 / CD 34 "Impulse" practicing, p. 41 / CD 34

"Learning the Piece" Practice Strategies: (choose any)

"Smart" fingering, p. 13 / CD 26	Slow vs. fast practicing (3x1 rule), p. 76 / CD 43	"Unit" practicing p. 58 / CD 39, p. 80 / CD 44	Improving muscle memory, p. 30 / CD 31	"8 times to perfection," p. 64

"Once the Piece Is Learned" Practice Strategies: (choose any)

Learning to "Follow the leader," p. 45 / CD 35	Practicing back to front, p. 22 / CD 29	"Inner listening," p. 54 / CD 38	Practicing cadence points, p. 64 / CD 41	Shaping irregular phrases, p. 86-87 / CD 46

Incorporate these concepts from **Succeeding with the Masters®, Romantic Era, Volume Two:**

<u>Title</u>	<u>Characteristic</u>	<u>Practice Strategy from SWTM</u>
FC - Prelude in E minor, Op. 28, No. 4, p. 68 / CD 23	The romantic interest in emotional expression, p. 52	Creating your own interpretation through listening, p. 81
FC - Morning Bell, Op. 109, No. 9, p. 72-73 / CD 26	Melody and accompaniment in the same hand, p. 28 Programmatic piece, p. 41	Voicing the melody, p. 10 / CD 33 Balancing melody with accompaniment, p. 64 / CD 45
FC - The Storm, Op. 109, No. 13, p. 82-83 / CD 31	Drama as an important Romantic element, p. 34 Programmatic piece, p. 41	Contrast in music to create drama, p. 34 / CD 38 Strong sense of rhythm defining a piece, p. 41 / CD 39

"Learning the Piece" Practice Strategies: (choose any)

Improving muscle memory, p. 24 / CD 36	Unit, section, and performance practice, p. 24-25 / CD 36	The importance of hands-alone practice, p. 77	How to play a piece faster, p. 68

"Once the Piece Is Learned" Practice Strategies: (choose any)

"Follow the leader," p. 60 / CD 44	Shaping phrases, p. 14 / CD 34 p. 52 / CD 42	Practicing with forward direction, p. 20 / CD 35
Finding places to relax for better facility, p. 44 / CD 40	Keen listening, p. 48 / CD 41	The importance of a singing *legato*, p. 86-87 / CD 50

Next: **Succeeding with the Masters®, Baroque Era and Romantic Era, Volume Two**

Succeeding with the Masters®, Baroque Era, Volume Two and Succeeding with the Masters®, Romantic Era, Volume Two

Correlated with **The Festival Collection®, Book 6**

- *Listen to the pieces in this unit on the CD's.*

Succeeding with the Masters®, Baroque Repertoire:

Composer	Characteristic	Practice Strategy from SWTM
Bach		
Prelude in D minor, p. 35-37 / CD 7	Use of broken chord and scale passages, p. 34	Playing in an improvisatory style, p. 34 / CD 32
Scarlatti		
Sonata in A major, p. 92-95 / CD 21	Binary form sonatas, p. 90	Complete rhythmic accuracy, p. 90 / CD 47 Learning to play faster, p. 91

Succeeding with the Masters®, Romantic Repertoire:

Composer	Characteristic	Practice Strategy from SWTM
Tchaikovsky		
Chanson Triste, p. 73-75 / CD 21	_____	Interpreting a phrase, p. 72 / CD 47 Voicing the melody, p. 72 / CD 47
Chopin		
Prelude in C minor, Op. 28, No. 20, p. 83 / CD 24	Emotion is a strong aspect of the music, p. 80	Conveying the mood and using the pedal, p. 80 / CD 49 Creating your own interpretation through listening, p. 81 / CD 49

Supplement from these pieces in **The Festival Collection®, Book 6.** *Refer to the "About the Pieces and Composers" sections for interesting and insightful information on each piece.*

Page	Era	Title
42-45	Classical	Sonatina in C major, Op. 55, No. 3 (1st Mvt.)
64-65	Classical	Rondo Grazioso
76-77	Romantic	Fantasy Dance, Op. 124 , No. 5
114-115	20th/21st Cent.	Petit Musique, Op. 33, No. 8

<u>*Suggested Teaching Order (both books)*</u>

Group 1: Prelude in D minor
    SWTM Baroque, p. 35-37/ CD 7
Fantasy Dance, Op. 124, No. 5
    FC, p. 76-77 / CD 28
Sonatina in C major, Op. 55, No. 3 (1st Mvt.)
    FC, p. 42-45 / CD 14
Prelude in C minor, Op. 28, No. 20
    SWTM Romantic, p. 83 / CD 24

Group 2: Sonata in A major
    SWTM Baroque, p. 92-95 / CD 21
Rondo Grazioso
    FC, p. 64-65 / CD 21
Chanson Triste
    SWTM Romantic, p. 73-75 / CD 21
Petit Musique, Op. 33, No. 8
    FC, p. 114-115 / CD 44

FJH2050

Incorporate these concepts from **Succeeding with the Masters®, Classical Era, Volume Two:**

Title	Characteristic	Practice Strategy from SWTM
FC - Sonata in C major, Op. 55, No. 3 (1st Mvt.) p. 42-45 / CD 14	Sonata form, p. 32 Straightforward, simple harmonies, p. 82	_____
FC - Rondo Grazioso, p. 64-65 / CD 21	Rondo form, p. 86 Melodies that are elegant, graceful, and easy to sing, p. 36	Practicing *Alberti* basses, p. 66 / CD 39

"Learning the Piece" Practice Strategies: (choose any)

Improving muscle memory, p. 47 / CD 34	"Smart" fingering, p. 70 / CD 40	Creating clear passagework, p. 52 / CD 36	Practicing with the metronome, p. 78-79	Slow vs. fast practicing (3x1 rule), p. 36 / CD 31

"Once the Piece Is Learned" Practice Strategies: (choose any)

Communicating a piece to an audience, p. 44	Practicing in different rhythms, p. 71	"Regrouping," p. 75 / CD 41
Bringing the piece to life, p. 25	Finding places to relax for better facility, p. 83	

Incorporate these concepts from **Succeeding with the Masters®, Romantic Era, Volume Two:**

Title	Characteristic	Practice Strategy from SWTM
FC - Fantasy Dance, Op. 124, No. 5, p. 76-77 / CD 28	Character piece, p. 24 The romantic interest in the fantastic, p. 52	Voicing the melody, p. 10 / CD 33 Strong sense of rhythm defining a piece, p. 41 / CD 39

"Learning the Piece" Practice Strategies: (choose any)

Improving muscle memory, p. 24 / CD 36	Unit, section, and performance practice, p. 24-25 / CD 36	The importance of hands-alone practice, p. 77	How to play a piece faster, p. 68

"Once the Piece Is Learned" Practice Strategies: (choose any)

"Follow the leader," p. 60 / CD 44	Shaping phrases, p. 14 / CD 34 p. 52 / CD 42	Practicing with forward direction, p. 20 / CD 35
Finding places to relax for better facility, p. 44 / CD 40	Keep listening, p. 48 / CD 41	The importance of a singing *legato*, p. 86-87 / CD 50

Next: **Succeeding with the Masters®, Classical Era and Romantic Era, Volume Two**

Succeeding with the Masters®, Classical Era, Volume Two and Succeeding with the Masters®, Romantic Era, Volume Two

*Correlated with **The Festival Collection®, Book 6***

Reviewing the Classical Era, Volume Two:

• *Use the pictures on p. 37 for further discussion of Haydn and the Classical era.*

Reviewing the Romantic Era, Volume Two:

• *Discuss "The Piano During the Romantic Era" on p. 40.*
• *Listen to the pieces in this unit on the CD's.*

Succeeding with the Masters®, Classical Repertoire:

Composer	Characteristic	Practice Strategy from SWTM
Haydn		
Presto in C major, p. 38-39 / CD 8	Elegant and graceful classical melodies, p. 36	Slow vs. fast practicing (3x1 rule), p. 36 / CD 31
Beethoven		
Für Elise, p. 88-91 / CD 21	Rondo form, p. 86 Contrast of mood, p. 87	Using the *una corda* pedal, p. 87 / CD 44

Succeeding with the Masters®, Romantic Repertoire:

Composer	Characteristic	Practice Strategy from SWTM
Schumann		
Little Hunting Song, p. 42-43 / CD 13	Example of a programmatic piece, p. 41	Strong sense of rhythm helping to define a piece, p. 41 / CD 39
The Horseman, p. 45-47 / CD 14	Example of a programmatic piece, p. 44	Creating the mood for a successful performance, p. 44 Finding places to relax for better facility, p. 44 / CD 40
Chopin		
Prelude in B minor, Op. 28, No. 6, p. 84-85 / CD 25	Emotion is a strong aspect of the music, p. 80	Conveying the mood and using the pedal, p. 80 / CD 49 Creating your own interpretation through listening, p. 81 / CD 49

FJH2050

Supplement from these pieces in **The Festival Collection®, Book 6.** *Refer to the "About the Pieces and Composers" sections for interesting and insightful information on each piece.*

Page	Era	Title
14-15	Baroque	Invention No. 8 in F major
28-29	Baroque	Divertimento
102-104	20th/21st Cent.	On the Farm

Suggested Teaching Order (both books)

Group 1: Presto in C major
    SWTM Classical, p. 38-39 / CD 8
  Little Hunting Song
    SWTM Romantic, p. 42-43 / CD 13
  Invention No. 8 in F major
    FC, p. 14-15 / CD 4
  On the Farm
    FC, p. 102-104 / CD 39

Group 2: Divertimento
    FC, p. 28-29 / CD 10
  The Horseman
    SWTM Romantic, p. 45-47 / CD 14
  Prelude in B minor, Op. 28, No. 6
    SWTM Romantic, p. 84-85 / CD 25
  Für Elise
    SWTM Classical, p. 88-91 / CD 21

Incorporate these concepts from **Succeeding with the Masters®, Baroque Era, Volume Two:**

Title	Characteristic	Practice Strategy from SWTM
FC - Invention No. 8 in F major, p. 14-15 / CD 4	Perpetual motion, p. 16, 26, and 69 Recurring rhythmic or melodic patterns, p. 22 Polyphonic texture, p. 45	Detached-note practicing p. 41 / CD 34 "Impulse" practicing, p. 41 / CD 34
FC - Divertimento, p. 28-29 / CD 10	Perpetual motion, p. 16, 26, and 69 Use of a pedal point, p. 16	"Blocking," p. 16-17 / CD 27

"Learning the Piece" Practice Strategies: (choose any)

"Smart" fingering, p. 13 / CD 26	Slow vs. fast practicing (3x1 rule), p. 76 / CD 43	"Unit" practicing p. 58 / CD 39 p. 80 / CD 44	Improving muscle memory, p. 30 / CD 31	"8 times to perfection," p. 64

"Once the Piece Is Learned" Practice Strategies: (choose any)

Learning to "Follow the leader," p. 45 / CD 35	Practicing back to front, p. 22 / CD 29	"Inner listening," p. 54 / CD 38	Practicing cadence points, p. 64 / CD 41	Shaping irregular phrases, p. 86-87 / CD 46

Next: **Succeeding with the Masters®, Baroque Era and Romantic Era, Volume Two**

Succeeding with the Masters®, Baroque Era, Volume Two and Succeeding with the Masters®, Romantic Era, Volume Two

*Correlated with **The Festival Collection®, Book 6***

Reviewing the Romantic Era, Volume Two:

- *Use the picture on p. 88 for further discussion of Chopin and the Romantic era.*
- *Listen to the pieces in this unit on the CD's.*

Succeeding with the Masters®, Baroque Repertoire:

Composer	Characteristic	Practice Strategy from SWTM
Bach Gavotte, p. 39-40 / CD 8	Rhythm as a distinctive element of the era, p. 38	Establishing an "inner pulse," p. 38 / CD 33
Handel Sonata, p. 70-73 / CD 17	Perpetual motion, p. 69	Bringing a piece to life, p. 69 / CD 42
Scarlatti Sonata in D minor, p. 97-99 / CD 23	Small details repeated; slightly changed, p. 96 Binary form, p. 96	Playing expressively, p. 96 "Regrouping," p. 96 / CD 48

Succeeding with the Masters®, Romantic Repertoire:

Composer	Characteristic	Practice Strategy from SWTM
Schumann Solitary Flowers, p. 49-51 / CD 15	_____	Playing seamlessly, p. 48 Keen listening, p. 48 / CD 41
Chopin Cantabile in B flat major, p. 89 / CD 26	_____	The importance of a singing *legato*, p. 86 / CD 50
Mazurka in F major, Op. 68, No. 3, p. 92-93 / CD 27	An example of nationalism, p. 90 Trills as part of the melodic line, p. 90	Playing trills written during the Romantic era, p. 90 / CD 51 Applying Chopin's *rubato*, p. 91 / CD 51

FJH2050

Supplement from these pieces in **The Festival Collection®***, Book 6. Refer to the "About the Pieces and Composers" sections for interesting and insightful information on each piece.*

Page	Era	Title
46-49	Classical	Rondo, Op. 18
98-99	20th/21st Cent.	Joc cu bâtă

<u>Suggested Teaching Order (both books)</u>

Group 1: Sonata in D minor
    SWTM Baroque, p. 97-99 / CD 23
  Rondo, Op. 18
    FC, p. 46-49 / CD 15
  Cantabile in B flat major
    SWTM Romantic, p. 89 / CD 26
  Solitary Flowers
    SWTM Romantic, p. 49-51 / CD 15

Group 2: Gavotte
    SWTM Baroque, p. 39-40 / CD 8
  Sonata
    SWTM Baroque, p. 70-73 / CD 17
  Mazurka in F major, Op. 68, No. 3
    SWTM Romantic, p. 92-93 / CD 27
  Joc cu bâtă
    FC, p. 98-99 / CD 37

Incorporate these concepts from **Succeeding with the Masters®***, Classical Era, Volume Two:*

<u>*Title*</u>	<u>*Characteristic*</u>	<u>*Practice Strategy from SWTM*</u>
FC - Rondo, Op. 18, p. 46-49 / CD 15	Rondo form, p. 86 Homophonic texture, p. 70	Balancing the melody with the accompaniment, p. 9 "Blocking," p. 60 / CD 38 Using the *una corda* pedal, p. 87 / CD 44

"Learning the Piece" Practice Strategies: (choose any)

Improving muscle memory, p. 47 / CD 34	"Smart" fingering, p. 70 / CD 40	Creating clear passagework, p. 52 / CD 36	Practicing with the metronome, p. 78-79	Slow vs. fast practicing (3x1 rule), p. 36 / CD 31

"Once the Piece Is Learned" Practice Strategies: (choose any)

Communicating a piece to an audience, p. 44	Practicing in different rhythms, p. 71	"Regrouping," p. 75 / CD 41
Bringing the piece to life, p. 25	Finding places to relax for better facility, p. 83	Shaping the phrases, p. 61

Next: **Succeeding with the Masters®***, Baroque Era, Volume Two*

Succeeding with the Masters®, Baroque Era, Volume Two

Correlated with **The Festival Collection®, Book 6**

Reviewing the Baroque Era, Volume Two:

- *Use the picture on p. 100 for further discussion of Scarlatti and the Baroque era.*
- *Listen to the pieces in this unit on the CD's.*

Succeeding with the Masters®, Baroque Repertoire:

Composer	Characteristic	Practice Strategy from SWTM
Bach Minuet in B minor, p. 42-43 / CD 9	_____	Detached-note practicing, p. 41 / CD 34 "Impulse" practicing, p. 41 / CD 34
Scarlatti Minuet in B flat major, p. 102-105 / CD 24	Sections ending with a trill, p. 101 Recurring rhythmic or melodic patterns, p. 101	Practicing arpeggios, p. 101 / CD 49
Gigue, p. 107-109 / CD 25	_____	Adding pedal for brilliance, p. 106 / CD 50

Supplement from these pieces in **The Festival Collection®, Book 6.** *Refer to the "About the Pieces and Composers" sections for interesting and insightful information on each piece.*

Page	Era	Title
50-52	Classical	Sonatina in C major, Op. 88, No. 1 (1st Mvt.)
52-53	Classical	Sonatina in C major, Op. 88, No. 1 (2nd Mvt.)
53-56	Classical	Sonatina in C major, Op. 88, No. 1 (3rd Mvt.)
70-71	Romantic	Prelude, Op. 40, No. 3
105-107	20th/21st Cent.	Run, Run!

Suggested Teaching Order (both books)

Group 1: Minuet in B flat major
    SWTM Baroque, p. 102-105/ CD 24
    Prelude, Op. 40, No. 3
    FC, p. 70-71 / CD 25

Group 2: Gigue
    SWTM Baroque, p. 107-109 / CD 25
    Sonatina in C major, Op. 88,
    No. 1 (1st Mvt.)
    FC, p. 50-52 / CD 16
    Sonatina in C major, Op. 88,
    No. 1 (2nd Mvt.)
    FC, p. 52-53 / CD 17

Group 3: Minuet in B minor
    SWTM Baroque, p. 42-43 / CD 9
    Sonatina in C major, Op. 88,
    No. 1 (3rd Mvt.)
    FC, p. 53-56 / CD 18
    Run, Run!
    FC, p. 105-107 / CD 40

Incorporate these concepts from **Succeeding with the Masters®, Classical Era, Volume Two:**

Title	Characteristic	Practice Strategy from SWTM
FC - Sonata in C major, Op. 88, No. 1 (1st Mvt.), p. 50-52 / CD 16	Sonata form, p. 32 Varied rhythmic motives	Voicing the melody, p. 28-29 / CD 29 Playing sixteenth notes evenly, p. 83 / CD 43
FC - Sonatina in C major, Op. 88, No. 1 (2nd Mvt.), p. 52-53 / CD 17	Well-balanced and symmetrical phrases, p. 12 Homophonic texture, p. 70	"Finger pedaling," p. 44 / CD 33 Incorporating the pedal, p. 57 / CD 37 Creating long phrases, p. 57 / no CD
FC - Sonatina in C major, Op. 88, No. 1 (3rd Mvt.), p. 53-56 / CD 18	Rondo form, p. 86 Straightforward, simple harmonies, p. 82	Tonic and dominant chords, p. 17 / CD 26 Playing sixteenth notes evenly, p. 83 / CD 43

"Learning the Piece" Practice Strategies: (choose any)

Improving muscle memory, p. 47 / CD 34	"Smart" fingering, p. 70 / CD 40	Creating clear passagework, p. 52 / CD 36	Practicing with the metronome, p. 78-79	Slow vs. fast practicing (3x1 rule), p. 36 / CD 31

"Once the Piece Is Learned" Practice Strategies: (choose any)

Communicating a piece to an audience, p. 44	Practicing in different rhythms, p. 71	"Regrouping," p. 75 / CD 41
Bringing the piece to life, p. 25	Finding places to relax for better facility, p. 83	Shaping the phrases, p. 61

Incorporate these concepts from **Succeeding with the Masters®, Romantic Era, Volume Two:**

Title	Characteristic	Practice Strategy from SWTM
FC - Prelude, Op. 40, No. 3, p. 70-71 / CD 25	Expansion of the harmonic language, p. 57 Use of *rubato*, p. 29	Applying *rubato*, p. 29 and p. 77 / CD 48

"Learning the Piece" Practice Strategies: (choose any)

Improving muscle memory, p. 24 / CD 36	Unit, section, and performance practice, p. 24-25 / CD 36	The importance of hands-alone practice, p. 77	How to play a piece faster, p. 68

"Once the Piece Is Learned" Practice Strategies: (choose any)

"Follow the leader," p. 60 / CD 44	Shaping phrases p. 14 / CD 34 p. 52 / CD 42	Practicing with forward direction, p. 20 / CD 35	Finding places to relax for better facility, p. 44 / CD 40
Keen listening, p. 48 / CD 41	The importance of a singing *legato*, p. 86-87 / CD 50	"80% practice," p. 100 / CD 52	Using imagery to create a successful performance, p. 104 / CD 53

Next: **Succeeding with the Masters®, Classical Era, Volume Two**

Succeeding with the Masters®, Classical Era, Volume Two

*Correlated with **The Festival Collection®**, Book 6*

Reviewing the Classical Era, Volume Two:

- Use the picture on p. 96 for further discussion of Beethoven and the Classical era.
- Listen to the pieces in this unit on the CD's.

Succeeding with the Masters®, Classical Repertoire:

Composer	Characteristic	Practice Strategy from SWTM
Beethoven Minuet in D major, p. 94-95 / CD 22	Establishment of the Classical orchestra, p. 92	"Orchestrating" a piece, p. 92 / CD 45
Six Variations on a Swiss Song, p. 98-101 / CD 23	Melodies that are elegant, graceful, and easy to sing, p. 97 Theme and variations, p. 97 Varied rhythmic motives, p. 97	Playing portato articulations, p. 97 / CD 46 Learning musical interpretation, p. 97 / CD 46

Supplement from these pieces in **The Festival Collection®**, *Book 6. Refer to the "About the Pieces and Composers" sections for interesting and insightful information on each piece.*

Page	Era	Title
12-13	Baroque	Invention No. 1 in C major
26-27	Baroque	The Grape Pickers
69	Romantic	From Foreign Lands and People, Op. 15, No. 1
78-79	Romantic	Mazurka in B flat major, Op. 7, No. 1
94-95	20th/21st Cent.	No fundo do meu quintal

<u>Suggested Teaching Order (both books)</u>

Group 1: The Grape Pickers
FC, p. 26-27/ CD 9
Minuet in D major
SWTM, p. 94-95 / CD 22
From Foreign Lands and People,
Op. 15, No. 1
FC, p. 69/ CD 24
No fundo do meu quintal
FC, p. 94-95/ CD 35

Group 2: Invention No. 1 in C major
FC, p. 12-13 / CD 3
Six Variations on a Swiss Song
SWTM, p. 98-101 / CD 23
Mazurka in B flat major, Op. 7, No. 1
FC, p. 78-79 / CD 29

FJH2050

Incorporate these concepts from **Succeeding with the Masters®, Baroque Era, Volume Two:**

Title	Characteristic	Practice Strategy from SWTM
FC - Invention No. 1 in C major, p. 12-13 / CD 3	Recurring rhythmic or melodic patterns, p. 22 Polyphonic texture, p. 45 Single mood or affect, p. 30 and 86	Detached-note practicing "Impulse" practicing, p. 41 / CD 34
FC - The Grape Pickers, p. 26-27 / CD 9	Melodies made up of short phrase fragments of irregular lengths, p. 86	"Finger *legato*," p. 20 / CD 28 Establishing an "inner pulse," p. 38 / CD 33

"Learning the Piece" Practice Strategies: (choose any)

"Smart" fingering, p. 13 / CD 26	Slow vs. fast practicing (3x1 rule), p. 76 / CD 43	"Unit" practicing p. 58 / CD 39, p. 80 / CD 44	Improving muscle memory, p. 30 / CD 31	"8 times to perfection," p. 64

"Once the Piece Is Learned" Practice Strategies: (choose any)

Learning to "Follow the leader," p. 45 / CD 35	Practicing back to front, p. 22 / CD 29	"Inner listening," p. 54 / CD 38	Practicing cadence points, p. 64 / CD 41
Shaping irregular phrases, p. 86-87 / CD 46	Bringing a piece to life, p. 69 / CD 42	"Regrouping," p. 96 / CD 48	Adding pedal for brilliance, p. 106 / CD 50

Incorporate these concepts from **Succeeding with the Masters®, Romantic Era, Volume Two:**

Title	Characteristic	Practice Strategy from SWTM
FC - From Foreign Lands and People, Op. 15, No. 1, p. 69 / CD 24	Character piece, p. 24 Phrases of varying length, p. 77	Balancing melody with accompaniment, p. 64 / CD 45
FC - Mazurka in B flat major, Op. 7, No. 1, p. 78-79 / CD 29	Nationalism, p. 90	Playing dotted rhythms, p. 57 / CD 43 Trills as part of the melodic line, p. 90-91 / CD 51 Applying Chopin's *rubato*, p. 91 / CD 51

"Learning the Piece" Practice Strategies: (choose any)

Improving muscle memory, p. 24 / CD 36	Unit, section, and performance practice, p. 24-25 / CD 36	The importance of hands-alone practice, p. 77	How to play a piece faster, p. 68

"Once the Piece Is Learned" Practice Strategies: (choose any)

"Follow the leader," p. 60 / CD 44	Shaping phrases, p. 14 / CD 34 p. 52 / CD 42	Practicing with forward direction, p. 20 / CD 35	Finding places to relax for better facility, p. 44 / CD 40
Keen listening, p. 48 / CD 41	The importance of a singing *legato*, p. 86-87 / CD 50	"80% practice," p. 100 / CD 52	Using imagery to create a successful performance, p. 104 / CD 53

Next: **Succeeding with the Masters®, Romantic Era, Volume Two**

Succeeding with the Masters®, Romantic Era, Volume Two

Correlated with *The Festival Collection®, Book 6*

Reviewing the Romantic Era, Volume Two:

- Use the picture on p. 97 for further discussion of Chopin and the Romantic era.
- Listen to the pieces in this unit on the CD's.

Succeeding with the Masters®, Romantic Repertoire:

Composer	Characteristic	Practice Strategy from SWTM
Chopin Mazurka in G minor, Op. 67, No. 2, p. 95-97 / CD 28	An example of nationalism, p. 90 Trills as part of the melodic line, p. 90	Playing trills written during the Romantic era, p. 90 / CD 51 Applying Chopin's *rubato*, p. 91 / CD 51
Mazurka in C major, Op. 67, No. 3, p. 98-99 / CD 29	An example of nationalism, p. 90 Trills as part of the melodic line, p. 90	Playing trills written during the Romantic era, p. 90 / CD 51 Applying Chopin's *rubato*, p. 91 / CD 51

*Supplement from these pieces in **The Festival Collection®, Book 6.** Refer to the "About the Pieces and Composers" sections for interesting and insightful information on each piece.*

Page	Era	Title
20-22	Baroque	Allegro
57-61	Classical	Sonata in C, K. 545 (2nd Mvt.)
61-63	Classical	Sonata in C, K. 545 (3rd Mvt.)
84-86	Romantic	Little Troll, Op. 71, No. 3
96-97	20th/21st Cent.	To the Rising Sun, Op. 4, No. 1

<u>Suggested Teaching Order (both books)</u>

Group 1: Sonata in C, K. 545 (2nd Mvt.)
  FC, p. 57-61 / CD 19
  Mazurka in G minor, Op. 67, No. 2
  SWTM, p. 95-97 / CD 28
  To the Rising Sun, Op. 4, No. 1
  FC, p. 96-97 / CD 36

Group 2: Allegro
  FC, p. 20-22 / CD 7
  Sonata in C, K. 545 (3rd Mvt.)
  FC, p. 61-63 / CD 20
  Mazurka in C major, Op. 67, No. 3
  SWTM, p. 98-99 / CD 29
  Little Troll, Op. 71, No. 3
  FC, p. 84-86 / CD 32

*Incorporate these concepts from **Succeeding with the Masters®, Baroque Era, Volume Two:***

Title	Characteristic	Practice Strategy from SWTM
FC - Allegro, p. 20-22	Recurring rhythmic or melodic patterns, p. 22 Single mood or affect, p. 30 and 86	Complete rhythmic accuracy, p. 90 / CD 47

"Learning the Piece" Practice Strategies: (choose any)

"Smart" fingering, p. 13 / CD 26	Slow vs. fast practicing (3x1 rule), p. 76 / CD 43	"Unit" practicing p. 58 / CD 39, p. 80 / CD 44	Improving muscle memory, p. 30 / CD 31	"8 times to perfection," p. 64

FJH2050

"Once the Piece Is Learned" Practice Strategies: (choose any)			
Learning to "Follow the leader," p. 45 / CD 35	Practicing back to front, p. 22 / CD 29	"Inner listening," p. 54 / CD 38	Practicing cadence points, p. 64 / CD 41
Shaping irregular phrases, p. 86-87 / CD 46	Bringing a piece to life, p. 69 / CD 42	"Regrouping," p. 96 / CD 48	Adding pedal for brilliance, p. 106 / CD 50

Incorporate these concepts from **Succeeding with the Masters®, Classical Era, Volume Two:**

<u>Title</u>	<u>Characteristic</u>	<u>Practice Strategy from SWTM</u>
FC - Sonata in C, K. 545 (2nd Mvt.), p. 57-61 / CD 19	Well-balanced and symmetrical phrases, p. 12 Homophonic texture, p. 70	"Finger pedaling," p. 44 / CD 33 Incorporating the pedal, p. 57 / CD 37 Creating long phrases, p. 57
FC - Sonata in C, K. 545 (3rd Mvt.), p. 61-63 / CD 20	Rondo form, p. 86 Many dynamic changes	Practicing *Alberti* basses, p. 66 / CD 39

"Learning the Piece" Practice Strategies: (choose any)				
Improving muscle memory, p. 47 / CD 34	"Smart" fingering, p. 70 / CD 40	Creating clear passagework, p. 52 / CD 36	Practicing with the metronome, p. 78-79	Slow vs. fast practicing (3x1 rule), p. 36 / CD 31

"Once the Piece Is Learned" Practice Strategies: (choose any)			
Communicating a piece to an audience, p. 44	Practicing in different rhythms, p. 71	"Regrouping," p. 75 / CD 41	Bringing the piece to life, p. 25
Finding places to relax for better facility, p. 83	Shaping the phrases, p. 61	"Orchestrating" a piece, CD 45 (picture on p. 92)	

Incorporate these concepts from **Succeeding with the Masters®, Romantic Era, Volume Two:**

<u>Title</u>	<u>Characteristic</u>	<u>Practice Strategy from SWTM</u>
FC - Little Troll, Op. 71, No. 3, p. 84-86 / CD 32	Drama as an important Romantic element, p. 34 Programmatic piece, p. 41	Strong sense of rhythm defining a piece, p. 41 / CD 39 Playing with a supple wrist, p. 68 / CD 46

"Learning the Piece" Practice Strategies: (choose any)			
Improving muscle memory, p. 24 / CD 36	Unit, section, and performance practice, p. 24-25 / CD 36	The importance of hands-alone practice, p. 77	How to play a piece faster, p. 68

"Once the Piece Is Learned" Practice Strategies: (choose any)			
"Follow the leader," p. 60 / CD 44	Shaping phrases p. 14 / CD 34 p. 52 / CD 42	Practicing with forward direction, p. 20 / CD 35	Finding places to relax for better facility, p. 44 / CD 40
Keen listening, p. 48 / CD 41	The importance of a singing legato, p. 86-87 / CD 50	"80% practice," p. 100 / CD 52	Using imagery to create a successful performance, p. 104 / CD 53

Next: **The Festival Collection®, Book 6**

The Festival Collection®, Book 6

- *Listen to the pieces in this unit on the CD's.*

Supplement from these pieces in The Festival Collection®, Book 6. Refer to the "About the Pieces and Composers" sections for interesting and insightful information on each piece.

Page	Era	Title
6-7	Baroque	Solfeggietto
30-32	Classical	Sonata No. 18 in A major
66-67	Romantic	Cradle song, Op. 68, No. 5
74-75	Romantic	Chanson Triste
87-89	Romantic	Valse in A minor
113	20th/21st Cent.	Moment sérieux

Suggested Teaching Order (both books)

Group 1: Sonata No. 18 in A major
FC, p. 30-32 / CD 11
Valse in A minor
FC, p. 87-89 / CD 33
Cradle Song, Op. 68, No. 5
FC, p. 66-67 / CD 22

Group 2: Solfeggietto
FC, p. 6-7 / CD 1
Chanson Triste
FC, p. 74-75 / CD 27
Moment sérieux
FC, p. 113 / CD 43

Incorporate these concepts from **Succeeding with the Masters®, Baroque Era, Volume Two:**

Title	Characteristic	Practice Strategy from SWTM
FC - Solfeggietto, p. 6-7 / CD 1	Perpetual motion, p. 16, 26, and 69 Compelling energy, p. 22 and 54 Piece created from broken chords and scale passages, p. 34	

"Learning the Piece" Practice Strategies: (choose any)

"Smart" fingering, p. 13 / CD 26	Slow vs. fast practicing (3x1 rule), p. 76 / CD 43	"Unit" practicing p. 58 / CD 39, p. 80 / CD 44	Improving muscle memory, p. 30 / CD 31	"8 times to perfection," p. 64

"Once the Piece Is Learned" Practice Strategies: (choose any)

Learning to "Follow the leader," p. 45 / CD 35	Practicing back to front, p. 22 / CD 29	"Inner listening," p. 54 / CD 38	Practicing cadence points, p. 64 / CD 41
Shaping irregular phrases, p. 86-87 / CD 46	Bringing a piece to life, p. 69 / CD 42	"Regrouping," p. 96 / CD 48	Adding pedal for brilliance, p. 106 / CD 50

Incorporate these concepts from **Succeeding with the Masters®, Classical Era, Volume Two:**

Title	Characteristic	Practice Strategy from SWTM
FC - Sonata No. 18 in A major, p. 30-32	Varied rhythmic motives	

"Learning the Piece" Practice Strategies: (choose any)

Improving muscle memory, p. 47 / CD 34	"Smart" fingering, p. 70 / CD 40	Creating clear passagework, p. 52 / CD 36	Practicing with the metronome, p. 78-79	Slow vs. fast (3x1 rule), p. 36 / CD 31

"Once the Piece Is Learned" Practice Strategies: (choose any)

Communicating a piece to an audience, p. 44	Practicing in different rhythms, p. 71	"Regrouping," p. 75 / CD 41	Bringing the piece to life, p. 25
Finding places to relax for better facility, p. 83	Shaping the phrases, p. 61	"Orchestrating" a piece, CD 45 (picture on p. 92)	

FJH2050

Incorporate these concepts from **Succeeding with the Masters®, Romantic Era, Volume Two:**

<u>Title</u>	<u>Characteristic</u>	<u>Practice Strategy from SWTM</u>
FC - Cradle Song, Op. 68, No. 5, p.66-67 / CD 22	Trills as part of the melodic line, p. 90 Melody and accompaniment in the same hand, p. 28 Programmatic piece, p. 41	Voicing the melody, p. 10 / CD 33 Balancing the melody with accompaniment, p. 64 / CD 45 Applying *rubato*, p. 29 and 77 / CD 48 Trills as part of the melodic line, p. 90-91 / CD 51
FC - Chanson Triste, p. 74-75 / CD 27	Trills as part of the melodic line, p. 90 Character piece, p. 24 Use of *rubato*, p. 29	Applying *rubato*, p. 29 and 77 / CD 48 Trills as part of the melodic line, p. 90-91 / CD 51
FC - Valse in A minor, p. 87-89 / CD 33	Trills as part of the melodic line, p. 90 Use of *rubato*, p. 29	Applying *rubato*, p. 29 and 77 / CD 48 Trills as part of the melodic line, p. 90-91 / CD 51

<u>"Learning the Piece" Practice Strategies: (choose any)</u>

Improving muscle memory, p. 24 / CD 36	Unit, section, and performance practice, p. 24-25 / CD 36	The importance of hands-alone practice, p. 77	How to play a piece faster, p. 68

<u>"Once the Piece Is Learned" Practice Strategies: (choose any)</u>

"Follow the leader," p. 60 / CD 44	Shaping phrases, p. 14 / CD 34 p. 52 / CD 42	Practicing with forward direction, p. 20 / CD 35	Finding places to relax for better facility, p. 44 / CD 40
Keen listening, p. 48 / CD 41	The importance of a singing *legato*, p. 86-87 / CD 50	"80% practice," p. 100 / CD 52	Using imagery to create a successful performance, p. 104 / CD 53

Next: **Succeeding with the Masters®, Romantic Era, Volume Two**

Succeeding with the Masters®, Romantic Era, Volume Two

Correlated with *The Festival Collection®, Book 6*

Reviewing the Romantic Era, Volume Two:

- *Use the picture on p. 53 for further discussion of Schumann and the Romantic era.*
- *Use the picture on p. 101 for further discussion of Chopin and the Romantic era.*
- *Listen to the pieces in this unit on the CD's.*

Succeeding with the Masters®, Romantic Repertoire:

Composer	Characteristic	Practice Strategy from SWTM
Schumann Evening Song, p. 54-55 / CD 16	The romantic interest in nature, the fantastic and emotional expression, p. 52	Shaping phrases, p. 52 / CD 42 Voicing the melody, p. 52 / CD 42
Chopin Polonaise in G minor, p. 102-103 / CD 30	**Characteristic** The characteristics of a polonaise, p. 100	**Practice Strategy** "80% Practice," p. 100 / CD 52
Largo in E flat major, p. 105 / CD 31	Drama as an important romantic element, p. 104	Using imagery to create a successful performance, p. 104 / CD 53

Supplement from these pieces in **The Festival Collection®, Book 6.** *Refer to the "About the Pieces and Composers" sections for interesting and insightful information on each piece.*

Page	Era	Title
23-25	Baroque	Toccata in F minor
33-37	Classical	Sonata in G major, Hob. XVI: 27 (3rd Mvt.)
80-81	Romantic	Sketch
110-112	20th/21st Cent.	Busy Toccata

<u>Suggested Teaching Order (both books)</u>

Group 1: Sonata in G major, Hob. XVI: 27
(3rd Mvt.)
   FC, p. 33-37 / CD 12
Evening Song
   SWTM, p. 54-55 / CD 16
Polonaise in G minor
   SWTM, p. 102-103/ CD 30
Sketch
   FC, p. 80-81 / CD 30

Group 2: Toccata in F minor
   FC, p. 23-25 / CD 8
Largo in E flat major
   SWTM, p. 105 / CD 31
Busy Toccata
   FC, p. 110-112 / CD 42

Incorporate these concepts from **Succeeding with the Masters®, Baroque Era, Volume Two:**

Title	Characteristic	Practice Strategy from SWTM
FC - Toccata in F minor, p. 23-25 / CD 8	Perpetual motion, p. 16, 26, and 69 Recurring rhythmic or melodic patterns, p. 22 Compelling energy, p. 22 and 54	_____

"Learning the Piece" Practice Strategies: (choose any)

"Smart" fingering, p. 13 / CD 26	Slow vs. fast practicing (3x1 rule), p. 76 / CD 43	"Unit" practicing p. 58 / CD 39, p. 80 / CD 44	Improving muscle memory, p. 30 / CD 31	"8 times to perfection," p. 64

"Once the Piece Is Learned" Practice Strategies: (choose any)

Learning to "Follow the leader," p. 45 / CD 35	Practicing back to front, p. 22 / CD 29	"Inner listening," p. 54 / CD 38	Practicing cadence points, p. 64 / CD 41
Shaping irregular phrases, p. 86-87 / CD 46	Bringing a piece to life, p. 69 / CD 42	"Regrouping," p. 96 / CD 48	Adding pedal for brilliance, p. 106 / CD 50

Incorporate these concepts from **Succeeding with the Masters®, Classical Era, Volume Two:**

Title	Characteristic	Practice Strategy from SWTM
FC - Sonata in G major, Hob. XVI: 27 (3rd Mvt.), p. 33-37 / CD 12	Theme and variations, p. 97 Varied rhythmic motives, p. 97	Playing sixteenth notes evenly, p. 83 / CD 43

"Learning the Piece" Practice Strategies: (choose any)

Improving muscle memory, p. 47 / CD 34	"Smart" fingering, p. 70 . CD 40	Creating clear passagework, p. 52 / CD 36	Practicing with the metronome, p. 78-79	Slow vs. fast practicing (3x1 rule), p. 36 / CD 31

"Once the Piece Is Learned" Practice Strategies: (choose any)

Communicating a piece to an audience, p. 44	Practicing in different rhythms, p. 71	"Regrouping," p. 75 / CD 41	Bringing the piece to life, p. 25
Finding places to relax for better facility, p. 83	Shaping the phrases, p. 61	"Orchestrating" a piece, CD 45 (picture on p. 92)	

Incorporate these concepts from **Succeeding with the Masters®, Romantic Era, Volume Two:**

Title	Characteristic	Practice Strategy from SWTM
FC - Sketch, p. 80-81 / CD 30	Use of *rubato*, p. 29 Phrases of varying lengths, p. 77	Applying *rubato*, p. 29 and 77 / CD 48

"Learning the Piece" Practice Strategies: (choose any)

Improving muscle memory, p. 24 / CD 36	Unit, section, and performance practice, p. 24-25 / CD 36	The importance of hands-alone practice, p. 77	How to play a piece faster, p. 68

"Once the Piece Is Learned" Practice Strategies: (choose any)

"Follow the leader," p. 60 / CD 44	Shaping phrases, p. 14 / CD 34 p. 52 / CD 42	Practicing with forward direction, p. 20 / CD 35	Finding places to relax for better facility, p. 44 / CD 40
Keen listening, p. 48 / CD 41	The importance of a singing *legato*, p. 86-87 / CD 50	"80% practice," p. 100 / CD 52	Using imagery to create a successful performance, p. 104 / CD 53

Next: **Succeeding with the Masters®, Romantic Era, Volume Two**

Succeeding with the Masters®, Romantic Era, Volume Two

Correlated with *The Festival Collection®, Book 6*

- *Listen to the pieces in this unit on the CD's.*

Succeeding with the Masters®, Romantic Repertoire:

Composer	Characteristic	Practice Strategy from SWTM
Chopin		
Grand Valse Brillante in A minor, Op. 34, No. 2 p. 107-115 / CD 32	Use of varied rhythmic patterns and patterns with an unequal number of notes, p. 106	Playing *fioritura* embellishments, p. 106 / CD 54

Supplement from these pieces in **The Festival Collection®, Book 6.** *Refer to the "About the Pieces and Composers" sections for interesting and insightful information on each piece.*

Page	Era	Title
16-17	Baroque	Invention No. 13 in A minor
38-41	Classical	Sonatina in E flat major, WoO 47, No. 1 (1st Mvt.)
100-101	20th/21st Cent.	Golden Leaves
108-109	20th/21st Cent.	A Blown-Away Leaf

<u>Suggested Teaching Order (both books)</u>

Group 1: Sonatina in E flat major, WoO 47, No. 1 (3rd Mvt.)
    FC, p. 38-41 / CD 13
Golden Leaves
    FC, p. 100-101 / CD 38
A Blown-Away Leaf
    FC, p. 108-109 / CD 41

Group 2: Invention No. 13 in A minor
    FC, p. 16-17 / CD 5
Grand Valse Brillante in A minor, Op. 34, No. 2
    SWTM, p. 107-115 / CD 32

FJH2050

Incorporate these concepts from **Succeeding with the Masters®, Baroque Era, Volume Two:**

Title	_Characteristic_	_Practice Strategy from SWTM_
FC - Invention No. 13 in A minor, p. 16-17 / CD 5	Recurring rhythmic or melodic patterns, p. 22 Polyphonic texture, p. 45 Single mood or affect, p. 30 and 86	Detached-note practicing "Impulse" practicing, p. 41 / CD 34

"Learning the Piece" Practice Strategies: (choose any)

"Smart" fingering, p. 13 / CD 26	Slow vs. fast practicing (3x1 rule), p. 76 / CD 43	"Unit" practicing p. 58 / CD 39, p. 80 / CD 44	Improving muscle memory, p. 30 / CD 31	"8 times to perfection," p. 64

"Once the Piece Is Learned" Practice Strategies: (choose any)

Learning to "Follow the leader," p. 45 / CD 35	Practicing back to front, p. 22 / CD 29	"Inner listening," p. 54 / CD 38	Practicing cadence points, p. 64 / CD 41
Shaping irregular phrases, p. 86-87 / CD 46	Bringing a piece to life, p. 69 / CD 42	"Regrouping," p. 96 / CD 48	Adding pedal for brilliance, p. 106 / CD 50

Incorporate these concepts from **Succeeding with the Masters®, Classical Era, Volume Two:**

Title	_Characteristic_	_Practice Strategy from SWTM_
FC - Sonatina in E flat major, WoO 47, No. 1 (1st Mvt.) p. 38-41 / CD 13	Sonata form, p. 32 Contrast of mood, p. 28, 74 Many dynamic changes, p. 42	Practicing _Alberti_ bass, p. 66 / CD 39 Using the _una corda_ pedal, p. 87 / CD 44

"Learning the Piece" Practice Strategies: (choose any)

Improving muscle memory, p. 47 / CD 34	"Smart" fingering, p. 70 / CD 40	Creating clear passagework, p. 52 / CD 36	Practicing with the metronome, p. 78-79	Slow vs. fast (3x1 rule), p. 36 / CD 31

"Once the Piece Is Learned" Practice Strategies: (choose any)

Communicating a piece to an audience, p. 44	Practicing in different rhythms, p. 71	"Regrouping," p. 75 / CD 41	Bringing the piece to life, p. 25
Finding places to relax for better facility, p. 83	Shaping the phrases, p. 61	"Orchestrating" a piece, CD 45 (picture on p. 92)	

Next: **The Festival Collection®, Book 7**

PART II
SUGGESTED TEACHING ORDER of pieces by era:

The Festival Collection®, Preparatory

Baroque Era:

Page / CD Track	Title	Composer
6 / 1	Bagpipe (*Dudelsack*)	Unknown
7 / 3	Follow the Leader	John Playford
6 / 2	A Merry Dance	François Couperin

Classical Era:

Page / CD Track	Title	Composer
8 / 4	March	Daniel Gottlob Türk
8 / 5	Running the Race	Johann Christian Bach/Francesco Pasquale Ricci
9 / 6	Elegant Dance	Alexander Reinagle
10 / 7	A Day in the Country	Alexander Reinagle
12-13 / 11	At Play	Timothy Brown
10 / 8	Buying Potatoes	Alexander Reinagle
11 / 9	The Lively Boy	Daniel Gottlob Türk
11 / 10	Saturday Afternoon Walk	Daniel Gottlob Türk

Romantic Era:

Page / CD Track	Title	Composer
14 / 12	Two Penguins	Ferdinand Beyer
15 / 13	In a Hot Air Balloon	Hermann Berens
16 / 14	The Mermaid	Carl Czerny
17 / 15	Busy at Work	Hermann Berens
18 / 16	Going on a Road Trip	Louis Köhler

20th/21st Centuries:

Page / CD Track	Title	Composer
19 / 17	Having Fun on My Pogo Stick	Dianne Goolkasian Rahbee
20-21 / 18	The Peacock	Valerie Roth Roubos
22-23 / 19	Lightning Strike!	Timothy Brown
24-25 / 20	The Dance at the Village Square	Mary Leaf

FJH2050

SUGGESTED TEACHING ORDER *of pieces by era:*

The Festival Collection®, Book I

Baroque Era:

Page / CD Track	Title	Composer
6 / 1	Old German Dance	Michael Praetorius
8 / 3	Canary	Joachim van den Hove
10 / 5	Intrada	Paul Peuerl
7 / 2	Allemande	Johann Hermann Schein
9 / 4	Petit Minuet	Jean-Nicolas Geoffroy
11 / 6	Petit Rondo	Jean-Nicolas Geoffroy

Classical Era:

Page / CD Track	Title	Composer
17 / 14	Allegro	Alexander Reinagle
13 / 9	Minuet	James Hook
12 / 7	Minuet	Daniel Gottlob Türk
12 / 8	A Carefree Fellow	Daniel Gottlob Türk
16 / 13	Song	Anton Diabelli
18 / 15	Agitato	Johann Christian Bach/Francesco Pasquale Ricci
14 / 10	Sonatina (1st Mvt.)	Daniel Gottlob Türk
14 / 11	Sonatina (2nd Mvt.)	Daniel Gottlob Türk
15 / 12	Sonatina (3rd Mvt.)	Daniel Gottlob Türk

Romantic Era:

Page / CD Track	Title	Composer
20 / 17	The Young Dancer	Cornelius Gurlitt
19 / 16	A Song	Alexander Gedike
21 / 18	Kitten Play	Cornelius Gurlitt
24-25 / 20	Spring Waltz	Fritz Spindler
22-23 / 19	Valsette	Moritz Vogel

20th/21st Centuries:

Page / CD Track	Title	Composer
26 / 21	Trumpets	Martín Kutnowski
29 / 24	Hungarian Song	Béla Bartók
32 / 27	The Shepherd Plays	Tat'iana Salutrinskaya
30 / 25	Arabian Dance	Timothy Brown
27 / 22	Snowflakes Gently Falling	Dianne Goolkasian Rahbee
28 / 23	The Sparrows	A. Rubbach
31 / 26	Air for Southpaw	Arthur R. Frackenpohl

The Festival Collection®, Book 2

Baroque Era:

Page / CD Track	Title	Composer
9 / 4	Gavotte	Daniel Speer
6 / 1	King William's March	Jeremiah Clarke
12 / 6	Menuet en Rondeau	Jean-Philippe Rameau
10-11 / 5	Minuet in F major	Johann Kuhnau
13 / 7	Sarabande	Arcangelo Corelli
7 / 2	Rigaudon	Georg Philipp Telemann
8 / 3	Burleske	Unknown

Classical Era:

Page / CD Track	Title	Composer
27 / 16	Little Dance	Daniel Gottlob Türk
29 / 18	The Hunting Horns and the Echo	Daniel Gottlob Türk
28 / 17	Russian Folk song	Ludwig van Beethoven
24 / 13	Bagatelle	Anton Diabelli
25 / 14	Swabian Tune	Johann Christoph Friedrich Bach
26 / 15	Scotch Dance No. 1	Friedrich Kuhlau
22-23 / 12	Lesson I	James Hook
14-15 / 8	The Village Prophet	Jean-Jacques Rousseau
18-19 / 10	Allegro	Alexander Reinagle
16-17 / 9	Sonatina in C major	Johann Anton André
20-21 / 11	Sonatina in G	Thomas Attwood

Romantic Era:

Page / CD Track	Title	Composer
33 / 22	Etude	Ferdinand Beyer
32 / 21	The Hunt	Cornelius Gurlitt
37 / 26	Hunting Horns	Theodore Oesten
31 / 20	Petite Prelude	Ludwig Schytte
35 / 24	Song Without Words	Fritz Spindler
36 / 25	Theme and Variation	Louis Köhler
34 / 23	Mazurka	Alexander Gedike
30 / 19	A Hymn	Ludwig Schytte
38 / 27	Night Journey	Cornelius Gurlitt
39 / 28	Timid Little Heart	Robert Fuchs

20th/21st Centuries:

Page / CD Track	Title	Composer
43 / 33	The Bear	Vladimir Rebikov
48 / 36	Una Capricciosa Nuvola Estiva	Federico Ermirio
42 / 31	Mister Czerny in New Orleans	Manfred Schmitz
42 / 32	Waltz Time	Manfred Schmitz
41 / 30	Rippling Waters	Dianne Goolkasian Rahbee
40 / 29	To the Garden	Alexandre Tansman
46-47 / 35	Two's Company	Alec Rowley
44-45 / 34	Long Gone Blues	George Frederick McKay

SUGGESTED TEACHING ORDER of pieces by era:

The Festival Collection®, Book 3

Baroque Era:

Page / CD Track	Title	Composer
8-9 / 3	Fantasie	Georg Philipp Telemann
11 / 5	Minuet in C major	Carlos de Seixas
6 / 1	Minuet in A minor	Johann Krieger
10 / 4	Minuet in E minor	Henry Purcell (attributed to)
7 / 2	Minuet in G major	Wilhelm Friedemann Bach
13 / 7	Gigue	Georg Philipp Telemann
12 / 6	Minuet in A minor	Henry Purcell
18-19 / 10	The Fifers	Jean-François Dandrieu
16-17 / 9	Minuet in D minor	Johann Heinrich Buttstett
14-15 / 8	Minuet in G minor, BWV 115	Christian Pezold

Classical Era:

Page / CD Track	Title	Composer
20-21 / 11	Never a Dull Moment	Daniel Gottlob Türk
24-25 / 13	Sonatina in G, (1st Mvt. Moderato)	Ludwig van Beethoven
26-27 / 14	Sonatina in G, (2nd Mvt. Romanze)	Ludwig van Beethoven
22-23 / 12	Adagio	Daniel Steibelt
28-29 / 15	Sonatina in G major	Anton Diabelli
37 / 20	Dance	Christian Gottlob Neefe
30-31 / 16	Sonata in F major, Hob. XVI: 9	Franz Joseph Haydn
32-33 / 17	Sonatina in C major, (1st Mvt.)	Muzio Clementi
34 / 18	Sonatina in C major, (2nd Mvt.)	Muzio Clementi
35-36 / 19	Sonatina in C major, (3rd Mvt.)	Muzio Clementi

Romantic Era:

Page / CD Track	Title	Composer
40-41 / 23	Through Forest and Field	Cornelius Gurlitt
48-49 / 27	Hunting Music	Cornelius Gurlitt
46-47 / 26	Arabesque, Op. 100, No. 2	Johann Friedrich Burgmüller
52 / 29	Romantic Study, Op. 139, No. 49	Carl Czerny
53 / 30	Romantic Study, Op. 261, No. 54	Carl Czerny
50-51 / 28	Praeludium	Carl Reinecke
38 / 21	Innocence, Op. 100, No. 6	Johann Friedrich Burgmüller
42-43 / 24	In the Garden	Cornelius Gurlitt
39 / 22	Progress, Op. 100, No. 6	Johann Friedrich Burgmüller
44-45 / 25	Song	Carl Reinecke
55-57 / 32	Kamarinskaya	Pyotr Ilyich Tchaikovsky
54 / 31	Andantino	Theodor Furchtegott Kirchner

20th/21st Centuries:

Page / CD Track	Title	Composer
71 / 40	Playing Soldiers	Vladimir Rebikov
58 / 33	Highwayman's Tune	Béla Bartók
70 / 39	Little Shepherd	Samuel Maykapar
62-65 / 36	Five Variations on a Russian Folk Song	Dmitri Kabalevsky
72 / 41	Waves	Emma Lou Diemer
68-69 / 38	Waltz	Dianne Goolkasian Rahbee
66-67 / 37	The Elegant Toreador	Seymour Bernstein
59 / 34	Play It Again	Christopher Norton
60-61 / 35	Machines on the Loose	Kevin Olson

SUGGESTED TEACHING ORDER *of pieces by era:*

The Festival Collection®, Book 4

Baroque Era:

Page / CD Track	Title	Composer
6-7 / 1	The Little Trifle	François Couperin
8 / 2	Fantasia in G major	Georg Philipp Telemann
9 / 3	Polonaise	Unknown (from the Anna Magdalena Bach Notebook)
10-11 / 4	Minuet in G minor	Jean-Philippe Rameau
16-17 / 6	Loure	Georg Philipp Telemann
22-24 / 9	Intrada	Christoph Graupner
18-19 / 7	Bourée in A minor	Johann Ludwig Krebs
20-21 / 8	Verso in E minor	Domenico Zipoli
25 / 10	Dedicated Most Humbly to the Right-Hand Little Finger	Daniel Gottlob Türk
12-15 / 5	Ciaccona with Five Variatons	Johann Pachelbel

Classical Era:

Page / CD Track	Title	Composer
32-33 / 13	Rondo in B flat major	Ignace Joseph Pleyel
36-37 / 15	Sonatina in G major, Op. 83, No. 1 (1st Mvt.)	Jacob Schmitt
38-39 / 16	Rondo in F major	James Hook
26-28 / 11	Sonatina in G, Op. 36, No. 2 (1st Mvt.)	Muzio Clementi
29-31 / 12	La Caroline	Carl Philipp Emanuel Bach
40-42 / 17	Sonatina in C major, Op. 168, No. 3 (3rd Mvt.)	Anton Diabelli
43 / 18	Strong, Sturdy Character	Daniel Gottlob Türk
44-45 / 19	Minuet in F major, K. 5	Wolfgang Amadeus Mozart
46-47 / 20	Capriccio	Johann Wilhelm Hässler
34-35 / 14	Angloise in D major	Johann Christoph Friedrich Bach
48-50 / 21	Sonatina in G major, Op. 55, No. 2 (1st Mvt.)	Friedrich Kuhlau

Romantic Era:

Page / CD Track	Title	Composer
54-57 / 23	Spinning Song, Op. 14, No. 4	Albert Ellmenreich
58-59 / 24	The Shepherdess, Op. 100, No. 11	Johann Friedrich Burgmüller
60-61 / 25	Polka, Op. 39	Pyotr Ilyich Tchaikovsky
62-63 / 26	Allemande in E flat	Carl Maria von Weber
64-65 / 27	Sicilienne, Op. 68, No. 11	Robert Schumann
68-69 / 29	Little Flower, Op. 205	Cornelius Gurlitt
74-75 / 32	Etude in A minor, Op. 47, No. 3	Stephen Heller
72-73 / 31	Turkish March, Op. 101, No. 9	Cornelius Gurlitt
66-67 / 28	Miniature Waltz, Op. 10, No. 10	Vladimir Rebikov
70-71 / 30	Mazurka	Mikhail Glinka
51-53 / 22	Boys Round Dance, Op. 36, No. 3B	Niels W. Gade

20th/21st Centuries:

Page / CD Track	Title	Composer
76 / 33	Elephant Tune	Nina Perry
77 / 34	Tango in C minor	Martín Kutnowski
78 / 35	Song of the Range Rider	George Frederick McKay
84-85 / 39	Rustic Dance, Op. 24, No. 1	Paul Creston
86-87 / 40	Ivan's Song	Aram Khachaturian
79 / 36	Prelude, Op. 138	Dianne Goolkasian Rahbee
80-81 / 37	Two Roosters	Sergey Razorenov
88 / 41	Oriental Flower	Christopher Norton
82-83 / 38	Daydreaming	Timothy Brown

FJH2050

The Festival Collection®, Book 5

Baroque Era:

Page / CD Track	Title	Composer
12-13 / 3	The Prince of Denmark's March	Jeremiah Clarke
14-15 / 4	Marche	Carl Philipp Emanuel Bach
16-17 / 5	Hornpipe	Henry Purcell
18-19 / 6	Passepied	Johann Philipp Kirnberger
22-23 / 8	Bourée in G minor	Gottfried Heinrich Stölzel
20-21 / 7	Rigaudon	Jean-Philippe Rameau
6-8 / 1	Bourée in F major	Georg Philipp Telemann
9-11 / 2	Aire	Jean-Baptiste Loeillet

Classical Era:

Page / CD Track	Title	Composer
30-33 / 11	Allegro, Op. 52, No. 2	Johann Nepomuk Hummel
38-40 / 13	Sonata in G major, Hob. XVI:8 (1st Mvt.)	Franz Joseph Haydn
24-26 / 9	Sonatina in G major, Op. 20, No. 1 (1st Mvt.)	Jan Ladislav Dussek
41-45 / 14	Sonatina in C major, Op. 36, No. 3 (1st Mvt.)	Muzio Clementi
45 / 15	Sonatina in C major, Op. 36, No. 3 (2nd Mvt.)	Muzio Clementi
27-29 / 10	Sonatina in F major, Op. 168, No. 1 (3rd Mvt.)	Anton Diabelli
46-48 / 16	Arietta with Variations, Hob, XVII: 2	Franz Joseph Haydn
34-37 / 12	Sonatina in E flat major, Op. 37, No. 1 (1st Mvt.)	Muzio Clementi

Romantic Era:

Page / CD Track	Title	Composer
58-59 / 20	The Avalanche, Op. 45, No. 2	Stephen Heller
55-57 / 19	Pantalon	Amy Marcy Cheney Beach
66-67 / 23	Waltz, Op. 12, No. 2	Edvard Grieg
68-69 / 24	Elves' Dance, Op. 12, No. 4	Edvard Grieg
52-54 / 18	L'adieu, (The Farewell) Op. 100, No. 12	Johann Friedrich Burgmüller
72-73 / 26	Prelude in C minor, Op. 8, No. 1	Henryk Pachulski
60-63 / 21	Minuet, Op. 23, No. 1	Erkki Melartin
49-51 / 17	Romance, Op. 31, No. 7	Reyngol'd Glier
70-71 / 25	Improvisation, Op. 18	Max Reger
64-65 / 22	Vals sentimental	Enrique Granados

20th/21st Centuries:

Page / CD Track	Title	Composer
94-96 / 35	Toccatina No. 1	Dianee Goolkasian Rahbee
86-87 / 31	Russian Dance	Alexandre Tansman
80-81 / 29	The Banjo Player	Fritz Kaylor
92-93 / 34	Moonlit Meadows, Op. 65, No. 12	Sergei Prokofiev
90-91 / 33	Caravan	Alexei Machavariani
88-89 / 32	Play: for Piano	Andrei Eshpai
74-76 / 27	Evening at the Village	Béla Bartók
82-85 / 30	First Gymnopédie	Erik Satie
77-79 / 28	Le petit nègre	Claude Debussy

SUGGESTED TEACHING ORDER of pieces by era:

The Festival Collection®, Book 6

Baroque Era:

Page / CD Track	Title	Composer
8-11 / 2	Sonata in D minor, K. 89, L. 211	Domenico Scarlatti
18-19 / 6	Toccata in G minor	Leonardo Leo
14-15 / 4	Invention No. 8 in F major	Johann Sebastian Bach
28-29 / 10	Divertimento	Georg Christoph Wagenseil
26-27 / 9	The Grape Pickers	François Couperin
12-13 / 3	Invention No. 1 in C major	Johann Sebastian Bach
20-22 / 7	Allegro	Giovanni Battista Pergolesi
6-7 / 1	Solfeggietto	Carl Philipp Emanuel Bach
23-25 / 8	Toccata in F minor	Carlos de Seixas
16-17 / 5	Invention No. 13 in A minor	Johann Sebastian Bach

Classical Era:

Page / CD Track	Title	Composer
42-45 / 14	Sonatina in C major, Op. 55, No. 3 (1st Mvt.)	Friedrich Kuhlau
64-65 / 21	Rondo Grazioso	Joseph Ignace Pleyel
46-49 / 15	Rondo, Op. 18	Jan Václav Voříšek
50-52 / 16	Sonatina in C major, Op. 88, No. 1 (1st Mvt.)	Friedrich Kuhlau
52-53 / 17	Sonatina in C major, Op. 88, No. 1 (2nd Mvt.)	Friedrich Kuhlau
53-56 / 18	Sonatina in C major, Op. 88, No. 1 (3rd Mvt.)	Friedrich Kuhlau
57-61 / 19	Sonata in C, K. 545 (2nd Mvt.)	Wolfgang Amadeus Mozart
61-63 / 20	Sonata in C, K. 545 (3rd Mvt.)	Wolfgang Amadeus Mozart
30-32 / 11	Sonata No. 18 in A major	Domenico Cimarosa
33-37 / 12	Sonata in G major, Hob. XVI: 27 (3rd Mvt.)	Franz Joseph Haydn
38-41 / 13	Sonatina in E flat major, WoO 47, No. 1 (1st Mvt.)	Ludwig van Beethoven

Romantic Era:

Page / CD Track	Title	Composer
82-83 / 31	The Storm, Op. 109, No. 13	Johann Friedrich Burgmüller
68 / 23	Prelude in E minor	Frédéric Chopin
72-73 / 26	Morning Bell, Op. 109, No. 9	Johann Friedrich Burgmüller
76-77 / 28	Fantasy Dance, Op. 124, No. 5	Robert Schumann
70-71 / 25	Prelude, Op. 40, No. 3	Anatol Liadov
69 / 24	From Foreign Lands and People, Op. 15, No. 1	Robert Schumann
78-79 / 29	Mazurka in B flat major, Op. 7, No. 1	Frédéric Chopin
84-86 / 32	Little Troll, Op. 71, No. 3	Edvard Grieg
87-89 / 33	Valse in A minor	Frédéric Chopin
66-67 / 22	Cradle Song, Op. 68, No. 5	Edvard Grieg
74-75 / 27	Chanson Triste	Vasili Kalinnikov
80-81 / 30	Sketch	César Franck

20th/21st Centuries:

Page / CD Track	Title	Composer
90-93 / 34	Rondo Toccata, Op. 60, No. 4	Dmitri Kabalevsky
114-115 / 44	Petit Musique, Op. 33, No. 8	Florent Schmitt
102-104 / 39	On the Farm	Bohuslav Martinů
98-99 / 37	Joc cu bătă	Béla Bartók
105-107 / 40	Run, Run!	Octavio Pinto
94-95 / 35	No fundo do meu quintal	Heitor Villa-Lobos
96-97 / 36	To the Rising Sun, Op. 4, No. 1	Trygve Torjussen
113 / 43	Moment sérieux	Alexandre Tansman
110-112 / 42	Busy Toccata	Emma Lou Diemer
100-101 / 38	Golden Leaves	Dimitar Ninov
108-109 / 41	A Blown-Away Leaf	Leoš Janáček

The Festival Collection®, Book 7

Baroque Era:

Page / CD Track	Title	Composer
8 / 2	Sarabande in D minor	Johann Sebastian Bach
6-7 / 1	Allemande in D minor	Johann Sebastian Bach
12-13 / 4	Allemande in E flat major	Johann Sebastian Bach
18-19 / 7	Prelude No. 4 in D major	Johann Sebastian Bach
9-11 / 3	Allegro in G minor	George Frideric Handel
14-15 / 5	Giga	Baldassare Galuppi
16-17 / 6	Sinfonia No. 6 in E major	Johann Sebastian Bach
20-21 / 8	Sinfonia No. 15 in B minor	Johann Sebastian Bach
22-24 / 9	Sonata in C major, K. 159/L. 104	Domenico Scarlatti

Classical Era:

Page / CD Track	Title	Composer
37-40 / 13	Sonata in B flat major	Muzio Clementi
34-36 / 12	Moonlight Sonata, Op. 27, No. 2 (1st Mvt.)	Ludwig van Beethoven
46-49 / 15	Sonata in C major, K. 545 (1st Mvt.)	Wolfgang Amadeus Mozart
41-45 / 14	Sonata in E minor, Hob. XV: 34 (3rd Mvt.)	Franz Joseph Haydn
25-29 / 10	Fantasie in D minor	Wolfgang Amadeus Mozart
30-33 / 11	Sonata in G, K. 283 (1st Mvt.)	Wolfgang Amadeus Mozart
50-55 / 16	Variations in G major, WoO 77	Ludwig van Beethoven

Romantic Era:

Page / CD Track	Title	Composer
58 / 2	Waltz in G sharp minor, Op. 39, No. 3	Johannes Brahms
91-93 / 11	Venetian Boat Song, Op. 30, No. 6	Felix Mendelssohn
88-90 / 10	Forest Birds	Adolf Jensen
58-59 / 3	Waltz in E minor, Op. 39, No. 4	Johannes Brahms
60-63 / 4	Waltz in A flat major, Op. 70, No. 2	Frederic Chopin
56-57 / 1	Moments musicaux, Op. 94, No. 3	Franz Schubert
94 / 12	Study in D minor, Op. 45, No. 15	Stephen Heller
76-79 / 8	Notturno, Op. 54, No. 4	Edvard Grieg
72-75 / 7	April, Op. 37b, No. 4	Pyotr Ilyich Tchaikovsky
64-66 / 5	Romanze in F sharp major, Op. 28, No. 2	Robert Schumann
80-87 / 9	Tarantella	Albert Pieczonka
67-71 / 6	The Bamboula, Op. 59, No. 8	Samuel Coleridge-Taylor

20th/21st Centuries:

Page / CD Track	Title	Composer
102-103 / 15	Fantastic Dance No. 1	Dmitri Shostakovich
104-107 / 16	Playera, Op. 5, No. 5	Enrique Granados
108-110 / 17	Cris dans la rue	Federico Mompou
100-101 / 14	Galop final	Alfredo Casella
96-99 / 13	O Polichinello	Heitor Villa-Lobos
111-115 / 18	First Arabesque	Claude Debussy
116-120 / 19	Sonatina in C major (1st Mvt.)	Aram Khachaturian

SUGGESTED TEACHING ORDER *of pieces by era:*

The Festival Collection®, Book 8

Baroque Era:

Page / CD Track	Title	Composer
6-7 / 1	Allemande in G major from French Suite No. 5, BWV 816	Johann Sebastian Bach
8-9 / 2	Courante in G major from French Suite No. 5, BWV 816	Johann Sebastian Bach
10-11 / 3	Sonata in B minor, K. 87, L. 33	Domenico Scarlatti
24-27 / 9	Air with Variations in E minor (The Harmonious Blacksmith from Suite No. 5, HWV 430)	George Frideric Handel
16-19 / 5,6	Prelude and Fugue No. 2 in C minor, BWV 847	Johann Sebastian Bach
20-23 / 7,8	Prelude and Fugue No. 9 in E major, BWV 854	Johann Sebastian Bach
12-15 / 4	Sonata in F sharp minor, K. 25, L. 481	Domenico Scarlatti

Classical Era:

Page / CD Track	Title	Composer
67-74 / 17	Sonata in B flat major, K. 570 (1st Mvt.)	Wolfgang Amadeus Mozart
57-62 / 15	Sonata in D Major, Hob. XVI: 37 (1st Mvt.)	Franz Joseph Haydn
28-41 / 10,11,12	Sonata in F Major, Hob. XVI: 23 (1st, 2nd, and 3rd Mvt.)	Franz Joseph Haydn
63-66 / 16	Rondo alla Turca, KV. 331 (3rd Mvt.)	Wolfgang Amadeus Mozart
42-56 / 13,14	Sonata in C minor, Op. 13 (1st and 2nd Mvt.)	Ludwig van Beethoven

Romantic Era:

Page / CD Track	Title	Composer
94-97 / 22	Mazurka in A flat major, Op. 59, No. 2	Frédéric Chopin
92-93 / 21	Consolation No. 5	Franz Liszt
98-104 / 23	Wedding Day at Troldhaugen, Op. 65, No. 6	Edvard Grieg
86-91 / 20	Nocturne in B flat minor, Op. 9, No. 1	Frédéric Chopin
80-85 / 19	Intermezzo in A major Op. 118, No. 2	Johannes Brahms
75-79 / 18	Dreaming, Op. 15, No. 3	Amy Marcy Cheney Beach

Late Romantic Era:

Page / CD Track	Title	Composer
114-117 / 26	Capriccio, Op. 84, No. 1	Gabriel Urbain Fauré
118-123 / 27	Romance, Op. 24, No. 9	Jean Sibelius
105-109 / 24	Prelude in C sharp minor, Op. 3, No. 2	Sergei Rachmaninov
110-113 / 25	Poem No. 1, Op. 32	Alexander Nikolayevich Scriabin

20th/21st Centuries:

Page / CD Track	Title	Composer
134-139 / 30	The Cat and the Mouse	Aaron Copland
140-143 / 31	Rialto Ripples	George Gershwin/Will Donaldson
146-148 / 33	Bulgarian Dance No. 2	Béla Bártok
144-145 / 32	Minuet on the Name of Haydn	Maurice Ravel
124-127 / 28	Etude de Sonorite No. 1	Francois Morel
128-133 / 29	Clair de lune	Claude Debussy

FJH2050

SUGGESTED TEACHING ORDER of pieces by book:

The Festival Collection®, Preparatory

March, p. 8 / CD 4
Bagpipe, p. 6 / CD 1
Follow the Leader, p. 7 / CD 3
Running the Race, p. 8 / CD 5
Elegant Dance, p. 9 / CD 6
A Day in the Country, p. 10 / CD 7
At Play, p. 12-13 / CD 11
Having Fun on My Pogo Stick,
    p. 19 / CD 17

Buying Potatoes, p. 10 / CD 8
Two Penguins, p. 14 / CD 12
A Merry Dance, p. 6 / CD 2
The Lively Boy, p. 11 / CD 9
Saturday Afternoon Walk,
    p. 11 / CD 10
In a Hot Air Balloon, p. 15 / CD 13
The Mermaid, p. 16 / CD 14
The Peacock, p. 20-21 / CD 18

Lightning Strike!, p. 22-23 / CD 19
Busy at Work, p. 17 / CD 15
Going on A Road Trip,
    p. 18 / CD 16
The Dance at the Village Square,
    p. 24-25 / CD 20

The Festival Collection®, Preparatory can be used when a student learns eighth notes in any method book, which is usually in Level 2. After the Preparatory level is finished, students can go on to On Your Way to Succeeding with the Masters® as well as The Festival Collection®, Book 1.

The Festival Collection®, Book 1

(with On Your Way to Succeeding with the Masters®)

Trumpets, p. 26 / CD 21
Hungarian Song, p. 29 / CD 24
Allegro, p. 17 / CD 14
Old German Dance, p. 6 / CD 1
Canary, p. 8 / CD 3
The Young Dancer, p. 20 / CD 17
A Song, p. 19 / CD 16
The Shepherd Plays, p. 32 / CD 27
Arabian Dance, p. 30 / CD 25
Minuet, p. 13 / CD 9

Minuet, p. 12 / CD 7
A Carefree Fellow, p. 12 / CD 8
Intrada, p. 10 / CD 5
Allemande, p. 7 / CD 2
Kitten Play, p. 21 / CD 18
Snowflakes Gently Falling,
    p. 27 / CD 22
Song, p. 16 / CD 13
Petit Minuet, p. 9 / CD 4
Spring Waltz, p. 24-25 / CD 20

The Sparrows, p. 28 / CD 23
Air for Southpaw, p. 31 / CD 26
Sonatina (1st Mvt.), p. 14 / CD 10
Sonatina (2nd Mvt.), p. 14 / CD 11
Sonatina (3rd Mvt.), p. 15 / CD 12
Petit Rondo, p. 11 / CD 6
Agitato, p. 18 / CD 15
Valsette, p. 22-23 / CD 19

SUGGESTED TEACHING ORDER of pieces by book:

The Festival Collection®, Book 2

(with *Succeeding with the Masters®, Volume One*)

The Festival Collection®, Book 3

(with *Succeeding with the Masters®, Volume One*)

FJH2050

SUGGESTED TEACHING ORDER *of pieces by book:*

The Festival Collection®, Book 4

(with *Succeeding with the Masters®, Volume One*)

Spinning Song, p. 54-57 / CD 23
Rondo in B flat major, p. 32-33 / CD 13
The Shepherdess, Op. 100, No. 11,
   p. 58-59 / CD 24
Sonatina in G, p. 36-37 / CD 15
Polka, p. 60-61 / CD 25
Rondo in F major, p. 38-39 / CD 16
Allemande in E flat, p. 62-63 / CD 26
Sonatina in G, Op. 36, No. 2,
   (1st Mvt.), p. 26-28 / CD 11

Sicilienne, Op. 68, No. 11,
   p. 64-65 / CD 27
La Caroline, p. 29-31 / CD 12
Little Flower, p. 68-69 / CD 29
The Little Trifle, p. 6-7 / CD 1
Elephant Tune, p. 76 / CD 33
Fantasia in G minor, p. 8 / CD 2
Tango in C minor, p. 77 / CD 34
Polonaise, p. 9 / CD 3
Song of the Range Rider, p. 78 / CD 35

Minuet in G minor,
   p. 10-11 / CD 4
Rustic Dance, Op. 24, No. 1,
   p. 84-85 / CD 39
Loure, p. 16-17 / CD 6
Ivan's Song, p. 86-87 / CD 40

(with *Succeeding with the Masters®, Volume Two*)

Sonatina in C major, Op. 168, No. 3,
   (3rd Mvt.), p. 40-42 / CD 17
Etude in A minor, Op. 47, No. 3,
   p. 74-75 / CD 32
Strong, Sturdy Character, p. 43 / CD 18
Turkish March, Op. 101, No. 9,
   p. 72-73 / CD 31
Prelude Op. 138, p. 79 / CD 36
Minuet in F major, K. 5,
   p. 44-45 / CD 19
Intrada, p. 22-24 / CD 9

Two Roosters, p. 80-81 / CD 37
Capriccio, p. 46-47 / CD 20
Verso in E minor, p. 20-21 / CD 8
Miniature Waltz, Op. 10, No. 10,
   p. 66-67 / CD 28
Dedicated Most Humbly to the
   Right-Hand Little Finger,
   p. 25 / CD 10
Mazurka, p. 70-71 / CD 30
Bourrée in A minor, p. 18-19 / CD 7

Boys Round Dance, Op. 36, No. 3B,
   p. 51-53 / CD 22
Oriental Flower, p. 88 / CD 41
Ciaccona with Five Variations,
   p. 12-15 / CD 5
Angloise in D major,
   p. 34-35 / CD 14
Daydreaming, p. 82-83 / CD 38
Sonatina in G major, Op. 55, No. 2
   (1st Mvt.), p. 48-50 / CD 21

SUGGESTED TEACHING ORDER of pieces by book:

The Festival Collection®, Book 5

(with *Succeeding with the Masters*®, *Volume Two*)

Toccatina No. 1, p. 94-96 / CD 35
The Prince of Denmark's March,
   p. 12-13 / CD 3
Marche, p. 14-15 / CD 4
The Avalanche, Op. 45, No. 2,
   p. 58-59 / CD 20
Russian Dance, p. 86-87 / CD 31
Allegro, Op. 52, No. 2,
   p. 30-33 / CD 11
Pantalon, p. 55-57 / CD 19
Sonata in G major, Hob. XVI:8
   (1st Mvt.), p. 38-40 / CD 13
Waltz, Op. 12, No. 2, p. 66-67 / CD 23
The Banjo Player, p. 80-81 / CD 29
Hornpipe, p. 16-17 / CD 5
Sonatina in G major, Op. 20, No. 1
   (1st Mvt.), p. 24-26 / CD 9
Moonlit Meadows, Op. 65, No. 12,
   p. 92-93 / CD 34

Sonatina in C major, Op. 36, No. 3,
   (1st Mvt.), p. 41-45 / CD 14
Sonatina in C major, Op. 36, No. 3,
   (2nd Mvt.), p. 45 / CD 15
Caravan, p. 90-91 / CD 33
Elves' Dance, Op. 12, No. 4,
   p. 68-69 / CD 24
L'adieu, Op. 100, No. 12,
   p. 52-54 / CD 18
Prelude in C minor, Op. 8, No. 1,
   p. 72-73 / CD 26
Sonatina in F major, Op. 168, No. 1
   (3rd Mvt.), p. 27-29 / CD 10
Play: for Piano, p. 88-89 / CD 32
Arietta with Variations, Hob, XVII:2,
   p. 46-47 / CD 16
Minuet, Op. 23, No. 1, p. 60-63 / CD 21
Passepied, p. 18-19 / CD 6

Evening at the Village,
   p. 74-76 / CD 27
Bourrée in G minor, p. 22-23 / CD 8
Rigaudon, p. 20-21 / CD 7
First Gymnopédie, p. 82-85 / CD 30
Bourrée in F major, p. 6-8 / CD 1
Le petit nègre, p. 77-79 / CD 28
Aire, p. 9-11 / CD 2
Sonatina in E flat major, Op. 37,
   No. 1 (1st Mvt.), p. 34-37 / CD 12
Romance, Op. 31, No. 7,
   p. 49-51 / CD 17
Improvisation, Op. 18,
   p. 70-71 / CD 25
Vals sentimental, p. 64-65 / CD 22

The Festival Collection®, Book 6

(with *Succeeding with the Masters*®, *Volume Two*)

Sonata in D minor, K. 89, L. 211,
   p. 8-11 / CD 2
The Storm, Op. 109, No. 13,
   p. 82-83 / CD 31
Prelude in E minor, Op. 28, No. 4,
   p. 68 / CD 23
Toccata in G minor, p. 18-19 / CD 6
Morning Bell, Op. 109, No. 9,
   p. 72-73 / CD 26
Rondo Toccata, Op. 60, No. 4,
   p. 90-93 / CD 34
Fantasy Dance, Op. 124, No. 5,
   p. 76-77 / CD 28
Sonatina in C major, Op. 55, No. 3
   (1st Mvt.), p. 42-45 / CD 14
Rondo Grazioso, p. 64-65 / CD 21
Petit Musique, Op. 33, No. 8,
   p. 114-115 / CD 44
Invention No. 8 in F major,
   p. 14-15 / CD 4
On the Farm, p. 102-104 / CD 39
Divertimento, p. 28-29 / CD 10
Rondo, Op. 18, p. 46-49 / CD 15
Joc cu bâtă, p. 98-99 / CD 37
Prelude, Op. 40, No. 3,
   p. 70-71 / CD 25

Sonatina in C major, Op. 88, No. 1
   (1st Mvt.), p. 50-52 / CD 16
Sonatina in C major, Op. 88, No. 1
   (2nd Mvt.), p. 52-53 / CD 17
Sonatina in C major, Op. 88, No. 1
   (3rd Mvt.), p. 53-56 / CD 18
Run, Run!, p. 105-107 / CD 40
The Grape Pickers, p. 26-27 / CD 9
From Foreign Lands and People,
   Op. 15, No. 1, p. 69 / CD 24
No fundo do meu quintal,
   p. 94-95 / CD 35
Invention No. 1 in C major,
   p. 12-13 / CD 3
Mazurka in B flat major, Op. 7,
   No. 1, p. 78-79 / CD 29
Sonata in C, K. 545 (2nd Mvt.),
   p. 57-61 / CD 19
To the Rising Sun, Op. 4, No. 1,
   p. 96-97 / CD 36
Allegro, p. 20-22 / CD 7
Sonata in C, K. 545 (3rd Mvt.),
   p. 61-63 / CD 20
Little Troll, Op. 71, No. 3,
   p. 84-86 / CD 32

Sonata No. 18 in A major,
   p. 30-32 / CD 11
Valse in A minor, p. 87-89 / CD 33
Cradle Song, Op. 68, No. 5,
   p. 66-67 / CD 22
Solfeggietto, p. 6-7 / CD 1
Chanson Triste, p. 74-75 / CD 27
Moment sérieux, p. 113 / CD 43
Sonata in G major, Hob. XVI: 27
   (3rd Mvt.), p. 33-37 / CD 12
Sketch, p. 80-81 / CD 30
Toccata in F minor, p. 23-25 / CD 8
Busy Toccata, p. 110-112 / CD 42
Sonatina in E flat major, WoO 47,
   No. 1 (1st Mvt.), p. 38-41 / CD 13
Golden Leaves, p. 100-101 / CD 38
A Blown-Away Leaf,
   p. 108-109 / CD 41
Invention No. 13 in A minor,
   p. 16-17 / CD 5

FJH2050

The Festival Collection®, Book 1

Correlated with **On Your Way to Succeeding with the Masters**®

FEATURES OF THIS CORRELATION:

1. *The Festival Collection*®, *Book 1* is considered the core curriculum and *On Your Way to Succeeding with the Masters*® is used for special focus on musical eras and Practice Strategies.

2. Each unit includes pieces from all 4 musical eras found in *The Festival Collection*®, *Book 1*. These pieces are listed in order of difficulty.

3. Each unit also features a special focus on 2 musical eras found in *On Your Way to Succeeding with the Masters*®. The musical eras are introduced in chronological order in Units 1-3 and then reviewed in Units 4-5. The pieces from *On Your Way to Succeeding with the Masters*® are listed in order of difficulty.

4. A complete list of Practice Strategies found in *On Your Way to Succeeding with the Masters*® is included in every unit. One Practice Strategy is suggested for each piece in the unit for a well-rounded curriculum that includes regular review and reinforcement.

5. The Practice Strategy assigned to each piece is a suggestion only. Teachers should feel free to change or adapt any Practice Strategy to the needs of the individual student.

6. The Practice Strategy "Getting Ready for a Performance" may be used with any piece at any time the student is preparing for an upcoming performance.

7. Much freedom is given for teachers and students to choose appropriate repertoire once the basic concepts of each era have been presented. The listening CD's provide a valuable resource to aid in the selection process.

8. The following abbreviations are used: FC = *The Festival Collection*®; SWTM = *Succeeding with the Masters*®; and Cent. = Centuries.

Succeeding with the Masters® *& The Festival Collection*® *Etudes with Technique Book 1*, can be used at the same time as *The Festival Collection*®, *Book 1* (See p. 4 for more details).

The Festival Collection®, Book 1

Correlated with **On Your Way to Succeeding with the Masters®**

Pieces from **The Festival Collection®**, *arranged in order of difficulty.*
The section "About the Pieces and the Composers" beginning on p. 33 provides further valuable information.

Era	Title, Page, and CD Track	Composer
20th/21st Cent.	Trumpets, p. 26 / CD 21	Martín Kutnowski
20th/21st Cent.	Hungarian Song, p. 29 / CD 24	Béla Bartók
Classical	Allegro, p. 17 / CD 14	Alexander Reinagle
Baroque	Old German Dance, p. 6 / CD 1	Michael Praetorius
Romantic	The Young Dancer, p. 20 / CD 17	Cornelius Gurlitt
Classical	Minuet, p. 13 / CD 9	James Hook

Pieces from **On Your Way to Succeeding with the Masters®**, *arranged in order of difficulty.*
The introduction and activities for this era are found on p. 4-5.

Era	Title, Page, and CD Track	Composer
Medieval	Trouvère, p. 6 / CD 1	Richard I, Coeur-de-lion
Medieval	Ballade, p. 7 / CD 2	Perrin d'Angicourt

Pieces from **On Your Way to Succeeding with the Masters®**, *arranged in order of difficulty.*
The introduction and activities for this era are found on p. 8-9.

Era	Title, Page, and CD Track	Composer
Renaissance	Hercules' Dance, p. 12 / CD 5	Attributed to Tielman Susato
Renaissance	Pavanne, p. 10 / CD 3	Claude Gervaise
Renaissance	Skipping Dance, p. 13 / CD 6	August Nörmiger
Renaissance	A Study in 5/4 Time, p. 11 / CD 4	Thomas Morley

Practice Strategies found in **On Your Way to Succeeding with the Masters®**

Practice Strategy	Page	CD
Learn and Practice	5	38
Chain-linking	9	39
Getting Ready for a Performance	15	40
Balancing the Melody with the Accompaniment	23	41
Careful Listening	33	42
3x1 Rule	41	43

Suggested Practice Strategies for each piece in Unit 1.
Reminders:

• *The Practice Strategy assigned to each piece is a suggestion only. These strategies can be used interchangeably with practically all of the repertoire pieces. The teacher should feel free to change or adapt any Practice Strategy to the needs of the individual student.*

• *The Practice Strategy "Getting Ready for a Performance" may be used with any piece at any time the student is preparing for an upcoming performance.*

Book	Title	Practice Strategy
FC	Trumpets	Balancing the Melody with the Accompaniment
FC	Hungarian Song	Chain-linking
FC	Allegro	Balancing the Melody with the Accompaniment
FC	Old German Dance	Learn and Practice
FC	The Young Dancer	Learn and Practice
FC	Minuet	Balancing the Melody with the Accompaniment

Book	Title	Practice Strategy
SWTM	Trouvère	Learn and Practice
SWTM	Ballade	Careful Listening
SWTM	Hercules' Dance	Chain-linking
SWTM	Pavanne	3x1 Rule
SWTM	Skipping Dance	Learn & Practice
SWTM	A Study in 5/4 Time	Learn & Practice

FJH2050

The Festival Collection®, Book 1

Correlated with **On Your Way to Succeeding with the Masters**®

Pieces from **The Festival Collection**®, *arranged in order of difficulty.*
The section "About the Pieces and the Composers" beginning on p. 33 provides further valuable information.

Era	Title, Page, and CD Track	Composer
Baroque	Canary, p. 8 / CD 3	Joachim van den Hove
Romantic	A Song, p. 19 / CD 16	Alexander Gedike
20th/21st Cent.	The Shepherd Plays, p. 32 / CD 27	Tat'iana Salutrinskaya
Classical	Minuet, p. 12 / CD 7	Daniel Gottlob Türk
Baroque	Intrada, p.10 / CD 5	Paul Peuerl

Pieces from **On Your Way to Succeeding with the Masters**®, *arranged in order of difficulty.*
The introduction and activities for this era are found on p. 14-15.

Era	Title, Page, and CD Track	Composer
Baroque	The Statues Are Dancing, p. 16 / CD 7	André Cardinal Destouches
Baroque	Two Baroque Musicians, p. 17 / CD 8	Attributed to Sébastien de Brossard
Baroque	Bourrée, p. 19 / CD 10	Maaghdalena Dakkert

Pieces from **On Your Way to Succeeding with the Masters**®, *arranged in order of difficulty.*
The introduction and activities for this era are found on p. 22-23.

Era	Title, Page, and CD Track	Composer
Classical	Allegro, p. 28 / CD 21	Alexander Reinagle
Classical	The Cobblestone Road, p. 31 / CD 24	Alexander Reinagle
Classical	Sunset at the Boardwalk, p. 29 / CD 22	Carl Czerny
Classical	Monday March, p. 30 / CD 23	Carl Czerny
Classical	Allegretto, p. 27 / CD 19	Alexander Reinagle
Classical	Children's Song, p. 27 / CD 20	Daniel Gottlob Türk

Practice Strategies found in **On Your Way to Succeeding with the Masters**®

Practice Strategy	Page	CD
Learn and Practice	5	38
Chain-linking	9	39
Getting Ready for a Performance	15	40
Balancing the Melody with the Accompaniment	23	41
Careful Listening	33	42
3x1 Rule	41	43

Suggested Practice Strategies for each piece in Unit 2.
Reminders:

- *The Practice Strategy assigned to each piece is a suggestion only. These strategies can be used interchangeably with practically all of the repertoire pieces. The teacher should feel free to change or adapt any Practice Strategy to the needs of the individual student.*

- *The Practice Strategy "Getting Ready for a Performance" may be used with any piece at any time the student is preparing for an upcoming performance.*

Book	Title	Practice Strategy
FC	Canary	Chain-linking
FC	A Song	Careful Listening
FC	The Shepherd Plays	3x1 Rule
FC	Minuet	3x1 Rule
FC	Intrada	Learn and Practice

Book	Title	Practice Strategy
SWTM	The Statues Are Dancing	Learn and Practice
SWTM	Two Baroque Musicians	Chain-linking
SWTM	Bourrée	Chain-linking
SWTM	Allegro	Balancing the Melody with the Accompaniment
SWTM	The Cobblestone Road	Learn and Practice
SWTM	Sunset at the Boardwalk	Careful Listening
SWTM	Monday March	3x1 Rule
SWTM	Allegretto	Balancing the Melody with the Accompaniment
SWTM	Children's Song	Balancing the Melody with the Accompaniment

The Festival Collection®, Book 1

Correlated with *On Your Way to Succeeding with the Masters®*

Pieces from *The Festival Collection®*, arranged in order of difficulty.
The section "About the Pieces and the Composers" beginning on p. 33 provides further valuable information.

Era	Title, Page, and CD Track	Composer
20th/21st Cent.	Arabian Dance, p. 30 / CD 25	Timothy Brown
Classical	A Carefree Fellow, p. 12 / CD 8	Daniel Gottlob Türk
Baroque	Allemande, p. 7 / CD 2	Johann Hermann Schein
Romantic	Kitten Play, p. 21 / CD 18	Cornelius Gurlitt
Classical	Song, p. 16 / CD 13	Anton Diabelli

Pieces from *On Your Way to Succeeding with the Masters®*, arranged in order of difficulty.
The introduction and activities for this era are found on p. 32-33.

Era	Title, Page, and CD Track	Composer
Romantic	In the Garden, p. 35 / CD 26	Louis Köhler
Romantic	The Mighty Hawk, p. 39 / CD 30	Cornelius Gurlitt
Romantic	Soldier's Song, p. 34 / CD 25	Moritz Vogel

Pieces from *On Your Way to Succeeding with the Masters®*, arranged in order of difficulty.
The introduction and activities for this era are found on p. 40-41.

Era	Title, Page, and CD Track	Composer
20th/21st Cent.	Polka, p. 44 / CD 34	Dmitri Kabalevsky
20th/21st Cent.	Study, p. 43 / CD 32	Béla Bartók
20th/21st Cent.	Gradus No. 8, p. 44 / CD 33	Samuel Adler
20th/21st Cent.	The Sparrow's Song, p. 42 / CD 31	Timothy Brown

Practice Strategies found in *On Your Way to Succeeding with the Masters®*

Practice Strategy	Page	CD
Learn and Practice	5	38
Chain-linking	9	39
Getting Ready for a Performance	15	40
Balancing the Melody with the Accompaniment	23	41
Careful Listening	33	42
3x1 Rule	41	43

Suggested Practice Strategies for each piece in Unit 3.
Reminders:

- The Practice Strategy assigned to each piece is a suggestion only. These strategies can be used interchangeably with practically all of the repertoire pieces. The teacher should feel free to change or adapt any Practice Strategy to the needs of the individual student.

- The Practice Strategy "Getting Ready for a Performance" may be used with any piece at any time the student is preparing for an upcoming performance.

Book	Title	Practice Strategy	Book	Title	Practice Strategy
FC	Arabian Dance	Careful Listening	SWTM	In the Garden	Careful Listening
FC	A Carefree Fellow	Chain-linking	SWTM	The Mighty Hawk	3x1 Rule
FC	Allemande	Chain-linking	SWTM	Soldier's Song	Chain-linking
FC	Kitten Play	Careful Listening	SWTM	Polka	3x1 Rule
FC	Song	Careful Listening	SWTM	Study	Careful Listening
			SWTM	Gradus No. 8	Balancing the Melody with the Accompaniment
			SWTM	The Sparrow's Song	Careful Listening

The Festival Collection®, Book 1

Correlated with **On Your Way to Succeeding with the Masters®**

Pieces from The Festival Collection®, arranged in order of difficulty.
The section "About the Pieces and the Composers" beginning on p. 33 provides further valuable information.

Era	Title, Page, and CD Track	Composer
20th/21st Cent.	Snowflakes Gently Falling, p. 27 / CD 22	Dianne Goolkasian Rahbee
Baroque	Petit Minuet, p. 9 / CD 4	Jean-Nicolas Geoffroy
Romantic	Spring Waltz, p. 24-25 / CD 20	Fritz Spindler
20th/21st Cent.	The Sparrows, p. 28 / CD 23	A. Rubbach
Classical	Agitato, p. 18 / CD 15	Johann Christian Bach/Francesco Pasquale Ricci
Classical	Sonatina (1st Mvt.), p. 14 / CD 10	Daniel Gottlob Türk

Pieces from On Your Way to Succeeding with the Masters®, arranged in order of difficulty.

Era	Title, Page, and CD Track	Composer
Baroque	Noël, p. 21 / CD 12	arr. Jean François Dandrieu
Baroque	Minuet, p. 18 / CD 9	Maaghdalena Dakkert
Baroque	Minuet, p. 20 / CD 11	Marin Marais
Romantic	Happily Exercising, p. 38 / CD 29	Ferdinand Beyer
Romantic	Water Sprite, p. 37 / CD 28	Hermann Berens
Romantic	Going to School, p. 36 / CD 27	Cornelius Gurlitt

Practice Strategies found in On Your Way to Succeeding with the Masters®

Practice Strategy	Page	CD
Learn and Practice	5	38
Chain Linking	9	39
Getting Ready for a Performance	15	40
Balancing the Melody with the Accompaniment	23	41
Careful Listening	33	42
3x1 Rule	41	43

Suggested Practice Strategies for each piece in Unit 4.
Reminders:

- The Practice Strategy assigned to each piece is a suggestion only. These strategies can be used interchangeably with practically all of the repertoire pieces. The teacher should feel free to change or adapt any Practice Strategy to the needs of the individual student.

- The Practice Strategy "Getting Ready for a Performance" may be used with any piece at any time the student is preparing for an upcoming performance.

Book	Title	Practice Strategy
FC	Snowflakes Gently Falling	Learn and Practice
FC	Petit Minuet	Learn and Practice
FC	Spring Waltz	Balancing the Melody with the Accompaniment
FC	The Sparrows	3x1 Rule
FC	Agitato	Learn and Practice
FC	Sonatina (1st Mvt.)	Balancing the Melody with the Accompaniment

Book	Title	Practice Strategy
SWTM	Noël	Chain-linking
SWTM	Minuet, p. 18	Learn and Practice
SWTM	Minuet, p. 20	Careful Listening
SWTM	Happily Exercising	Learn and Practice
SWTM	Water Sprite	Careful Listening
SWTM	Going to School	Careful Listening

FJH2050

The Festival Collection®, Book 1

Correlated with On Your Way to Succeeding with the Masters®

Pieces from The Festival Collection®, arranged in order of difficulty.
The section "About the Pieces and the Composers" beginning on p. 33 provides further valuable information.

Era	Title, Page, and CD Track	Composer
20th/21st Cent.	Air for Southpaw, p. 31 / CD 26	Arthur R. Frackenpohl
Classical	Sonatina (2nd Mvt.), p. 14 / CD 11	Daniel Gottlob Türk
Classical	Sonatina (3rd Mvt.), p. 15 / CD 12	Daniel Gottlob Türk
Baroque	Petit Rondo, p. 11 / CD 6	Jean-Nicolas Geoffroy
Romantic	Valsette, p. 22-23 / CD 19	Moritz Vogel

Pieces from On Your Way to Succeeding with the Masters®, arranged in order of difficulty.

Era	Title, Page, and CD Track	Composer
Classical	Prelude, p. 26 / CD 18	Samuel Arnold
Classical	A Little Waltz, p. 26 / CD 17	Daniel Gottlob Türk
Classical	Softly, Like the Wind, p. 25 / CD 16	Daniel Gottlob Türk
Classical	The Scale Ladder, p. 25 / CD 15	Daniel Gottlob Türk
Classical	Scherzo, p. 24 / CD 13	Johann Andreas Kauchlitz Colizzi
Classical	The Bohemian, p. 24 / CD 14	Johann Andreas Kauchlitz Colizzi
20th/21st Cent.	Tiresome Prank, p. 45 / CD 35	Erik Satie
20th/21st Cent.	The Old Gypsy Violin, p. 47 / CD 37	Kevin Olson
20th/21st Cent.	Playing, p. 46 / CD 36	Dmitri Kabalevsky

Practice Strategies found in On Your Way to Succeeding with the Masters®

Practice Strategy	Page	CD
Learn and Practice	5	38
Chain-linking	9	39
Getting Ready for a Performance	15	40
Balancing the Melody with the Accompaniment	23	41
Careful Listening	33	42
3x1 Rule	41	43

Suggested Practice Strategies for each piece in Unit 5.
Reminders:

• *The Practice Strategy assigned to each piece is a suggestion only. These strategies can be used interchangeably with practically all of the repertoire pieces. The teacher should feel free to change or adapt any Practice Strategy to the needs of the individual student.*

• *The Practice Strategy "Getting Ready for a Performance" may be used with any piece at any time the student is preparing for an upcoming performance.*

Book	Title	Practice Strategy	Book	Title	Practice Strategy
FC	Air for Southpaw	Balancing the Melody with the Accompaniment	SWTM	Prelude	3x1 Rule
			SWTM	A Little Waltz	3x1 Rule
FC	Sonatina (2nd Mvt.)	Careful Listening	SWTM	Softly, Like the Wind	Balancing the Melody with the Accompaniment
FC	Sonatina (3rd Mvt.)	3x1 Rule			
FC	Petit Rondo	Chain-linking	SWTM	The Scale Ladder	Learn and Practice
FC	Valsette	Balancing the Melody with the Accompaniment	SWTM	Scherzo	3x1 Rule
			SWTM	The Bohemian	Chain-linking
			SWTM	Tiresome Prank	3x1 Rule
			SWTM	The Old Gypsy Violin	Balancing the Melody with the Accompaniment
			SWTM	Playing	Chain-linking

The Festival Collection®, Books 2, 3, and easier selections from Book 4

Correlated with *Succeeding with the Masters®, Volume One*
Baroque, Classical, and Romantic Eras.

Using *The Festival Collection®* as the core series and *Succeeding with the Masters®, Volume One* as a pedagogical and historical guide to the master composers. Using both series together is the most beneficial way for students to learn repertoire—through a pedagogical, social, and historical perspective.

FEATURES OF THIS CORRELATION:

1. *The Festival Collection®* is considered the core curriculum and *Succeeding with the Masters®, Volume One* is used for special focus on musical eras, composers, and Practice Strategies.

2. Each unit includes pieces from all 4 musical eras found in *The Festival Collection®*. These pieces are listed in order of difficulty.

3. Each unit also features a special focus on master composers found in *Succeeding with the Masters®, Volume One*. The pieces by the composers are listed in order of difficulty.

4. One of the teacher's goals is to make student practicing more efficient. Students can easily apply the Practice Strategies from *Succeeding with the Masters®, Volume One* to the pieces in *The Festival Collection®*. One Practice Strategy is suggested for each piece in the unit for a well-rounded curriculum that includes regular review and reinforcement.

5. The Practice Strategies found in *On Your Way to Succeeding with the Masters®* can also be used with all the pieces in *The Festival Collection®*. These Practice Strategies include: "Learn and Practice;" "Chain-linking;" "Getting Ready for a Performance;" "Careful Listening;" and "Slow vs. fast practice (3x1rule)."

6. The Practice Strategy assigned to each piece is a suggestion only. Teachers should feel free to change or adapt any Practice Strategy to the needs of the individual student.

7. Much freedom is given for teachers and students to choose appropriate repertoire once the basic concepts of each era have been presented. The listening CD's provide a valuable resource to aid in the selection process.

8. For a general overview of the Baroque era and Baroque performance practice, see p. 2-3 and 7-9 of *Succeeding with the Masters®, Baroque Era, Volume One*. For a general overview of the Classical era, see p. 2-3 of *Succeeding with the Masters®, Classical Era, Volume One*. For a general overview of the Romantic era, see p. 2-3 of *Succeeding with the Masters®, Romantic Era, Volume One*.

9. The following abbreviations are used: FC = *The Festival Collection®*; SWTM = *Succeeding with the Masters®*; and Cent. = Centuries.

FJH2050

The Festival Collection®, Book 2

*Correlated with **Succeeding with the Masters®,** Volume One*
Baroque, Classical, and Romantic Eras

Pieces from The Festival Collection®, arranged in order of difficulty.
The section "About the Pieces and the Composers" beginning on p. 50 provides further valuable information.

Era	Title, Page, and CD Track	Composer
Romantic	Etude, p. 33 / CD 22	Ferdinand Beyer
Baroque	Gavotte, p. 9 / CD 4	Daniel Speer
Romantic	The Hunt, p. 32 / CD 21	Cornelius Gurlitt
Classical	Little Dance, p. 27 / CD 16	Daniel Gottlob Türk
20th/21st Cent.	The Bear, p. 43 / CD 33	Vladimir Rebikov

Practice Strategies for The Festival Collection®, arranged in chronological order.
*Refer to the corresponding era in **Succeeding with the Masters®,** Volume One for a complete description of each Practice Strategy.*

Era	Title, Page, and CD Track	Practice Strategies from SWTM
Baroque	Gavotte, p. 9 / CD 4	• 8 times to perfection, p. 35 / CD 30 • Slow vs. fast practicing (3 x 1 rule), p. 52 / CD 36
Classical	Little Dance, p. 27 / CD 16	• Balancing a melody with an accompaniment, p. 14 / CD 30 • Breathing at the ends of phrases, p. 42 / CD 39
Romantic	The Hunt, p. 32 / CD 21	• Blocking, p. 54 • Energizing the melody, p. 50 / CD 37
Romantic	Etude, p. 33 / CD 22	• 8 times to perfection, p. 22 / CD 29 • Practicing with the metronome, p. 75 / CD 43
20th/21st Cent.	The Bear, p. 43 / CD 33	• Baroque era: Creating the mood of the piece, p. 59 • Romantic era: Getting ready for a performance, p. 81 / CD 44

Pieces from Succeeding with the Masters®, Classical Era, Volume One.
The biographical information on Wolfgang Amadeus Mozart is found on p. 32.

Composer	Title, Page, and CD Track	Characteristics and Practice Strategies
Wolfgang Amadeus Mozart	Minuet in F, p. 36 / CD 10	p. 34-35 / CD 36
Wolfgang Amadeus Mozart	Minuet in C, K. 6, p. 39 / CD 11	p. 38 / CD 37

Baroque Era

*For a general overview of Baroque performance practice, see p. 7-9 of **Succeeding with the Masters®,** Baroque Era, Volume One. For a general overview of the Baroque era, see p. 2-3.*

Classical Era

*For a general overview of Classical era, see p. 2-3 of **Succeeding with the Masters®,** Classical Era, Volume One.*

Romantic Era

*For a general overview of Romantic era, see p. 2-3 of **Succeeding with the Masters®,** Romantic Era, Volume One.*

Succeeding with the Masters® & The Festival Collection® Etudes with Technique Book 2, can be used at the same time as The Festival Collection®, Book 2.

The Festival Collection®, Book 2

Correlated with **Succeeding with the Masters®, Volume One**
Baroque, Classical, and Romantic Eras

Pieces from **The Festival Collection®**, *arranged in order of difficulty.*
The section "About the Pieces and the Composers" beginning on p. 50 provides further valuable information.

Era	Title, Page, and CD Track	Composer
Romantic	Hunting Horns, p. 37 / CD 26	Theodore Oesten
Baroque	King William's March, p. 6 / CD 1	Jeremiah Clarke
Classical	The Hunting Horns and the Echo, p. 29 / CD 18	Daniel Gottlob Türk
20th/21st Cent.	Una Capricciosa Nuvola Estiva, p. 48 / CD 36	Federico Ermirio

Practice Strategies for **The Festival Collection®**, *arranged in chronological order.*
Refer to the corresponding era in **Succeeding with the Masters®, Volume One** *for a complete description of each Practice Strategy.*

Era	Title, Page, and CD Track	Practice Strategies from SWTM
Baroque	King William's March, p. 6 / CD 1	• Adding ornamentation, p. 13 / CD 24 • Practicing the first measure, p. 17
Classical	The Hunting Horns and the Echo, p. 29 / CD 18	• Shaping the phrases, p. 38 • Romantic era: Perfect rhythm, p. 18 / CD 28 • Romantic era: Playing dotted rhythms, p. 80
Romantic	Hunting Horns, p. 37 / CD 26	• Chain-linking, p. 66 / CD 41 • Blocking, p. 54 / CD 38. Students can block all of the chords and their inversions throughout the piece.
20th/21st Cent.	Una Capricciosa Nuvola Estiva, p. 48 / CD 36	• This piece must sound impressionistic, like the works by Debussy. Students can think about summer clouds and a storm that comes rolling by. The piece should be played freely.

Pieces from **Succeeding with the Masters®, Classical Era, Volume One.**
The biographical information on Ludwig van Beethoven is found on p. 60.

Composer	Title, Page, and CD Track	Characteristics and Practice Strategies
Ludwig van Beethoven	German Dance in C major, p. 63 / CD 19	p. 62 / CD 45
Ludwig van Beethoven	Ecossaise in G major, p. 65 / CD 20	p. 64 / CD 46

Baroque Era

For a general overview of Baroque performance practice, see p. 7-9 of **Succeeding with the Masters®, Baroque Era, Volume One**. *For a general overview of the Baroque era, see p. 2-3.*

Classical Era

For a general overview of Classical era, see p. 2-3 of **Succeeding with the Masters®, Classical Era, Volume One.**

Romantic Era

For a general overview of Romantic era, see p. 2-3 of **Succeeding with the Masters®, Romantic Era, Volume One.**

FJH2050

The Festival Collection®, Book 2

*Correlated with **Succeeding with the Masters®, Volume One***
Baroque, Classical, and Romantic Eras

Pieces from The Festival Collection®, arranged in order of difficulty.
The section "About the Pieces and the Composers" beginning on p. 50 provides further valuable information.

Era	Title, Page, and CD Track	Composer
Romantic	Petite Prelude, p. 31 / CD 20	Ludwig Schytte
Baroque	Menuet en Rondeau, p. 12 / CD 6	Jean-Philippe Rameau
Romantic	Song Without Words, p. 35 / CD 24	Fritz Spindler
Classical	Russian Folk Song, p. 28 / CD 17	Ludwig van Beethoven
20th/21st Cent.	Mister Czerny in New Orleans, p. 42 / CD 31	Manfred Schmitz

Practice Strategies for The Festival Collection®, arranged in chronological order.
*Refer to the corresponding era in **Succeeding with the Masters®, Volume One** for a complete description of each Practice Strategy.*

Era	Title, Page, and CD Track	Practice Strategies from SWTM
Baroque	Menuet en Rondeau, p. 12 / CD 6	• Focusing on forward motion, p. 35 • Creating the mood, p. 59
Classical	Russian Folk Song, p. 28 / CD 17	• Practicing two-note slurs, p. 8 / CD 27 • Use the Characteristics of the era as well as the Practice Strategy on p. 73 as a starting point for discussion of the information on the page.
Romantic	Petite Prelude, p. 31 / CD 20	• Blocking, p. 54 • Practicing to perform with the utmost evenness, p. 54 / CD 38
Romantic	Song Without Words, p. 35 / CD 24	• Blocking, p. 54 / CD 38 • Balancing melody with accompaniment, p. 70 / CD 42
20th/21st Cent.	Mister Czerny in New Orleans, p. 42 / CD 31	• Baroque era: Learning to "Follow the leader," p. 71 • Romantic era: Practicing scale patterns, p. 12 / CD 25. As a variant on this Practice Strategy, the student can practice the scale patterns in the left hand forwards as well as backwards. Each pattern is to be played detached, except for the very last measure.

*Pieces from **Succeeding with the Masters®, Classical Era, Volume One**.*
The biographical information on Franz Joseph Haydn is found on p. 7.

Composer	Title, Page, and CD Track	Characteristics and Practice Strategies
Franz Joseph Haydn	German Dance No. 8 in G major, p. 9 / CD 1	p. 8 / CD 27
Franz Joseph Haydn	German Dance No. 1 in G major, p. 11 / CD 2	p. 10 / CD 28

Baroque Era

*For a general overview of Baroque performance practice, see p. 7-9 of **Succeeding with the Masters®, Baroque Era, Volume One**. For a general overview of the Baroque era, see p. 2-3.*

Classical Era

*For a general overview of Classical era, see p. 2-3 of **Succeeding with the Masters®, Classical Era, Volume One**.*

Romantic Era

*For a general overview of Romantic era, see p. 2-3 of **Succeeding with the Masters®, Romantic Era, Volume One**.*

The Festival Collection®, Book 2

Correlated with **Succeeding with the Masters®, Volume One**
Baroque, Classical, and Romantic Eras

Pieces from The Festival Collection®, *arranged in order of difficulty.*
The section "About the Pieces and the Composers" beginning on p. 50 provides further valuable information.

Era	Title, Page, and CD Track	Composer
Classical	Bagatelle, p. 24 / CD 13	Anton Diabelli
20th/21st Cent.	Waltz Time, p. 42 / CD 32	Manfred Schmitz
Classical	Swabian Tune, p. 25 / CD 14	Johann Christoph Friedrich Bach
Romantic	Theme and Variation, p. 36 / CD 25	Louis Köhler
Baroque	Minuet in F major, p. 10-11 / CD 5	Johann Kuhnau

Practice Strategies for The Festival Collection®, *arranged in chronological order.*
Refer to the corresponding era in **Succeeding with the Masters®, Volume One** *for a complete description of each Practice Strategy.*

Era	Title, Page, and CD Track	Practice Strategies from SWTM
Baroque	Minuet in F major, p. 10-11 / CD 5	• Creating clear passagework, p. 59 / CD 38 • Balancing the melody with an equally important bass line, p. 74 / CD 43
Classical	Bagatelle, p. 24 / CD 13	• Blocking, p. 56 / CD 44 • Slow vs fast practicing (3 x 1 rule), p. 70 / CD 49
Classical	Swabian Tune, p. 25 / CD 14	• Practicing with the metronome, p. 40 / CD 38 • Practicing contrapuntal phrases, p. 40 / CD 34
Romantic	Theme and Variation, p. 36 / CD 25	• "Blocking" Practice Strategy, p. 54 / CD 38 • Balancing melody with accompaniment, p. 70 / CD 42
20th/21st Cent.	Waltz Time, p. 42 / CD 32	• Romantic era: Practicing with the metronome, p. 75 / CD 43 • Baroque era: Learning to "Follow the leader," p. 71

Pieces from Succeeding with the Masters®, Classical Era, Volume One.
The biographical information on Wolfgang Amadeus Mozart is found on p. 32.

Composer	Title, Page, and CD Track	Characteristics and Practice Strategies
Wolfgang Amadeus Mozart	Minuet in C, p. 41 / CD 12	p. 40 / CD 38
Wolfgang Amadeus Mozart	Air, p. 44 / CD 13	p. 42-43 / CD 39
Wolfgang Amadeus Mozart	Minuet in F, K. 2, p. 47 / CD 14	p. 45-46 / CD 40

Baroque Era

For a general overview of Baroque performance practice, see p. 7-9 of **Succeeding with the Masters®, Baroque Era, Volume One**. *For a general overview of the Baroque era, see p. 2-3.*

Classical Era

For a general overview of Classical era, see p. 2-3 of **Succeeding with the Masters®, Classical Era, Volume One**.

Romantic Era

For a general overview of Romantic era, see p. 2-3 of **Succeeding with the Masters®, Romantic Era, Volume One**.

The Festival Collection®, Book 2

Correlated with *Succeeding with the Masters®*, Volume One
Baroque, Classical, and Romantic Eras

Pieces from The Festival Collection®, arranged in order of difficulty.
The section "About the Pieces and the Composers" beginning on p. 50 provides further valuable information.

Era	Title, Page, and CD Track	Composer
Classical	Scotch Dance No. 1, p. 26 / CD 15	Friedrich Kuhlau
Romantic	Mazurka, p. 34 / CD 23	Alexander Gedike
Baroque	Sarabande, p. 13 / CD 7	Arcangelo Corelli
Classical	Lesson I, p. 22-23 / CD 12	James Hook
20th/21st Cent.	Rippling Waters, p. 41 / CD 30	Dianne Goolkasian Rahbee

Practice Strategies for The Festival Collection®, arranged in chronological order.
Refer to the corresponding era in Succeeding with the Masters®, Volume One for a complete description of each Practice Strategy.

Era	Title, Page, and CD Track	Practice Strategies from SWTM
Baroque	Sarabande, p. 13 / CD 7	• Practicing two-note slurs, p. 54 / CD 37 • First-beat practice, p. 55
Classical	Lesson I, p. 22-23 / CD 12	• Chain-linking, p. 38 / CD 37 • Regrouping, p. 70 / CD 49
Classical	Scotch Dance No. 1, p. 26 / CD 15	• Blocking, p. 56 / CD 44 • Bringing a piece to life musically after it is learned, p. 54 / CD 43
Romantic	Mazurka, p. 34 / CD 23	• Play-prepare, p. 10 / CD 24 • Keen listening, p. 37 / CD 33
20th/21st Cent.	Rippling Waters, p. 41 / CD 30	• Classical era: Impulse practicing, p. 62 / CD 45 • Baroque era: Focusing on forward motion, p. 35

Pieces from Succeeding with the Masters®, Classical Era, Volume One.
The biographical information on Franz Joseph Haydn is found on p. 7.

Composer	Title, Page, and CD Track	Characteristics and Practice Strategies
Franz Joseph Haydn	Minuet in C major, p. 13 / CD 3	p. 12 / CD 29
Franz Joseph Haydn	German Dance in F major, p. 15 / CD 4	p. 14 / CD 30
Franz Joseph Haydn	German Dance in C major, p. 18 / CD 5	p. 16-17 / CD 31

Baroque Era

*For a general overview of Baroque performance practice, see p. 7-9 of **Succeeding with the Masters®, Baroque Era, Volume One**. For a general overview of the Baroque era, see p. 2-3.*

Classical Era

*For a general overview of Classical era, see p. 2-3 of **Succeeding with the Masters®, Classical Era, Volume One**.*

Romantic Era

*For a general overview of Romantic era, see p. 2-3 of **Succeeding with the Masters®, Romantic Era, Volume One**.*

The Festival Collection®, Book 2

Correlated with **Succeeding with the Masters®, Volume One**
Baroque, Classical, and Romantic Eras

Pieces from **The Festival Collection®**, *arranged in order of difficulty.*
The section "About the Pieces and the Composers" beginning on p. 50 provides further valuable information.

Era	Title, Page, and CD Track	Composer
Romantic	A Hymn, p. 30 / CD 19	Ludwig Schytte
Baroque	Rigaudon, p. 7 / CD 2	Georg Philipp Telemann
Classical	The Village Prophet, p. 14-15 / CD 8	Jean-Jacques Rousseau
20th/21st Cent.	To the Garden, p. 40 / CD 29	Alexandre Tansman

Practice Strategies for **The Festival Collection®**, *arranged in chronological order.*
Refer to the corresponding era in **Succeeding with the Masters®, Volume One** *for a complete description of each Practice Strategy.*

Era	Title, Page, and CD Track	Practice Strategies from SWTM
Baroque	Rigaudon, p. 7 / CD 2	• Learn and Practice, p. 5 of *On Your Way to Succeeding with the Masters®* • Shaping phrases, p. 11 / CD 23 • Shaping the left-hand phrases, p. 25 / CD 27
Classical	The Village Prophet, p. 14-15 / CD 8	• Playing three-note slurs, p. 45 / CD 40 • Bringing a piece to life musically after it is learned, p. 54 / CD 43
Romantic	A Hymn, p. 30 / CD 19	• Practicing chordal pieces, p. 40 / CD 34 • Chain-linking, p. 66 / CD 41
20th/21st Cent.	To the Garden, p. 40 / CD 29	• Romantic era: Blocking, p. 54 • Classical era: Shaping phrases, p. 38 / CD 37. Discuss with students where each phrase begins and ends, and where the phrase goal is in each phrase.

Pieces from **Succeeding with the Masters®, Classical Era, Volume One.**
The biographical information on Ludwig van Beethoven is found on p. 60.

Composer	Title, Page, and CD Track	Characteristics and Practice Strategies
Ludwig van Beethoven	Country Dance No. 2 in D major, p. 67 / CD 21	p. 66 / CD 47
Ludwig van Beethoven	Ecossaise in E flat major, p. 69 / CD 22	p. 68 / CD 48

Baroque Era

For a general overview of Baroque performance practice, see p. 7-9 of **Succeeding with the Masters®, Baroque Era, Volume One**. *For a general overview of the Baroque era, see p. 2-3.*

Classical Era

For a general overview of Classical era, see p. 2-3 of **Succeeding with the Masters®, Classical Era, Volume One**.

Romantic Era

For a general overview of Romantic era, see p. 2-3 of **Succeeding with the Masters®, Romantic Era, Volume One**.

The Festival Collection®, Book 2

*Correlated with **Succeeding with the Masters®, Volume One***
Baroque, Classical, and Romantic Eras

*Pieces from **The Festival Collection®**, arranged in order of difficulty.*
The section "About the Pieces and the Composers" beginning on p. 50 provides further valuable information.

Era	Title, Page, and CD Track	Composer
Romantic	Night Journey, p. 38 / CD 27	Cornelius Gurlitt
Baroque	Burleske, p. 8 / CD 3	Unknown composer
Classical	Allegro, p. 18-19 / CD 10	Alexander Reinagle
20th/21st Cent.	Two's Company, p. 46-47 / CD 35	Alec Rowley

*Practice Strategies for **The Festival Collection®**, arranged in chronological order.*
*Refer to the corresponding era in **Succeeding with the Masters®, Volume One** for a complete description of each Practice Strategy.*

Era	Title, Page, and CD Track	Practice Strategies from SWTM
Baroque	Burleske, p. 8 / CD 3	• Creating clear sixteenth-note patterns, p. 24 / CD 27 • Creating a dance feel, p. 41 / CD 32 • Practicing with the metronome, p. 21 / CD 26
Classical	Allegro, p. 18-19 / CD 10	• Impulse practicing, p. 62 and p. 80 / CD 26 • Balancing a melody with an accompaniment, p. 48
Romantic	Night Journey, p. 38 / CD 27	• Practicing to perform with the utmost evenness, p. 54 / CD 38. Students can count out loud while they play, stopping on every third beat of the measure. Then they can practice stopping on every first beat of the measure. • "Learn and Practice" from *On Your Way to Succeeding with the Masters®*, p. 5. Students can work on playing from one measure to the next downbeat, and then two measures to the next downbeat.
20th/21st Cent.	Two's Company, p. 46-47 / CD 35	• Baroque era: "Smart" fingering, p. 62 / CD 39 • Baroque era: The importance of "hands-alone" work, p. 68 • Baroque era: Activating rhythmic patterns, p. 28 / CD 28

*Pieces from **Succeeding with the Masters®, Baroque Era, Volume One**.*
The biographical information on Johann Sebastian Bach is found on p. 10.

Composer	Title, Page, and CD Track	Characteristics and Practice Strategies
Johann Sebastian Bach	Theme in F major, BWV Anh. 131, p. 12 / CD 1	p. 11 / CD 23
Johann Sebastian Bach	Minuet in G major, BWV Anh. 114, p. 14-15 / CD 2	p. 13 / CD 24

Baroque Era

*For a general overview of Baroque performance practice, see p. 7-9 of **Succeeding with the Masters®, Baroque Era, Volume One**. For a general overview of the Baroque era, see p. 2-3.*

Classical Era

*For a general overview of Classical era, see p. 2-3 of **Succeeding with the Masters®, Classical Era, Volume One**.*

Romantic Era

*For a general overview of Romantic era, see p. 2-3 of **Succeeding with the Masters®, Romantic Era, Volume One**.*

The Festival Collection®, Book 2

Correlated with **Succeeding with the Masters®, Volume One**
Baroque, Classical, and Romantic Eras

Pieces from **The Festival Collection®**, *arranged in order of difficulty.*
The section "About the Pieces and the Composers" beginning on p. 50 provides further valuable information.

Era	Title, Page, and CD Track	Composer
Romantic	Timid Little Heart, p. 39 / CD 28	Robert Fuchs
Classical	Sonatina in C major, p. 16-17 / CD 9	Johann Anton André
20th/21st Cent.	Long Gone Blues, p. 44-45 / CD 34	George Frederick McKay
Classical	Sonatina in G, p. 20-21 / CD 11	Thomas Attwood

Practice Strategies for **The Festival Collection®**, *arranged in chronological order.*
Refer to the corresponding era in **Succeeding with the Masters®, Volume One** *for a complete description of each Practice Strategy.*

Era	Title, Page, and CD Track	Practice Strategies from SWTM
Classical	Sonatina in C major, p. 16-17 / CD 9	• Playing double thirds, p. 62 • Slow vs. fast practicing (3 x 1 rule), p. 70 / CD 49
Classical	Sonatina in G, p. 20-21 / CD 11	• Blocking, p. 56 / CD 44 • Regrouping, p. 70 / CD 49
Romantic	Timid Little Heart, p. 39 / CD 28	• Practicing with the metronome, p. 75 / CD 43 • Careful Listening from *On Your Way to Succeeding with the Masters®*, p. 33 / CD 42
20th/21st Cent.	Long Gone Blues, p. 44-45 / CD 34	• Romantic era: Applying *rubato*, p. 59 / CD 39 • Romantic era: Using imagery to create a successful performance, p. 51

Pieces from **Succeeding with the Masters®, Baroque Era, Volume One.**
The biographical information on Johann Sebastian Bach is found on p. 10.

Composer	Title, Page, and CD Track	Characteristics and Practice Strategies
Johann Sebastian Bach	Musette in D major, BWV Anh. 126, p. 18-19 / CD 3	p. 16-17 / CD 25
Johann Sebastian Bach	Minuet in G minor, BWV 822, p. 22-23 / CD 4	p. 21 / CD 26

Baroque Era

For a general overview of Baroque performance practice, see p. 7-9 of **Succeeding with the Masters®, Baroque Era, Volume One**. *For a general overview of the Baroque era, see p. 2-3.*

Classical Era

For a general overview of Classical era, see p. 2-3 of **Succeeding with the Masters®, Classical Era, Volume One**.

Romantic Era

For a general overview of Romantic era, see p. 2-3 of **Succeeding with the Masters®, Romantic Era, Volume One**.

The Festival Collection®, Book 3

Correlated with *Succeeding with the Masters*®, *Volume One*
Baroque, Classical, and Romantic Eras

Pieces from *The Festival Collection*®, *arranged in order of difficulty.*
The section "About the Pieces and the Composers" beginning on p. 74 provides further valuable information.

Era	Title, Page, and CD Track	Composer
Classical	Never A Dull Moment, p. 20-21 / CD 11	Daniel Gottlob Türk
20th/21st Cent.	Playing Soldiers, p. 71 / CD 40	Vladimir Rebikov
Romantic	Through Forest and Field, p. 40-41 / CD 23	Cornelius Gurlitt
Baroque	Fantasie, p. 8-9 / CD 3	Georg Philipp Telemann
Romantic	Hunting Music, p. 48-49 / CD 27	Cornelius Gurlitt

Practice Strategies for **The Festival Collection**®, *arranged in chronological order.*
Refer to the corresponding era in **Succeeding with the Masters**®, **Volume One** *for a complete description of each Practice Strategy.*

Era	Title, Page, and CD Track	Practice Strategies from SWTM
Baroque	Fantasie, p. 8-9 / CD 3	• 8 times to perfection, p. 35 / CD 30 • Playing baroque articulations, p. 44 / CD 33
Classical	Never A Dull Moment, p. 20-21 / CD 11	• Practicing two-note slurs, p. 8 / CD 27 • Playing notes marked by wedges, p. 17 / CD 31
Romantic	Through Forest and Field, p. 40-41 / CD 23	• Chain-linking, p. 66 / CD 41 • Blocking, p. 54 / CD 38
Romantic	Hunting Music, p. 48-49 / CD 27	• Balancing melody with accompaniment, p. 70-71 / CD 42 • "8 times to perfection" Practice Strategy, p. 22 / CD 29
20th/21st Cent.	Playing Soldiers, p. 71 / CD 40	• Baroque era: Activating rhythmic patterns, p. 28 / CD 28 • Baroque era: Creating clear sixteenth-note patterns, p. 24 / CD 27

Pieces from *Succeeding with the Masters*®, *Baroque Era, Volume One.*
The biographical information on George Frideric Handel is found on p. 40.

Composer	Title, Page, and CD Track	Characteristics and Practice Strategies
George Frideric Handel	Minuet in G major, p. 42-43 / CD 10	p. 41 / CD 32
George Frideric Handel	Impertinence, HWV 494, p. 45 / CD 11	p. 44 / CD 33

The Festival Collection®, Book 3

Correlated with *Succeeding with the Masters*®, *Volume One*
Baroque, Classical, and Romantic Eras

Pieces from *The Festival Collection*®, arranged in order of difficulty.
The section "About the Pieces and the Composers" beginning on p. 74 provides further valuable information.

Era	Title, Page, and CD Track	Composer
Classical	Sonatina in G (1st Mvt.), p. 24-25 / CD 13	Ludwig van Beethoven
20th/21st Cent.	Highwayman's Tune, p. 58 / CD 33	Béla Bartók
Baroque	Minuet in C major, p. 11 / CD 5	Carlos de Seixas
Romantic	Arabesque, p. 46-47 / CD 26	Johann Friedrich Burgmüller

Practice Strategies for *The Festival Collection*®, arranged in chronological order.
Refer to the corresponding era in **Succeeding with the Masters**®, **Volume One** for a complete description of each Practice Strategy.

Era	Title, Page, and CD Track	Practice Strategies from SWTM
Baroque	Minuet in C major, p. 11 / CD 5	• "Smart" fingering, p. 62 / CD 39 • Creating clear passagework, p. 59 / CD 38
Classical	Sonatina in G (1st Mvt.), p. 24-25 / CD 13	• Blocking, p. 56 / CD 44 (Especially for left-hand broken chords) • Bringing a piece to life musically, p. 54 / CD 43
Romantic	Arabesque, p. 46-47 / CD 26	• Energizing the melody, p. 50 / CD 37 • Getting ready for a performance, p. 81 / CD 44
20th/21st Cent.	Highwayman's Tune, p. 58 / CD 33	• Baroque era: Practicing with the metronome, p. 21 / CD 26 • Baroque era: "Smart" fingering, p. 62 / CD 39

Pieces from *Succeeding with the Masters*®, *Baroque Era, Volume One.*
The biographical information on Domenico Scarlatti is found on p. 64.

Composer	Title, Page, and CD Track	Characteristics and Practice Strategies
Domenico Scarlatti	Minuet in G minor, K. 88/L. 36, p. 66-67 / CD 18	p. 65 / CD 40

The Festival Collection®, Book 3

Correlated with **Succeeding with the Masters®, Volume One**
Baroque, Classical, and Romantic Eras

Pieces from **The Festival Collection®**, *arranged in order of difficulty.*
The section "About the Pieces and the Composers" beginning on p. 74 provides further valuable information.

Era	Title, Page, and CD Track	Composer
Classical	Sonatina in G (2nd Mvt.), p. 26-27 / CD 14	Ludwig van Beethoven
20th/21st Cent.	Little Shepherd, p. 70 / CD 39	Samuel Maykapar
Baroque	Minuet in A minor, p. 6 / CD 1	Johann Krieger
Romantic	Romantic Study, Op. 139, No. 49, p. 52 / CD 29	Carl Czerny
Romantic	Romantic Study, Op. 261, No. 54, p. 53 / CD 30	Carl Czerny

Practice Strategies for **The Festival Collection®**, *arranged in chronological order.*
Refer to the corresponding era in **Succeeding with the Masters®, Volume One** *for a complete description of each Practice Strategy.*

Era	Title, Page, and CD Track	Practice Strategies from SWTM
Baroque	Minuet in A minor, p. 6 / CD 1	• Practicing two-note slurs, p. 54 / CD 37 • Practicing with the metronome, p. 21 / CD 26
Classical	Sonatina in G (2nd Mvt.), p. 26-27 / CD 14	• Blocking, p. 56 / CD 44 (Especially for left-hand broken chords) • Breathing at the ends of phrases, p. 42 / CD 39 • Impulse practicing, p. 62 / CD 45
Romantic	Romantic Study, Op. 139, No. 49, p. 52 / CD 29	• Play-prepare, p. 10 / CD 24 • Classical era: Marking phrases by breathing, p. 10 / CD 28
Romantic	Romantic Study, Op. 261, No. 54, p. 53 / CD 30	• Blocking, p. 54 / CD 38 • Classical era: Balancing the melody with an accompaniment, p. 14 / CD 30
20th/21st Cent.	Little Shepherd, p. 70 / CD 39	• Classical era: Impulse practicing, p. 62 and 80 / CD 45 • Baroque era: Creating the mood, p. 59 / CD 38 • Baroque era: Play-prepare, p.16 and 17 / CD 25. (In order to go from one pattern to the next pattern in the right hand, students can use "play-prepare" to be ready for the next note.)

Pieces from **Succeeding with the Masters®, Baroque Era, Volume One.**
The biographical information on Domenico Scarlatti is found on p. 64.

Composer	Title, Page, and CD Track	Characteristics and Practice Strategies
Domenico Scarlatti	Minuetto in C major, K. 73b/L. 217, p. 69 / CD 19	p. 68 / CD 41

The Festival Collection®, Book 3

*Correlated with **Succeeding with the Masters®, Volume One** Baroque, Classical, and Romantic Eras*

Pieces from *The Festival Collection®*, arranged in order of difficulty.
The section "About the Pieces and the Composers" beginning on p. 74 provides further valuable information.

Era	Title, Page, and CD Track	Composer
Classical	Adagio, p. 22-23 / CD 12	Daniel Steibelt
20th/21st Cent.	Five Variations on a Russian Folk Song, p. 62-65 / CD 36	Dmitri Kabalevsky
Baroque	Minuet in E minor, p. 10 / CD 4	Henry Purcell
Romantic	Praeludium, p. 50-51 / CD 28	Carl Reinecke

Practice Strategies for *The Festival Collection®*, arranged in chronological order.
Refer to the corresponding era in **Succeeding with the Masters®, Volume One** for a complete description of each Practice Strategy.

Era	Title, Page, and CD Track	Practice Strategies from SWTM
Baroque	Minuet in E minor, p. 10 / CD 4	• How to create a dance feel, p. 41 / CD 32 • Slow vs. fast practicing (3 x 1 rule), p. 52 / CD 36
Classical	Adagio, p. 22-23 / CD 12	• Practicing two-note slurs, p. 8 / CD 27 • Balancing the melody with the accompaniment, p. 14 / CD 30 • Voicing *legato* double notes within one hand, p. 28 / CD 35
Romantic	Praeludium, p. 50-51 / CD 28	• Applying *rubato*, p. 43 • Shaping phrases, p. 46 / CD 36 • Classical era: Practicing three-note slurs, p. 45 / CD 40
20th/21st Cent.	Five Variations on a Russian Folk Song, p. 62-65 / CD 36	• Romantic era: Practicing with the metronome, p. 75 / CD 43 • Romantic era: Getting ready for a performance, p. 81 / CD 44

Pieces from **Succeeding with the Masters®**, Baroque Era, Volume One.
The biographical information on George Frideric Handel is found on p. 40.

Composer	Title, Page, and CD Track	Characteristics and Practice Strategies
George Frideric Handel	Minuet in F major, p. 48-49 / CD 12	p. 47 / CD 34
George Frideric Handel	Aria, HWV 449, p. 51 / CD 13	p. 50 / CD 35

FJH2050

The Festival Collection®, Book 3

Correlated with **Succeeding with the Masters®, Volume One**
Baroque, Classical, and Romantic Eras

Pieces from **The Festival Collection®**, *arranged in order of difficulty.*
The section "About the Pieces and the Composers" beginning on p. 74 provides further valuable information.

Era	Title, Page, and CD Track	Composer
Classical	Sonatina in G major, p. 28-29 / CD 15	Anton Diabelli
Baroque	Minuet in G major, p. 7 / CD 2	Wilhelm Friedemann Bach
Romantic	Innocence, p. 38 / CD 21	Johann Friedrich Burgmüller

Practice Strategies for **The Festival Collection®**, *arranged in chronological order.*
Refer to the corresponding era in **Succeeding with the Masters®, Volume One** *for a complete description of each Practice Strategy.*

Era	Title, Page, and CD Track	Practice Strategies from SWTM
Baroque	Minuet in G major, p. 7 / CD 2	• Activating rhythmic patterns, p. 28 / CD 28 • Shaping phrases, p. 11 / CD 23
Classical	Sonatina in G major, p. 28-29 / CD 15	• Practicing sf, p. 66 / CD 47 • Using a "play-prepare" Practice Strategy, p. 68 / CD 48 • Slow vs. fast practicing (3 x 1 rule), p. 70 / CD 49
Romantic	Innocence, p. 38 / CD 21	• Classical era: "Impulse" practicing, p. 51 / CD 42 • Keen listening, p. 37 / CD 33

Pieces from **Succeeding with the Masters®, Romantic Era, Volume One.**
The biographical information on Robert Schumann is found on p. 28.

Composer	Title, Page, and CD Track	Characteristics and Practice Strategies
Robert Schumann	Soldiers' March, Op. 68, No. 2, p. 30-31 / CD 9	p. 29 / CD 31
Robert Schumann	The Wild Rider, Op. 68, No. 8, p. 34-35 / CD 10	p. 32-33 / CD 32

The Festival Collection®, Book 3

Correlated with **Succeeding with the Masters®, Volume One**
Baroque, Classical, and Romantic Eras

Pieces from **The Festival Collection®**, *arranged in order of difficulty.*
The section "About the Pieces and the Composers" beginning on p. 74 provides further valuable information.

Era	Title, Page, and CD Track	Composer
Classical	Dance, p. 37 / CD 20	Christian Gottlob Neefe
Romantic	In the Garden, p. 42-43 / CD 24	Cornelius Gurlitt
20th/21st Cent.	Waves, p. 72 / CD 41	Emma Lou Diemer
Baroque	Gigue, p. 13 / CD 7	Georg Philipp Telemann

Practice Strategies for **The Festival Collection®**, *arranged in chronological order.*
Refer to the corresponding era in **Succeeding with the Masters®, Volume One** *for a complete description of each Practice Strategy.*

Era	Title, Page, and CD Track	Practice Strategies from SWTM
Baroque	Gigue, p. 13 / CD 7	• Balancing the melody with an equally important bass line, p. 74 / CD 43 • Unit practicing, p. 75 / CD 43 • "Follow the leader," p. 71 / CD 42
Classical	Dance, p. 37 / CD 20	• Playing three-note slurs, p. 45 / CD 40 • Blocking, p. 56 and 57 / CD 44 • Regrouping, p. 70 / CD 49
Romantic	In the Garden, p. 42-43 / CD 24	• Practicing two-note slurs, p. 14 / CD 26 • Practicing to perform with the utmost evenness, p. 54 / CD 38 • Classical era: Voicing the melody, p. 49 / CD 41, with the following variation: Play the outer two voices alone, *mf*. Then, slowly, play the outer melodies *mf* while adding the inner accompaniment *pp*, and *staccato*. Once students hear the difference, they can play the inner accompaniment as written.
20th/21st Cent.	Waves, p. 72 / CD 41	• Romantic era: Applying *rubato*, p. 43

Pieces from **Succeeding with the Masters®, Romantic Era, Volume One.**
The biographical information on Franz Schubert is found on p. 7.

Composer	Title, Page, and CD Track	Characteristics and Practice Strategies
Franz Schubert	Ecossaise in C major, D. 299, No. 8, p. 9 / CD 1	p. 8 / CD 23
Franz Schubert	German Dance in A major, D. 972, No. 3, p. 11 / CD 2	p. 10 / CD 24
Franz Schubert	Ecossaise in G major, D. 145, No. 4, p. 13 / CD 3	p. 12 / CD 25

FJH2050

The Festival Collection®, Book 3

Correlated with Succeeding with the Masters®, Volume One
Baroque, Classical, and Romantic Eras

Pieces from The Festival Collection®, arranged in order of difficulty.
The section "About the Pieces and the Composers" beginning on p. 74 provides further valuable information.

Era	Title, Page, and CD Track	Composer
Classical	Sonata in F major, Hob. XVI: 9, p. 30-31 / CD 16	Franz Joseph Haydn
Romantic	Progress, p. 39 / CD 22	Johann Friedrich Burgmüller
20th/21st Cent.	Waltz, p. 68-69 / CD 38	Dianne Goolkasian Rahbee
Baroque	Minuet in A minor, p. 12 / CD 6	Henry Purcell

Practice Strategies for The Festival Collection®, arranged in chronological order.
Refer to the corresponding era in Succeeding with the Masters®, Volume One for a complete description of each Practice Strategy.

Era	Title, Page, and CD Track	Practice Strategies from SWTM
Baroque	Minuet in A minor, p. 12 / CD 6	• First-beat practice, p. 55 • How to practice different voices within the same hand, p. 78 / CD 44
Classical	Sonata in F major, Hob. XVI: 9, p. 30-31 / CD 16	• Impulse practicing, p. 51 / CD 42 • Practicing with the metronome, p. 23 / CD 33 • Playing double-third, two-note slurs, p. 62
Romantic	Progress, p. 39 / CD 22	• Practicing two-note slurs, p. 14 / CD 26 • Energizing the melody, p. 50 / CD 37
20th/21st Cent.	Waltz, p. 68-69 / CD 38	• Classical era: Balancing a melody with an accompaniment, p. 48 • Classical era: Bringing the piece to life musically, p. 54 / CD 43

Pieces from Succeeding with the Masters®, Romantic Era, Volume One.
The biographical information on Peter Tchaikovsky is found on p. 58.

Composer	Title, Page, and CD Track	Characteristics and Practice Strategies
Peter Tchaikovsky	The Sick Doll, Op. 39, No. 7, p. 60-61 / CD 17	p. 59 / CD 39
Peter Tchaikovsky	The New Doll, Op. 39, No. 6, p. 63-65 / CD 18	p. 62 / CD 40

The Festival Collection®, Book 3

Correlated with **Succeeding with the Masters®, Volume One**
Baroque, Classical, and Romantic Eras

Pieces from The Festival Collection®, *arranged in order of difficulty.*
The section "About the Pieces and the Composers" beginning on p. 74 provides further valuable information.

Era	Title, Page, and CD Track	Composer
Classical	Sonatina in C major (1st Mvt.) p. 32-33 / CD 17	Muzio Clementi
Romantic	Song, p. 44-45 / CD 25	Carl Reinecke
20th/21st Cent.	The Elegant Toreador, p. 66-67 / CD 37	Seymour Bernstein
Baroque	The Fifers, p. 18-19 / CD 10	Jean-François Dandrieu

Practice Strategies for The Festival Collection®, *arranged in chronological order.*
Refer to the corresponding era in **Succeeding with the Masters®, Volume One** *for a complete description of each Practice Strategy.*

Era	Title, Page, and CD Track	Practice Strategies from SWTM
Baroque	The Fifers, p. 18-19 / CD 10	• Play-prepare, p. 16 / CD 25 • Slow vs. fast practicing (3 x 1 rule), p. 52 / CD 36
Classical	Sonatina in C major (1st Mvt.) p. 32-33 / CD 17	• Practicing *Alberti* basses, p. 77 / CD 51 • Balancing the melody with the accompaniment, p. 14 and 48 / CD 30
Romantic	Song, p. 44-45 / CD 25	• Using half and quarter pedal, p. 16 and 47 / CD 27 and 36 • Bringing a piece to life musically after it is learned, p. 26 / CD 30 • Keen listening, p. 37 / CD 33
20th/21st Cent.	The Elegant Toreador, p. 66-67 / CD 37	• Romantic era: Using imagery to create a successful performance, p. 51 / CD 37 • Romantic era: How to play repeated notes quickly and lightly, p. 62 / CD 40

Pieces from **Succeeding with the Masters®, Romantic Era, Volume One.**
The biographical information on Robert Schumann is found on p. 28.

Composer	Title, Page, and CD Track	Characteristics and Practice Strategies
Robert Schumann	Melody, Op. 68, No. 1, p. 38 / CD 11	p. 36-37 / CD 33
Robert Schumann	A Hymn, Op. 68, No. 4, p. 41 / CD 12	p. 40 / CD 34

FJH2050

The Festival Collection®, Book 3

Correlated with **Succeeding with the Masters®, Volume One**
Baroque, Classical, and Romantic Eras

Pieces from **The Festival Collection®,** *arranged in order of difficulty.*
The section "About the Pieces and the Composers" beginning on p. 74 provides further valuable information.

Era	Title, Page, and CD Track	Composer
Classical	Sonatina in C major (2nd Mvt.) p. 34 / CD 18	Muzio Clementi
Romantic	Kamarinskaya, p. 55-57 / CD 32	Pyotr Ilyich Tchaikovsky
20th/21st Cent.	Play It Again, p. 59 / CD 34	Christopher Norton
Baroque	Minuet in D minor, p. 16-17 / CD 9	Johann Heinrich Buttstett

Practice Strategies for **The Festival Collection®,** *arranged in chronological order.*
Refer to the corresponding era in **Succeeding with the Masters®, Volume One** *for a complete description of each Practice Strategy.*

Era	Title, Page, and CD Track	Practice Strategies from SWTM
Baroque	Minuet in D minor, p. 16-17 / CD 9	• Creating clear sixteenth-note patterns, p. 24 / CD 27 • How to create a baroque *ritardando (rit.)*, p. 47 / CD 34
Classical	Sonatina in C major (2nd Mvt.) p. 34 / CD 18	• Chain-linking practice, p. 38 / CD 37 • Voicing a melody, p. 49 / CD 41
Romantic	Kamarinskaya, p. 55-57 / CD 32	• Play-prepare, p. 10 / CD 24 • Classical era: Shaping phrases, p. 38 / CD 37 • Classical era: Slow vs. fast practicing (3 x 1 rule), p. 70 / CD 49
20th/21st Cent.	Play It Again, p. 59 / CD 34	• Baroque era: Slow vs. fast practicing (3 x 1 rule), p. 52 / CD 36 • Classical era: Voicing a melody, p. 49 / CD 41

Pieces from **Succeeding with the Masters®, Romantic Era, Volume One.**
The biographical information on Peter Tchaikovsky is found on p. 58.

Composer	Title, Page, and CD Track	Characteristics and Practice Strategies
Peter Tchaikovsky	Russian Song, Op. 39, No. 12, p. 68-69 / CD 19	p. 66-67 / CD 41
Peter Tchaikovsky	Old French Song, Op. 39, No. 16, p. 72-73 / CD 20	p. 70-71 / CD 42

The Festival Collection®, Book 3

*Correlated with **Succeeding with the Masters®, Volume One***
Baroque, Classical, and Romantic Eras

*Pieces from **The Festival Collection®**, arranged in order of difficulty.*
The section "About the Pieces and the Composers" beginning on p. 74 provides further valuable information.

Era	Title, Page, and CD Track	Composer
Classical	Sonatina in C major (3rd Mvt.) p. 35-36 / CD 19	Muzio Clementi
Romantic	Andantino, p. 54 / CD 31	Theodor Furchtegott Kirchner
20th/21st Cent.	Machines on the Loose, p. 60-61 / CD 35	Kevin Olson
Baroque	Minuet in G minor, BWV 115, p. 14-15 / CD 8	Christian Pezold

*Practice Strategies for **The Festival Collection®**, arranged in chronological order.*
*Refer to the corresponding era in **Succeeding with the Masters®, Volume One** for a complete description of each Practice Strategy.*

Era	Title, Page, and CD Track	Practice Strategies from SWTM
Baroque	Minuet in G minor, BWV 115, p. 14-15 / CD 8	• The importance of hands-alone work, p. 68 • Creating the mood, p. 59 / CD 38
Classical	Sonatina in C major (3rd Mvt.), p. 35-36 / CD 19	• Impulse practicing, p. 62 / CD 35 • Playing three-note slurs, p. 45 / CD 40
Romantic	Andantino, p. 54 / CD 31	• Classical era: Shaping phrases, p. 38 / CD 37 • Balancing melody with accompaniment, p. 70 / CD 42
20th/21st Cent.	Machines on the Loose, p. 60-61 / CD 35	• Classical era: Practicing two-note slurs, p. 8 / CD 27 • Classical era: Blocking, p. 56 / CD 44 • Romantic era: 8 times to perfection, p. 22 / CD 29

*Pieces from **Succeeding with the Masters®**, Romantic Era, Volume One.*
The biographical information on Franz Schubert is found on p. 7.

Composer	Title, Page, and CD Track	Characteristics and Practice Strategies
Franz Schubert	Ländler in G major, D. 365, No. 21, p. 15 / CD 4	p. 14 / CD 26
Franz Schubert	Ländler in B flat major, D. 378, No. 3, p. 17 / CD 5	p. 16 / CD 27

The Festival Collection®, Book 4 (easier selections)

Correlated with *Succeeding with the Masters*®, *Volume One*
Baroque, Classical, and Romantic Eras

Pieces from *The Festival Collection*®, arranged in order of difficulty.
The section "About the Pieces and the Composers" beginning on p. 90 provides further valuable information.

Era	Title, Page, and CD Track	Composer
Romantic	Spinning Song, p. 54-57 / CD 23	Albert Elimenreich
Classical	Rondo in B flat major, p. 32-33 / CD 13	Ignace Joseph Pleyel
Baroque	The Little Trifle, p. 6-7 / CD 1	François Couperin
20th/21st Cent.	Elephant Tune, p. 76 / CD 33	Nina Perry

Practice Strategies for *The Festival Collection*®, arranged in chronological order.
Refer to the corresponding era in *Succeeding with the Masters*®, *Volume One* for a complete description of each Practice Strategy.

Era	Title, Page, and CD Track	Practice Strategies from SWTM
Baroque	The Little Trifle, p. 6-7 / CD 1	• Focus on forward motion, p. 35 / CD 30 • 8 times to perfection, p. 35 / CD 30
Classical	Rondo in B flat major, p. 32-33 / CD 13	• Straightforward, simple harmonies, p. 22 • Impulse practicing, p. 51 / CD 42
Romantic	Spinning Song, p. 54-57 / CD 23	• How to play repeated notes quickly and lightly, p. 62 / CD 40 • Bringing a piece to life musically, p. 26 / CD 30
20th/21st Cent.	Elephant Tune, p. 76 / CD 33	• Romantic era: The importance of "hands-alone" work, p. 8 / CD 23 • Baroque era: Play-prepare, p. 16 / CD 25 • Classical era: Chain-linking, p. 38 / CD 37

Pieces from *Succeeding with the Masters*®, *Baroque Era*, *Volume One*. Choose from the following.
The biographical information on Johann Sebastian Bach is found on p. 10.

Composer	Title, Page, and CD Track	Characteristics and Practice Strategies
Johann Sebastian Bach	Minuet in D minor, p. 26-27 / CD 5	p. 24-25 / CD 27
Johann Sebastian Bach	Minuet in G major, p. 30-31 / CD 6	p. 28-29 / CD 28
Johann Sebastian Bach	Minuet in G major, p. 33-34 / CD 7	p. 32 / CD 29

Pieces from *Succeeding with the Masters*®, *Classical Era*, *Volume One*. Choose from the following.
The biographical information on Franz Joseph Haydn is found on p. 7.

Composer	Title, Page, and CD Track	Characteristics and Practice Strategies
Franz Joseph Haydn	German Dance in B flat major, p. 21 / CD 6	p. 20 / CD 32
Franz Joseph Haydn	Minuet in B flat major, p. 24 / CD 7	p. 22-23 / CD 33
Franz Joseph Haydn	Minuet and Trio in F major, p. 26-27 / CD 8	p. 25 / CD 34
Franz Joseph Haydn	Dance in B flat major, p. 30 / CD 9	p. 28-29 / CD 35

The Festival Collection®, Book 4 (easier selections)

Correlated with Succeeding with the Masters®, Volume One
Baroque, Classical, and Romantic Eras

Pieces from The Festival Collection®, arranged in order of difficulty.
The section "About the Pieces and the Composers" beginning on p. 90 provides further valuable information.

Era	Title, Page, and CD Track	Composer
Romantic	The Shepherdess, Op. 100, No. 11, p. 58-59 / CD 24	Johann Friedrich Burgmüller
Classical	Sonatina in G, p. 36-37 / CD 15	Jacob Schmitt
Romantic	Polka, p. 60-61 / CD 25	Pyotr Ilyich Tchaikovsky
Baroque	Fantasia in G major, p. 8 / CD 2	Georg Philipp Telemann
20th/21st Cent.	Tango in C minor, p. 77 / CD 34	Martín Kutnowski

Practice Strategies for The Festival Collection®, arranged in chronological order.
Refer to the corresponding era in Succeeding with the Masters®, Volume One for a complete description of each Practice Strategy.

Era	Title, Page, and CD Track	Practice Strategies from SWTM
Baroque	Fantasia in G major, p. 8 / CD 2	• Creating the mood of the piece, p. 59 / CD 38 • "Smart" fingering, p. 62 / CD 39 • Balancing the melody with an equally important bass line, p. 50 / CD 35
Classical	Sonatina in G, p. 36-37 / CD 15	• Practicing ornaments, p. 12 / CD 29 • Impulse practicing, p. 51 / CD 42
Romantic	The Shepherdess, Op. 100, No. 11, p. 58-59 / CD 24	• Energizing the melody, p. 50 / CD 37 • Using imagery, p. 51 / CD 37 • Chain-linking, p. 66 / CD 41
Romantic	Polka, p. 60-61 / CD 25	• 8 times to perfection, p. 22 / CD 29 • Blocking, p. 54
20th/21st Cent.	Tango in C minor, p. 77 / CD 34	• Baroque era: Play-prepare, p. 16 / CD 25 • Baroque era: Focusing on forward motion, p. 35. Even though this piece has rests in it, students need to feel that there is always a forward drive to the high point of each phrase. • Romantic era: Getting ready for a performance, p. 81 / CD 44

Pieces from Succeeding with the Masters®, Classical Era, Volume One. Choose from the following.
The biographical information on Wolfgang Amadeus Mozart is found on p. 32.

Composer	Title, Page, and CD Track	Characteristics and Practice Strategies
Wolfgang Amadeus Mozart	Andante and Maestoso, p. 50 / CD 15	p. 48-49 / CD 41
Wolfgang Amadeus Mozart	Minuet and Trio, K. 1, p. 52-53 / CD 16	p. 51 / CD 42
Wolfgang Amadeus Mozart	Allegro Moderato, p. 55 / CD 17	p. 54 / CD 43
Wolfgang Amadeus Mozart	Allegro, K. 3, p. 58 / CD 18	p. 56-57 / CD 44

The biographical information on Robert Schumann is found on p. 28.

Composer	Title, Page, and CD Track	Characteristics and Practice Strategies
Robert Schumann	First Loss, p. 48-49 / CD 14	p. 46-47 / CD 36
Robert Schumann	The Merry Farmer, p. 52-53 / CD 15	p. 50-51 / CD 37
Robert Schumann	Little Study, p. 55-57 / CD 16	p. 54 / CD 38

FJH2050

The Festival Collection®, Book 4 (easier selections)

Correlated with Succeeding with the Masters®, Volume One
Baroque, Classical, and Romantic Eras

Pieces from The Festival Collection®, arranged in order of difficulty.
The section "About the Pieces and the Composers" beginning on p. 90 provides further valuable information.

Era	Title, Page, and CD Track	Composer
Classical	Rondo in F major, p. 38-39 / CD 16	James Hook
Romantic	Allemande in E flat, p. 62-63 / CD 26	Carl Maria von Weber
Baroque	Polonaise, p. 9 / CD 3	Unknown (from the Anna Magdalena Bach Notebook)
20th/21st Cent.	Song of the Range Rider, p. 78 / CD 35	George Frederick McKay

Practice Strategies for The Festival Collection®, arranged in chronological order.
*Refer to the corresponding era in **Succeeding with the Masters®, Volume One** for a complete description of each Practice Strategy.*

Era	Title, Page, and CD Track	Practice Strategies from SWTM
Baroque	Polonaise, p. 9 / CD 3	• Creating clear sixteenth-note patterns, p. 24 / CD 27 • "Activating" rhythmic patterns, p. 28 / CD 28
Classical	Rondo in F major, p. 38-39 / CD 16	• Voicing *legato* double notes within one hand, p. 28 / CD 35 • Shaping the phrases, p. 38 / CD 37
Romantic	Allemande in E flat, p. 62-63 / CD 26	• Practicing scale patterns, p. 12 / CD 25 • Shaping phrases, p. 62 / CD 40. Students can decide the length of each phrase and where the phrase goal is within each phrase.
20th/21st Cent.	Song of the Range Rider, p. 78 / CD 35	• Classical era: Balancing a melody with an accompaniment, p. 14 / CD 30 • Classical era: Practicing two-note slurs, p. 8 / CD 27 • Romantic era: Perfect rhythm, p. 18 / CD 28. Students need to be sure to play the sixteenth notes like sixteenth notes and not like triplets.

Pieces from Succeeding with the Masters®, Baroque Era, Volume One. Choose from the following.
The biographical information on George Frideric Handel is found on p. 40.

Composer	Title, Page, and CD Track	Characteristics and Practice Strategies
George Frideric Handel	Gavotte in G major, p. 53 / CD 14	p. 52 / CD 36
George Frideric Handel	Sarabande, p. 56-57 / CD 15	p. 54-55 / CD 37
George Frideric Handel	Air in B flat major, p. 60-61 / CD 16	p. 59 / CD 38
George Frideric Handel	Sonatina in G major, p. 63 / CD 17	p. 62 / CD 39

Pieces from Succeeding with the Masters®, Romantic Era, Volume One. Choose from the following.
The biographical information on Peter Tchaikovsky is found on p. 58.

Composer	Title, Page, and CD Track	Characteristics and Practice Strategies
Peter Tchaikovsky	Waltz, p. 76-79 / CD 21	p. 74-75 / CD 43
Peter Tchaikovsky	March of the Wooden Soldiers, p. 82-84 / CD 22	p. 80-81 / CD 44

The Festival Collection®, Book 4 (easier selections)

*Correlated with **Succeeding with the Masters®, Volume One***
Baroque, Classical, and Romantic Eras

*Pieces from **The Festival Collection®**, arranged in order of difficulty.*
The section "About the Pieces and the Composers" beginning on p. 90 provides further valuable information.

Era	Title, Page, and CD Track	Composer
Classical	Sonatina in G, Op. 36, No. 2 (1st Mvt.), p. 26-28 / CD 11	Muzio Clementi
Romantic	Sicilienne, Op. 68, No. 11, p. 64-65 / CD 27	Robert Schumann
Baroque	Minuet in G minor, p. 10-11 / CD 4	Jean-Philippe Rameau
20th/21st Cent.	Rustic Dance, Op. 24, No. 1, p. 84-85 / CD 39	Paul Creston

*Practice Strategies for **The Festival Collection®**, arranged in chronological order.*
*Refer to the corresponding era in **Succeeding with the Masters®, Volume One** for a complete description of each Practice Strategy.*

Era	Title, Page, and CD Track	Practice Strategies from SWTM
Baroque	Minuet in G minor, p. 10-11 / CD 4	• How to create a baroque *ritardando*, p. 47 / CD 34 • Adding embellishments, p. 70 / CD 42 • Learning to "Follow the leader," p. 71 / CD 42
Classical	Sonatina in G , Op. 36, No. 2 (1st Mvt.), p. 26-28 / CD 11	• Regrouping, p. 70 / CD 49 • Slow vs. fast practicing (3 x 1 rule), p. 70 / CD 49 • Shaping phrases, p. 73 / CD 50
Romantic	Sicilienne, Op. 68, No. 11, p. 64-65 / CD 27	• Bringing a piece to life musically, p. 26 / CD 30 • Practicing to perform with the utmost evenness, p. 54 / CD 38
20th/21st Cent.	Rustic Dance, Op. 24, No. 1, p. 84-85 / CD 39	• Romantic era: Blocking, p. 54 • Romantic era: Chain-linking, p. 66 / CD 41 • Classical era: Voicing the melody, p. 49 / CD 41. Students will need to understand that even though this entire piece is played strongly, the alto voice in the right hand is to be voiced louder than the soprano voice in measures 1-13 and then again in measures 31-32 and 39-42. The rest of the piece calls for the soprano voice to be voiced over the alto voice.

*Pieces from **Succeeding with the Masters®, Baroque Era, Volume One**. Choose from the following.*
The biographical information on Johann Sebastian Bach is found on p. 10.

Composer	Title, Page, and CD Track	Characteristics and Practice Strategies
Johann Sebastian Bach	Minuet in C minor, p. 36-37 / CD 8	p. 35 / CD 30
Johann Sebastian Bach	Prelude in C major, p. 39 / CD 9	p. 38 / CD 31

*Pieces from **Succeeding with the Masters®, Classical Era, Volume One**. Choose from the following.*
The biographical information on Ludwig van Beethoven is found on p. 60.

Composer	Title, Page, and CD Track	Characteristics and Practice Strategies
Ludwig van Beethoven	Country Dance No. 1 in D major, p. 71 / CD 23	p. 70 / CD 49
Ludwig van Beethoven	Minuet and Trio in G major, p. 74-75 / CD 24	p. 73 / CD 50
Ludwig van Beethoven	German Dance in G major, p. 78-79 / CD 25	p. 77 / CD 51
Ludwig van Beethoven	Country Dance in D minor, p. 81 / CD 26	p. 80

The Festival Collection®, Book 4 (easier selections)

Correlated with *Succeeding with the Masters®, Volume One*
Baroque, Classical, and Romantic Eras

Pieces from *The Festival Collection®*, arranged in order of difficulty.
The section "About the Pieces and the Composers" beginning on p. 90 provides further valuable information.

Era	Title, Page, and CD Track	Composer
Classical	La Caroline, p. 29-31 / CD 12	Carl Philipp Emanuel Bach
Romantic	Little Flower, p. 68-69 / CD 29	Cornelius Gurlitt
Baroque	Loure, p. 16-17 / CD 6	Georg Philipp Telemann
20th/21st Cent.	Ivan's Song, p. 86-87 / CD 40	Aram Khachaturian

Practice Strategies for *The Festival Collection®*, arranged in chronological order.
Refer to the corresponding era in **Succeeding with the Masters®, Volume One** for a complete description of each Practice Strategy.

Era	Title, Page, and CD Track	Practice Strategies from SWTM
Baroque	Loure, p. 16-17 / CD 6	• Practicing different voices within the same hand, p. 78 / CD 44 • Practicing the first measure, p. 17 / CD 25
Classical	La Caroline, p. 29-31 / CD 12	• Bringing a piece to life musically, p. 54 / CD 43 • Voicing a melody, p. 49 / CD 41
Romantic	Little Flower, p. 68-69 / CD 29	• Keen listening, p. 37 / CD 33 • How to practice a melody with an accompaniment and a countermelody, p. 42 / CD 35
20th/21st Cent.	Ivan's Song, p. 86-87 / CD 40	• Romantic era: Blocking, p. 54 / CD 38, for measures 18-26 in the left hand. • Romantic era: Keen listening, p. 37 / CD 33 • Baroque era: Practicing the first measure, p. 17 / CD 25, points 1 and 2 only. • Baroque era: First-beat practice, p. 55

Pieces from *Succeeding with the Masters®, Baroque Era, Volume One*. Choose from the following.
The biographical information on Domenico Scarlatti is found on p. 64.

Composer	Title, Page, and CD Track	Characteristics and Practice Strategies
Domenico Scarlatti	Larghetto in D minor, p. 72-73 / CD 20	p. 70-71 / CD 42
Domenico Scarlatti	Minuetto in B flat major, p. 76-77 / CD 21	p. 74-75 / CD 43
Domenico Scarlatti	Minuetto in C minor, p. 80-81 / CD 22	p. 78-79 / CD 44

Pieces from *Succeeding with the Masters®, Romantic Era, Volume One*. Choose from the following.
The biographical information on Franz Schubert is found on p. 7.

Composer	Title, Page, and CD Track	Characteristics and Practice Strategies
Franz Schubert	Waltz in B minor, p. 20-21 / CD 6	p. 18-19 / CD 28
Franz Schubert	Ländler in G major, p. 24-25 / CD 7	p. 22 / CD 29
Franz Schubert	Waltz in A major, p. 27 / CD 8	p. 26 / CD 30

The Festival Collection®, Books 4 (more difficult selections), 5, and 6

Correlated with *Succeeding with the Masters*®, *Volume Two*
Baroque, Classical, and Romantic Eras

FEATURES OF THIS CORRELATION:

1. *The Festival Collection*® is considered the core curriculum and *Succeeding with the Masters*®, *Volume Two* is used for special focus on musical eras, composers and Practice Strategies.

2. Each unit includes pieces from all 4 musical eras found in *The Festival Collection*®. These pieces are listed in order of difficulty.

3. Each unit also features a special focus on master composers found in *Succeeding with the Masters*®, *Volume Two*. The pieces by the composers are listed in order of difficulty.

4. One of the teacher's goals is to make student practicing more efficient. Students can easily apply the Practice Strategies from *Succeeding with the Masters*®, *Volume Two* to the pieces in *The Festival Collection*®. One Practice Strategy is suggested for each piece in the unit for a well-rounded curriculum that includes regular review and reinforcement.

5. The Practice Strategy assigned to each piece is a suggestion only. Teachers should feel free to change or adapt any Practice Strategy to the needs of the individual student.

6. Much freedom is given for the teachers and students to choose appropriate repertoire once the basic concepts of each era have been presented. The listening CD's provide a valuable resource to aid in the selection process.

7. For a general overview of the Baroque era and Baroque performance practice, see p. 2-3 and 7-9 of *Succeeding with the Masters*®, *Baroque Era, Volume Two*. For a general overview of the Classical era, see p. 2-3 of *Succeeding with the Masters*®, *Classical Era, Volume Two*. For a general overview of the Romantic era, see p. 2-3 of *Succeeding with the Masters*®, *Romantic Era, Volume Two*.

8. Looking at the musical characteristics of the era on p. 3 of each volume of *Succeeding with the Masters*® as well as on every text page will help guide teachers in presenting to the student what makes each era unique.

FJH2050

The Festival Collection®, Book 4 (more difficult selections)

Correlated with Succeeding with the Masters®, Volume Two
Baroque, Classical, and Romantic Eras

Pieces from The Festival Collection®, arranged in order of difficulty.
The section "About the Pieces and the Composers" beginning on p. 90 provides further valuable information.

Era	Title, Page, and CD Track	Composer
Classical	Sonatina in C major, Op. 168, No. 3 (3rd Mvt.), p. 40-42 / CD 17	Anton Diabelli
Romantic	Etude in A minor, Op. 47, No. 3, p. 74-75 / CD 32	Stephen Heller
20th/21st Cent.	Prelude, Op. 138, p. 79 / CD 36	Dianne Goolkasian Rahbee
Baroque	Intrada, p. 22-24 / CD 9	Christoph Graupner

Practice Strategies for The Festival Collection®, arranged in chronological order.
Refer to the corresponding era in Succeeding with the Masters®, Volume Two for a complete description of each Practice Strategy.

Era	Title, Page, and CD Track	Practice Strategies from SWTM
Baroque	Intrada, p. 22-24 / CD 9	• Baroque era, Volume One: Focusing on forward motion, p. 35 (Both parts of this piece can be practiced hands separately, each with forward motion.) • Creating clear passagework, p. 59 / CD 38
Classical	Sonatina in C major, Op. 168, No. 3 (3rd mvt.) p. 40-42 / CD 17	• Balancing the melody with the accompaniment, p. 9 • Slow vs. fast practicing (3 x 1 rule), pgs. 36-37 / CD 31
Romantic	Etude in A minor, Op. 47, No. 3, p. 74-75 / CD 32	• Improving muscle memory, p. 24 / CD 36 • Strong sense of rhythm defining a piece, p. 41 / CD 39
20th/21st Cent.	Prelude, Op. 138, p. 79 / CD 36	• Romantic era, Volume Two: Using imagery to create a successful performance, p. 104 / CD 53. In this metric piece, students enjoy the sounds of tones without counting. They can be very free and create their own interpretation after listening to the CD. They can also create an improvisation.

Pieces from Succeeding with the Masters®, Classical Era, Volume Two. Choose from the following.
The biographical information on Wolfgang Amadeus Mozart is found on p. 40-41.

Composer	Title, Page, and CD Track	Characteristics and Practice Strategies
Wolfgang Amadeus Mozart	Klavierstück in F, p. 43 / CD 9	p. 42 / CD 32
Wolfgang Amadeus Mozart	Andante in F, p. 45-46 / CD 10	p. 44 / CD 33
Wolfgang Amadeus Mozart	Minuet in F, p. 49 / CD 11	p. 47-48 / CD 34

The Festival Collection®, Book 4 (more difficult selections)

*Correlated with **Succeeding with the Masters®, Volume Two***
Baroque, Classical, and Romantic Eras

Pieces from The Festival Collection®, arranged in order of difficulty.
The section "About the Pieces and the Composers" beginning on p. 90 provides further valuable information.

Era	Title, Page, and CD Track	Composer
Classical	Strong, Sturdy Character, p. 43 / CD 18	Daniel Gottlob Türk
Romantic	Turkish March, Op. 101, No. 9, p. 72-73 / CD 31	Cornelius Gurlitt
20th/21st Cent.	Two Roosters, p. 80-81 / CD 37	Sergey Razorenov
Baroque	Verso in E minor, p. 20-21 / CD 8	Domenico Zipoli

Practice Strategies for The Festival Collection®, arranged in chronological order.
*Refer to the corresponding era in **Succeeding with the Masters®, Volume Two** for a complete description of each Practice Strategy.*

Era	Title, Page, and CD Track	Practice Strategies from SWTM
Baroque	Verso in E minor, p. 20-21 / CD 8	• Learning to "Follow the leader," p. 45 / CD 35 • "Smart" fingering, p. 13 / CD 26 • Practicing back to front, p. 22 / CD 29
Classical	Strong, Sturdy Character, p. 43 / CD 18	• Bringing the piece to life musically, p. 50 / CD 35 • Shaping phrases, p. 61 / CD 38. Students can listen to the recording and hear where the phrase goal is of each phrase, and where the end of each phrase is. They can mark it in the score and breathe when they reach the end of each phrase. Then, they can use the same questions listed on p. 50 for the piece by Türk.
Romantic	Turkish March, Op. 101, No. 9, p. 72-73 / CD 31	• Playing dotted rhythms, p. 57 / CD 43 • Contrast in music to create drama, p. 34 / CD 38 • Strong sense of rhythm defining a piece, p. 41 / CD 39 • Unit, section, and performance practice, p. 24-25 / CD 36
20th/21st Cent.	Two Roosters, p. 80-81 / CD 37	• Romantic era, Volume Two: Contrast in music to create drama, p. 34 / CD 38. This piece is all about the imagery related to the title. In order to create drama, students need to think about a story line and enjoy the many different sections of the piece. • How to play a piece faster, p. 68 / CD 46

Pieces from Succeeding with the Masters®, Baroque Era, Volume Two. Choose from the following.
The biographical information on Johann Sebastian Bach is found on p. 10-11.

Composer	Title, Page, and CD Track	Characteristics and Practice Strategies
Johann Sebastian Bach	Minuet in E major, p. 14-15 / CD 1	p. 13 / CD 26
Johann Sebastian Bach	Prelude in C major, p. 18-19 / CD 2	p. 16-17 / CD 27
Johann Sebastian Bach	Minuet in G minor, p. 21 / CD 3	p. 20 / CD 28

FJH2050

The Festival Collection®, Book 4 (more difficult selections)

*Correlated with **Succeeding with the Masters®**, Volume Two*
Baroque, Classical, and Romantic Eras

Pieces from The Festival Collection®, arranged in order of difficulty.
The section "About the Pieces and the Composers" beginning on p. 90 provides further valuable information.

Era	Title, Page, and CD Track	Composer
Classical	Minuet in F major, K. 5, p. 44-45 / CD 19	Wolfgang Amadeus Mozart
Classical	Capriccio, p. 46-47 / CD 20	Johann Wilhelm Hässler
Romantic	Miniature Waltz, Op.10, No. 10, p. 66-67 / CD 28	Vladimir Rebikov
Baroque	Dedicated Most Humbly to the Right-Hand Little Finger, p. 25 / CD 10	Daniel Gottlob Türk

Practice Strategies for The Festival Collection®, arranged in chronological order.
*Refer to the corresponding era in **Succeeding with the Masters®**, Volume Two for a complete description of each Practice Strategy.*

Era	Title, Page, and CD Track	Practice Strategies from SWTM
Baroque	Dedicated Most Humbly to the Right-Hand Little Finger, p. 25 / CD 10	• Slow vs. fast practicing (3 x 1 rule), p. 76 / CD 43 • Inner listening, p. 54 / CD 38
Classical	Minuet in F major, K. 5, p. 44-45 / CD 19	• Creating a dance-like accompaniment pattern, p. 42 / CD 32. (For all detached notes in the Minuet by Mozart.) • How to create clear passagework, p. 52 / CD 36
Classical	Capriccio, p. 46-47 / CD 20	• Blocking, p. 60 / CD 38 • Improving muscle memory, p. 47 / CD 34
Romantic	Miniature Waltz, Op.10, No. 10, p. 66-67 / CD 28	• Applying *rubato*, p. 29 and 77 / CD 48 • Playing seamlessly, p. 48

*Pieces from **Succeeding with the Masters®**, Romantic Era, Volume Two. Choose from the following.*
The biographical information on Pyotr (Peter) Tchaikovsky is found on p. 56.

Composer	Title, Page, and CD Track	Characteristics and Practice Strategies
Pyotr (Peter) Tchaikovsky	Mazurka, p. 58-59 / CD 17	p. 57 / CD 43
Pyotr (Peter) Tchaikovsky	Neapolitan Song, p. 61-63 / CD 18	p. 60 / CD 44

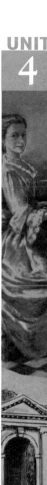

The Festival Collection®, Book 4 (more difficult selections)

Correlated with **Succeeding with the Masters®, Volume Two**
Baroque, Classical, and Romantic Eras

Pieces from **The Festival Collection®**, *arranged in order of difficulty.*
The section "About the Pieces and the Composers" beginning on p. 90 provides further valuable information.

Era	Title, Page, and CD Track	Composer
Romantic	Mazurka, p. 70-71 / CD 30	Mikhail Glinka
Baroque	Bourrée in A minor, p. 18-19 / CD 7	Johann Ludwig Krebs
20th/21st Cent.	Oriental Flower, p. 88 / CD 41	Christopher Norton
Classical	Angloise in D major, p. 34-35 / CD 14	Johann Christoph Friedrich Bach

Practice Strategies for **The Festival Collection®**, *arranged in chronological order.*
Refer to the corresponding era in **Succeeding with the Masters®, Volume Two** *for a complete description of each Practice Strategy.*

Era	Title, Page, and CD Track	Practice Strategies from SWTM
Baroque	Bourrée in A minor, p. 18-19 / CD 7	• Unit practicing, p. 58 / CD 39 • "Smart" fingering, p. 13 / CD 26
Classical	Angloise in D major, p. 34-35 / CD 14	• Practicing ornaments in classical repertoire, p. 20 / CD 27 • Playing sixteenth notes evenly, p. 83 / CD 43 • Shaping phrases, p. 61 / CD 38
Romantic	Mazurka, p. 70-71 / CD 30	• Keen listening, p. 48 / CD 41 • Romantic era, Volume One: How to practice a melody with an accompaniment and a countermelody, p. 42 / CD 35 • The importance of hands-alone practice, p. 77 / CD 48
20th/21st Cent.	Oriental Flower, p. 88 / CD 41	• Romantic era, Volume Two: Creating the mood, p. 44. Having students listen to the CD and teachers play it will guide students in discovering the mood of the piece, using the adjectives in the Practice Strategy.

Pieces from **Succeeding with the Masters®, Classical Era, Volume Two.** *Choose from the following.*
The biographical information on Franz Joseph Haydn is found on p. 7 and 16.

Composer	Title, Page, and CD Track	Characteristics and Practice Strategies
Franz Joseph Haydn	Minuet in D major, p. 10-11 / CD 1	p. 8-9 / CD 24
Franz Joseph Haydn	Minuet in B flat major, p. 14-15 / CD 2	p. 12-13 / CD 25
Franz Joseph Haydn	Gypsy Dance in C major, p. 18-19 / CD 3	p. 17 / CD 26

FJH2050

The Festival Collection®, Book 4 (more difficult selections)

Correlated with *Succeeding with the Masters®, Volume Two*
Baroque, Classical, and Romantic Eras

Pieces from The Festival Collection®, arranged in order of difficulty.
The section "About the Pieces and the Composers" beginning on p. 90 provides further valuable information.

Era	Title, Page, and CD Track	Composer
Romantic	Boys Round Dance, Op. 36, No. 3B, p. 51-53 / CD 22	Niels W. Gade
Baroque	Ciaccona with Five Variations, p. 12-15 / CD 5	Johann Pachelbel
20th/21st Cent.	Daydreaming, p. 82-83 / CD 38	Timothy Brown
Classical	Sonatina in G major, Op. 55, No. 2 (1st Mvt.), p. 48-50 / CD 21	Friedrich Kuhlau

Practice Strategies for The Festival Collection®, arranged in chronological order.
Refer to the corresponding era in Succeeding with the Masters®, Volume Two for a complete description of each Practice Strategy.

Era	Title, Page, and CD Track	Practice Strategies from SWTM
Baroque	Ciaccona with Five Variations, p. 12-15 / CD 5	• Baroque era, Volume One: Impulse practicing, p. 38 / CD 31 for Variations 2, 4, and 5. • Bringing a piece to life after it is learned, p. 65 / CD 40
Classical	Sonatina in G major, Op. 55, No. 2 (1st Mvt.), p. 48-50 / CD 21	• Balancing the melody with the accompaniment, p. 9 • Practicing *Alberti* rhythms, p. 66 / CD 39 • Tonic and dominant chords, p. 17 / CD 26
Romantic	Boys Round Dance, Op. 36, No. 3B, p. 51-53 / CD 22	• Contrast in music to create drama, p. 34 / CD 38 • Strong sense of rhythm defining a piece, p. 41 / CD 39 • How to play a piece faster, p. 68 / CD 46
20th/21st Cent.	Daydreaming, p. 82-83 / CD 38	• Romantic era, Volume Two: Keeping a continuous flow, p. 28 / CD 37 • The importance of hands-alone practice, p. 77 / CD 48

Pieces from Succeeding with the Masters®, Romantic Era, Volume Two. Choose from the following.
The biographical information on Franz Schubert is found on p. 8.

Composer	Title, Page, and CD Track	Characteristics and Practice Strategies
Franz Schubert	Melancholy Waltz in A flat major, Op. 9, No. 2, p. 11 / CD 1	p. 10 / CD 33
Franz Schubert	Waltz in A flat major, Op. 9, No. 3, p. 12 / CD 2	p. 10 / CD 33
Franz Schubert	Waltz in A flat major, Op. 9, No. 6, p. 13 / CD 3	p. 10 / CD 33

The Festival Collection®, Book 5

Correlated with **Succeeding with the Masters®, Volume Two**
Baroque, Classical, and Romantic Eras

Pieces from **The Festival Collection®**, *arranged in order of difficulty.*
The section "About the Pieces and the Composers" beginning on p. 98 provides further valuable information.

Era	Title, Page, and CD Track	Composer
20th/21st Cent.	Toccatina No. 1, p. 94-96 / CD 35	Dianne Goolkasian Rahbee
Baroque	The Prince of Denmark's March, p. 12-13 / CD 3	Jeremiah Clarke
Romantic	The Avalanche, Op. 45, No. 2, p. 58-59 / CD 20	Stephen Heller
20th/21st Cent.	Russian Dance, p. 86-87 / CD 31	Alexandre Tansman
Classical	Allegro, Op. 52, No. 2, p. 30-33 / CD 11	Johann Nepomuk Hummel

Practice Strategies for **The Festival Collection®**, *arranged in chronological order.*
Refer to the corresponding era in **Succeeding with the Masters®, Volume Two** *for a complete description of each Practice Strategy.*

Era	Title, Page, and CD Track	Practice Strategies from SWTM
Baroque	The Prince of Denmark's March, p. 12-13 / CD 3	• Finger *legato*, p. 20 / CD 28 • Establishing an "inner pulse," p. 38 / CD 33
Classical	Allegro, Op. 52, No. 2, p. 30-33 / CD 11	• Creating clear passagework, p. 52 / CD 36 • "Smart" fingering, p. 70 / CD 40
Romantic	The Avalanche, Op. 45, No. 2, p. 58-59 / CD 20	• Practicing with forward direction, p. 20 / CD 35. Listening to the CD, can students hear this forward direction and other points in the Practice Strategy that are useful in this piece? • Discovering the *espressivo* dynamic marking, p. 52
20th/21st Cent.	Russian Dance, p. 86-87 / CD 31	• Romantic era, Volume Two: Improving muscle memory, p. 24 / CD 36 • Practicing "slightly under tempo" or "80% practice," p. 100 / CD 52
20th/21st Cent.	Toccatina No. 1, p. 94-96 / CD 35	• Classical era, Volume Two: Creating a dance-like accompaniment pattern, p. 42 / CD 32 • Romantic era, Volume Two: Practicing "slightly under tempo" or "80% practice," p. 100 / CD 52

Pieces from **Succeeding with the Masters®, Baroque Era, Volume Two.** *Choose from the following.*
The biographical information on George Frideric Handel is found on p. 44.

Composer	Title, Page, and CD Track	Characteristics and Practice Strategies
George Frideric Handel	Minuet in A minor, p. 46 / CD 10	p. 45 / CD 35
George Frideric Handel	Minuet in G minor, p. 48-49 / CD 11	p. 47 / CD 36
George Frideric Handel	Sarabande, p. 51-53 / CD 12	p. 50 / CD 37

FJH2050

The Festival Collection®, Book 5

*Correlated with **Succeeding with the Masters®, Volume Two***
Baroque, Classical, and Romantic Eras

*Pieces from **The Festival Collection®**, arranged in order of difficulty.*
The section "About the Pieces and the Composers" beginning on p. 98 provides further valuable information.

Era	Title, Page, and CD Track	Composer
Baroque	Marche, p. 14-15 / CD 4	Carl Philip Emanuel Bach
Romantic	Pantalon, p. 55-57 / CD 19	Amy Marcy Cheney Beach
Classical	Sonata in G major, Hob. XVI:8 (1st Mvt.), p. 38-40 / CD 13	Franz Joseph Haydn
Romantic	Waltz, Op. 12, No. 2, p. 66-67 / CD 23	Edvard Grieg
20th/21st Cent.	The Banjo Player, p. 80-81 / CD 29	Fritz Kaylor

*Practice Strategies for **The Festival Collection®**, arranged in chronological order.*
*Refer to the corresponding era in **Succeeding with the Masters®, Volume Two** for a complete description of each Practice Strategy.*

Era	Title, Page, and CD Track	Practice Strategies from SWTM
Baroque	Marche, p. 14-15 / CD 4	• Practicing back to front, p. 22 / CD 29 • Inner listening, p. 54 / CD 38
Classical	Sonata in G major, Hob. XVI:8 (1st Mvt.), p. 38-40 / CD 13	• Practicing with the metronome, p. 78 • Finding places to relax for better facility, p. 83 / CD 43. Even though this movement is light and *allegro*, students can find places in the music to release any tension in their muscles.
Romantic	Pantalon, p. 55-57 / CD 19	• Finding places to relax for better facility, p. 44 / CD 40 • Follow the leader, p. 60 / CD 44
Romantic	Waltz, Op. 12, No. 2, p. 66-67 / CD 23	• Improving muscle memory, p. 24 / CD 36 • Follow the leader, p. 60 / CD 44
20th/21st Cent.	The Banjo Player, p. 80-81 / CD 29	• Classical era, Volume Two: Creating a dance-like accompaniment pattern, p. 42 / CD 32 • Baroque era, Volume Two: Detached-note practice, p. 41 / CD 34. Even though this spirited piece is not baroque in style, the Practice Strategy will work to make it very clean and clear.

*Pieces from **Succeeding with the Masters®, Classical Era, Volume Two**. Choose from the following.*
The biographical information on Ludwig van Beethoven is found on p. 64-65.

Composer	Title, Page, and CD Track	Characteristics and Practice Strategies
Ludwig van Beethoven	German Dance in E flat major, p. 68-69 / CD 16	p. 66 / CD 39
Ludwig van Beethoven	Bagatelle in A minor, p. 72 / CD 17	p. 70-71 / CD 40
Ludwig van Beethoven	Allemande in A, p. 76-77 / CD 18	p. 74-75 / CD 41

The Festival Collection®, Book 5

Correlated with **Succeeding with the Masters®, Volume Two**
Baroque, Classical, and Romantic Eras

Pieces from The Festival Collection®, *arranged in order of difficulty.*
The section "About the Pieces and the Composers" beginning on p. 98 provides further valuable information.

Era	Title, Page, and CD Track	Composer
Baroque	Hornpipe, p. 16-17 / CD 5	Henry Purcell
Classical	Sonatina in G major, Op. 20, No. 1 (1st Mvt.), p. 24-26 / CD 9	Jan Ladislav Dussek
20th/21st Cent.	Moonlit Meadows, Op. 65, No. 12, p. 92-93 / CD 34	Sergei Prokofiev
Romantic	Elves' Dance, Op. 12, No. 4, p. 68-69 / CD 24	Edvard Grieg

Practice Strategies for The Festival Collection®, *arranged in chronological order.*
Refer to the corresponding era in **Succeeding with the Masters®, Volume Two** *for a complete description of each Practice Strategy.*

Era	Title, Page, and CD Track	Practice Strategies from SWTM
Baroque	Hornpipe, p. 16-17 / CD 5	• Follow the leader, p. 45 / CD 35 • Learning to play faster, p. 91
Classical	Sonatina in G major, Op. 20, No. 1 (1st Mvt.), p. 24-26 / CD 9	• Playing *tenuto*, p. 9 • Practicing *Alberti* basses, p. 66 / CD 39
Romantic	Elves' Dance, Op. 12, No. 4, p. 68-69 / CD 24	• Strong sense of rhythm helping to define a piece, p. 41 / CD 39. Even though this piece is in a different time signature, the general information will still be valuable. • Playing with a supple wrist, p. 68 / CD 46 • How to play a piece faster, p. 68
20th/21st Cent.	Moonlit Meadows, Op. 65, No. 12, p. 92-93 / CD 34	• Classical era, Volume Two: Practicing with the metronome, p. 78 • Baroque era, Volume Two: Slow vs. fast practicing (3 x 1 rule), p. 76 / CD 43

Pieces from **Succeeding with the Masters®, Romantic Era, Volume Two.** *Choose from the following.*
The biographical information on Robert Schumann is found on p. 23.

Composer	Title, Page, and CD Track	Characteristics and Practice Strategies
Robert Schumann	Little Romance, p. 26-27 / CD 9	p. 24-25 / CD 36
Robert Schumann	Mignon, p. 30-31 / CD 10	p. 28-29 / CD 37
Robert Schumann	Little Cradle Song, p. 32-33 / CD 11	p. 28-29 / CD 37

FJH2050

The Festival Collection®, Book 5

Correlated with Succeeding with the Masters®, Volume Two
Baroque, Classical, and Romantic Eras

Pieces from The Festival Collection®, arranged in order of difficulty.
The section "About the Pieces and the Composers" beginning on p. 98 provides further valuable information.

Era	Title, Page, and CD Track	Composer
Classical	Sonatina in C major, Op. 36, No. 3 (1st Mvt.), p. 41-45 / CD 14	Muzio Clementi
20th/21st Cent.	Caravan, p. 90-91 / CD 33	Alexei Machavariani
Romantic	L'adieu, Op. 100, No. 12, p. 52-54 / CD 18	Johann Friedrich Burgmüller
Romantic	Prelude in C minor, Op. 8, No. 1, p. 72-73 / CD 26	Henryk Pachulski
Baroque	Passepied, p. 18-19 / CD 6	Johann Philipp Kirnberger

Practice Strategies for The Festival Collection®, arranged in chronological order.
*Refer to the corresponding era in **Succeeding with the Masters®, Volume Two** for a complete description of each Practice Strategy.*

Era	Title, Page, and CD Track	Practice Strategies from SWTM
Baroque	Passepied, p. 18-19 / CD 6	• Practicing cadence points, p. 64 / CD 41 • Playing contrapuntal pieces with success, p. 65
Classical	Sonatina in C major, Op. 36, No. 3 (1st Mvt.), p. 41-45 / CD 14	• Balancing the melody with the accompaniment, p. 9 • Thinking orchestrally to bring this piece to life, p. 92 / CD 45
Romantic	L'adieu, Op. 100, No. 12, p. 52-54 / CD 18	• Strong sense of rhythm helping to define a piece, p. 41 / CD 39. Even though this piece is in a different time signature, the general information will still be valuable. • How to play a piece faster, p. 68
Romantic	Prelude in C minor, Op. 8, No. 1, p. 72-73 / CD 26	• *Cantabile* playing, p. 24 The melody is clearly in the right hand of this prelude, but teachers can discuss *"cantabile"* playing with their students. • Applying *rubato*, p. 29
20th/21st Cent.	Caravan, p. 90-91 / CD 33	• Classical era, Volume Two: Regrouping, p. 75 / CD 41 • Baroque era, Volume Two: Attention to articulations, p. 26 / CD 30

*Pieces from **Succeeding with the Masters®**, Baroque Era, Volume Two. Choose from the following.*
The biographical information on Domenico Scarlatti is found on p. 74-75.

Composer	Title, Page, and CD Track	Characteristics and Practice Strategies
Domenico Scarlatti	Aria, p. 78-79 / CD 18	p. 76 / CD 43
Domenico Scarlatti	Minuet in A major, p. 82-83 / CD 19	p. 80 / CD 44
Domenico Scarlatti	Sonata in D minor, p. 85 / CD 20	p. 84 / CD 45

The Festival Collection®, Book 5

Correlated with **Succeeding with the Masters®, Volume Two**
Baroque, Classical, and Romantic Eras

Pieces from The Festival Collection®, *arranged in order of difficulty.*
The section "About the Pieces and the Composers" beginning on p. 98 provides further valuable information.

Era	Title, Page, and CD Track	Composer
Classical	Sonatina in C major, Op. 36, No. 3 (2nd Mvt.), p. 45 / CD 15	Muzio Clementi
20th/21st Cent.	Play: for Piano, p. 88-89 / CD 32	Andrei Eshpai
Romantic	Minuet, Op. 23, No. 1, p. 60-63 / CD 21	Erkki Melartin
Baroque	Bourrée in G minor, p. 22-23 / CD 8	Gottfried Heinrich Stölzel

Practice Strategies for The Festival Collection®, *arranged in chronological order.*
Refer to the corresponding era in **Succeeding with the Masters®, Volume Two** *for a complete description of each Practice Strategy.*

Era	Title, Page, and CD Track	Practice Strategies from SWTM
Baroque	Bourree in G minor, p. 22-23 / CD 8	• Make every note count, p. 26 • Blocking, p. 16 / CD 27
Classical	Sonatina in C major, Op. 36, No. 3 (2nd Mvt.), p. 45 / CD 15	• Balancing the melody with the accompaniment, p. 9 • Thinking orchestrally to bring this piece to life, p. 92 / CD 45
Romantic	Minuet, Op. 23, No. 1, p. 60-63 / CD 21	• Voicing the melody, p. 10 / CD 33 • Keeping a continuous flow, p. 28 / CD 37, very last paragraph underneath the music.
20th/21st Cent.	Play: for Piano, p. 88-89 / CD 32	• Romantic era, Volume Two: The importance of hands-alone practice, p. 77 / CD 48 • Classical era, Volume Two: Voicing the melody, p. 28 / CD 29

Pieces from Succeeding with the Masters®, Romantic Era, Volume Two. *Choose from the following.*
The biographical information on Pyotr (Peter) Tchaikovsky is found on p. 56.

Composer	Title, Page, and CD Track	Characteristics and Practice Strategies
Pyotr (Peter) Tchaikovsky	Sweet Dream, p. 65-67 / CD 19	p. 64 / CD 45

The biographical information on Frédéric Chopin is found on p. 76.

Composer	Title, Page, and CD Track	Characteristics and Practice Strategies
Frédéric Chopin	Sostenuto in E flat major, p. 78-79 / CD 22	p. 77 / CD 48

The Festival Collection®, Book 5

*Correlated with **Succeeding with the Masters®, Volume Two***
Baroque, Classical, and Romantic Eras

Pieces from The Festival Collection®, arranged in order of difficulty.
The section "About the Pieces and the Composers" beginning on p. 98 provides further valuable information.

Era	Title, Page, and CD Track	Composer
Classical	Sonatina in F major, Op. 168, No. 1 (3rd Mvt.), p. 27-29 / CD 10	Anton Diabelli
20th/21st Cent.	Evening at the Village, p. 74-76 / CD 27	Béla Bartók
Baroque	Rigaudon, p. 20-21 / CD 7	Jean-Philippe Rameau
Romantic	Romance, Op. 31, No. 7, p. 49-51 / CD 17	Reyngol'd Glier

Practice Strategies for The Festival Collection®, arranged in chronological order.
*Refer to the corresponding era in **Succeeding with the Masters®, Volume Two** for a complete description of each Practice Strategy.*

Era	Title, Page, and CD Track	Practice Strategies from SWTM
Baroque	Rigaudon, p. 20-21 / CD 7	• Unit practicing, p. 58 / CD 39 • Bringing a piece to life after it is learned, p. 69 / CD 42
Classical	Sonatina in F major, Op. 168, No. 1 (3rd Mvt.), p. 27-29 / CD 10	• Articulating wedges and *staccatos*, p. 53 / CD 36 • Slow vs. fast practicing (3 x 1 rule), p. 36 / CD 33
Romantic	Romance, Op. 31, No. 7, p. 49-51 / CD 17	• Voicing the melody, p. 10, for measures 17-32 / CD 33 • Shaping phrases, p. 14 / CD 34. The phrases in the A section of *Romance* are: two short phrases, followed by one long phrase; or one short phrase, followed by a longer phrase. Discuss with students how the phrasing in the B section is different and then discuss the phrase goals for each.
20th/21st Cent.	Evening at the Village, p. 74-76 / CD 27	• Romantic era, Volume Two: The importance of hands-alone practice, p. 77 • Classical era, Volume Two: Balancing the melody with the accompaniment, p. 9

Pieces from Succeeding with the Masters®, Classical Era, Volume Two. Choose from the following.
The biographical information on Wolfgang Amadeus Mozart is found on p. 40-41.

Composer	Title, Page, and CD Track	Characteristics and Practice Strategies
Wolfgang Amadeus Mozart	Little Funeral March, p. 51 / CD 12	p. 50 / CD 35
Wolfgang Amadeus Mozart	Moderato in F major, p. 54-55 / CD 13	p. 52-53 / CD 36

Pieces from Succeeding with the Masters®, Romantic Era, Volume Two. Choose from the following.
The biographical information on Franz Schubert is found on p. 8.

Composer	Title, Page, and CD Track	Characteristics and Practice Strategies
Franz Schubert	Ländler in A minor, p. 15 / CD 4	p. 14 / CD 34
Franz Schubert	Valse sentimentale in A major, p. 16-17 / CD 5	p. 14 / CD 34
Franz Schubert	Valse noble in A minor, p. 18-19 / CD 6	p. 14 / CD 34

The Festival Collection®, Book 5

Correlated with **Succeeding with the Masters®, Volume Two**
Baroque, Classical, and Romantic Eras

Pieces from The Festival Collection®, arranged in order of difficulty.
The section "About the Pieces and the Composers" beginning on p. 98 provides further valuable information.

Era	Title, Page, and CD Track	Composer
Classical	Arietta with Variations, Hob, XVII:2, p. 46-48 / CD 16	Franz Joseph Haydn
20th/21st Cent.	First Gymnopédie, p. 82-85 / CD 30	Erik Satie
Baroque	Bourrée in F major, p. 6-8 / CD 1	Georg Philipp Telemann
Romantic	Improvisation, Op. 18, p. 70-71 / CD 25	Max Reger

Practice Strategies for The Festival Collection®, arranged in chronological order.
Refer to the corresponding era in **Succeeding with the Masters®, Volume Two** *for a complete description of each Practice Strategy.*

Era	Title, Page, and CD Track	Practice Strategies from SWTM
Baroque	Bourrée in F major, p. 6-8 / CD 1	• Finger independence, p. 47 / CD 36 • Make every note count, p. 26
Classical	Arietta with Variations, Hob, XVII:2, p. 46-48 / CD 16	• Balancing the melody with the accompaniment, p. 9 • Impulse practicing, p. 47-48 / CD 34 for Variation I • Playing *tenuto*, p. 9 • Shaping phrases, p. 61 / CD 38 for Variation III • Bringing the piece to life after it is learned, p. 25. Students can use this Practice Strategy to create different moods in the variations.
Romantic	Improvisation, Op. 18, p. 70-71 / CD 25	• Keeping a continuous flow, p. 28 / CD 37, very last paragraph underneath the music. • Voicing the melody using two hands, p. 72
20th/21st Cent.	First Gymnopédie, p. 82-85 / CD 30	• Romantic era, Volume Two: The importance of a singing *legato*, p. 86 / CD 50. Like the music of Chopin, this *First Gymnopédie* also must have a singing *legato* in the right hand part. • Baroque era, Volume One: Play-prepare, p. 16 / CD 25

Pieces from **Succeeding with the Masters®, Classical Era, Volume Two.** *Choose from the following.*
The biographical information on Franz Joseph Haydn is found on p. 7 and 16.

Composer	Title, Page, and CD Track	Characteristics and Practice Strategies
Franz Joseph Haydn	Minuet in D major, p. 22-23 / CD 4	p. 20 / CD 27
Franz Joseph Haydn	Minuet in C major, p. 26-27 / CD 5	p. 24-25 / CD 28
Franz Joseph Haydn	Scherzo in F major, p. 30-31 / CD 6	p. 28-29 / CD 29

FJH2050

The Festival Collection®, Book 5

Correlated with **Succeeding with the Masters®, Volume Two**
Baroque, Classical, and Romantic Eras

Pieces from **The Festival Collection®**, *arranged in order of difficulty.*
The section "About the Pieces and the Composers" beginning on p. 98 provides further valuable information.

Era	Title, Page, and CD Track	Composer
20th/21st Cent.	Le petit nègre, p. 77-79 / CD 28	Claude Debussy
Baroque	Aire, p. 9-11 / CD 2	Jean-Baptiste Loeillet
Classical	Sonatina in E flat major, Op. 37, No. 1 (1st Mvt.), p. 34-37 / CD 12	Muzio Clementi
Romantic	Vals sentimental, p. 64-65 / CD 22	Enrique Granados

Practice Strategies for **The Festival Collection®**, *arranged in chronological order.*
Refer to the corresponding era in **Succeeding with the Masters®, Volume Two** *for a complete description of each Practice Strategy.*

Era	Title, Page, and CD Track	Practice Strategies from SWTM
Baroque	Aire, p. 9-11 / CD 2	• "Smart" fingering, p. 13 / CD 26 • Improving muscle memory, p. 30 / CD 31
Classical	Sonatina in E flat major, Op. 37, No. 1 (1st Mvt.), p. 34-37 / CD 12	• Shaping phrases, p. 61 / CD 38 • Bringing the piece to life musically, p. 50 / CD 35
Romantic	Vals sentimental, p. 64-65 / CD 22	• Applying *rubato*, p. 29 / CD 48 • Keen listening, p. 48 / CD 41
20th/21st Cent.	Le petit nègre, p. 77-79 / CD 28	• Romantic era, Volume Two: Improving muscle memory p. 24 / CD 36 • Practicing "slightly under tempo" or "80% practice," p. 100 / CD 52

Pieces from **Succeeding with the Masters®, Baroque Era, Volume Two.** *Choose from the following.*
The biographical information on George Frideric Handel is found on p. 44.

Composer	Title, Page, and CD Track	Characteristics and Practice Strategies
George Frideric Handel	Sonatina, p. 56-57 / CD 13	p. 54 / CD 38
George Frideric Handel	Prelude in F major, p. 60-61 / CD 14	p. 58 / CD 39
George Frideric Handel	Prelude in C minor, p. 63 / CD 15	p. 62 / CD 40

Pieces from **Succeeding with the Masters®, Romantic Era, Volume Two.** *Choose from the following.*
The biographical information on Franz Schubert is found on p. 8.

Composer	Title, Page, and CD Track	Characteristics and Practice Strategies
Franz Schubert	Ecossaise in D flat major, p. 21 / CD 7	p. 20 / CD 35
Franz Schubert	German Dance in B flat major, p. 22 / CD 8	p. 20 / CD 35

The Festival Collection®, Book 6

Correlated with Succeeding with the Masters®, Volume Two
Baroque, Classical, and Romantic Eras

Pieces from The Festival Collection®, arranged in order of difficulty.
The section "About the Pieces and the Composers" beginning on p. 116 provides further valuable information.

Era	Title, Page, and CD Track	Composer
Baroque	Sonata in D minor, K. 89, L. 211, p. 8-11 / CD 2	Domenico Scarlatti
Romantic	The Storm, Op. 109, No. 13, p. 82-83 / CD 31	Johann Friedrich Burgmüller
20th/21st Cent.	Rondo Toccata, Op. 60, No. 4, p. 90-93 / CD 34	Dmitri Kabalevsky
Classical	Sonatina in C major, Op. 55, No. 3 (1st Mvt.), p. 42-45 / CD 14	Friedrich Kuhlau

Practice Strategies for The Festival Collection®, arranged in chronological order.
Refer to the corresponding era in Succeeding with the Masters®, Volume Two for a complete description of each Practice Strategy.

Era	Title, Page, and CD Track	Practice Strategies from SWTM
Baroque	Sonata in D minor, K. 89, L. 211, p. 8-11 / CD 2	• "Smart" fingering, p. 13 / CD 26 • Learning to play faster, p. 91
Classical	Sonatina in C major, Op. 55, No. 3 (1st Mvt.), p. 42-45 / CD 14	• Slow vs. fast practicing (3 x 1 rule), p. 36 / CD 31 • Impulse practicing on p. 47-48 / CD 34 for all scale passages, and students should practice with the metronome.
Romantic	The Storm, Op. 109, No. 13, p. 82-83 / CD 31	• How to play a piece faster, p. 68 / CD 46 • Finding places to relax for better facility, p. 44 / CD 40
20th/21st Cent.	Rondo Toccata, Op. 60, No. 4, p. 90-93 / CD 34	• Romantic era, Volume Two: Unit, section, and performance practice, p. 24 / CD 36 • Baroque era, Volume Two: Slow vs. fast practicing (3 x 1 rule), p. 76 / CD 43

Pieces from Succeeding with the Masters®, Classical Era, Volume Two. Choose from the following.
The biographical information on Ludwig van Beethoven is found on p. 64-65.

Composer	Title, Page, and CD Track	Characteristics and Practice Strategies
Ludwig van Beethoven	Waltz in E flat major, p. 80-81 / CD 19	p. 78-79 / CD 42
Ludwig van Beethoven	Minuet in C major, p. 84-85 / CD 20	p. 82-83 / CD 43
Ludwig van Beethoven	Für Elise, p. 88-91 / CD 21	p. 86-87 / CD 44

FJH2050

The Festival Collection®, Book 6

Correlated with Succeeding with the Masters®, Volume Two
Baroque, Classical, and Romantic Eras

Pieces from *The Festival Collection®*, arranged in order of difficulty.
The section "About the Pieces and the Composers" beginning on p. 116 provides further valuable information.

Era	Title, Page, and CD Track	Composer
Romantic	Prelude in E minor, Op.28, No. 4, p. 68 / CD 23	Frédéric Chopin
Baroque	Toccata in G minor, p. 18-19 / CD 6	Leonardo Leo
Classical	Rondo Grazioso, p. 64-65 / CD 21	Joseph Ignace Pleyel
20th/21st Cent.	Petit Musique, Op. 33, No. 8, p. 114-115 / CD 44	Florent Schmitt

Practice Strategies for *The Festival Collection®*, arranged in chronological order.
Refer to the corresponding era in **Succeeding with the Masters®, Volume Two** for a complete description of each Practice Strategy.

Era	Title, Page, and CD Track	Practice Strategies from SWTM
Baroque	Toccata in G minor, p. 18-19 / CD 6	• Practicing back to front, p. 22 / CD 29 • Improving muscle memory, p. 30 / CD 31
Classical	Rondo Grazioso, p. 64-65 / CD 21	• Practicing *Alberti* basses, p. 66 / CD 39 • Shaping the phrases, p. 61
Romantic	Prelude in E minor, Op.28, No. 4, p. 68 / CD 23	• Conveying the mood and using the pedal, p. 80 / CD 49 • Creating your own interpretation through listening, p. 81 / CD 49
20th/21st Cent.	Petit Musique, Op. 33, No. 8, p. 114-115 / CD 44	• Romantic era, Volume Two: Follow the leader, p. 60 / CD 44. With this Practice Strategy, the tempo will be solid and students will be able to control all of the shifts and leaps. • Playing with a supple wrist, p. 68 / CD 46. This piece utilizes the same pianistic technique as the Tchaikovsky, but the overall character of the piece is different. Students will need to feel their wrists and arms lift up and move away up from the keyboard at the end of every short phrase and for all of the buoyant *staccato* accented notes. For all of the *staccato* notes that are followed by an accented note, (measures 1-2 and 24-25), it is best if students lift up from the *staccato* notes, and then drop down into the keys for the accented notes. In other words, throughout the piece, the downbeats are where pianists can drop into the keys, and the third beats are where pianists will lift off of the keys.

Pieces from *Succeeding with the Masters®, Baroque Era, Volume Two.* Choose from the following.
The biographical information on Johann Sebastian Bach is found on p. 10-11.

Composer	Title, Page, and CD Track	Characteristics and Practice Strategies
Johann Sebastian Bach	Prelude in F major, p. 24-25 / CD 4	p. 22-23 / CD 29
Johann Sebastian Bach	Prelude in C minor, p. 27-29 / CD 5	p. 26 / CD 30
Johann Sebastian Bach	Prelude in E minor, p. 32-33 / CD 6	p. 30 / CD 31

Pieces from *Succeeding with the Masters®, Romantic Era, Volume Two.* Choose from the following.
The biographical information on Pyotr (Peter) Tchaikovsky is found on p. 56.

Composer	Title, Page, and CD Track	Characteristics and Practice Strategies
Pyotr (Peter) Tchaikovsky	The Lark's Song, p. 70-71 / CD 20	p. 68 / CD 46
Pyotr (Peter) Tchaikovsky	Chanson Triste, p. 73-75 / CD 21	p. 72 / CD 47

The Festival Collection®, Book 6

Correlated with **Succeeding with the Masters®, Volume Two**
Baroque, Classical, and Romantic Eras

Pieces from **The Festival Collection®**, *arranged in order of difficulty.*
The section "About the Pieces and the Composers" beginning on p. 116 provides further valuable information.

Era	Title, Page, and CD Track	Composer
Romantic	Morning Bell, Op. 109, No. 9, p. 72-73 / CD 26	Johann Friedrich Burgmüller
Baroque	Invention No. 8 in F major, p. 14-15 / CD 4	Johann Sebastian Bach
20th/21st Cent.	On the Farm, p. 102-104 / CD 39	Bohuslav Martinu
Classical	Rondo, Op. 18, p. 46-49 / CD 15	Jan Václav Voříšek

Practice Strategies for **The Festival Collection®**, *arranged in chronological order.*
Refer to the corresponding era in **Succeeding with the Masters®, Volume Two** *for a complete description of each Practice Strategy.*

Era	Title, Page, and CD Track	Practice Strategies from SWTM
Baroque	Invention No. 8 in F major, p. 14-15 / CD 4	• Impulse practicing, p. 41 • Follow the leader, p. 45 / CD 35
Classical	Rondo, Op. 18, p. 46-49 / CD 15	• Playing repeated notes quickly, p. 29 • Practicing with the metronome, p. 78
Romantic	Morning Bell, Op. 109, No. 9, p. 72-73 / CD 26	• Voicing the melody, p. 10 / CD 33 • Keeping a continuous flow, p. 28 / CD 37, very last paragraph underneath the music
20th/21st Cent.	On the Farm, p. 102-104 / CD 39	• Romantic era, Volume Two: Practicing "slightly under tempo" or "80% practice," p. 100 / CD 52 • Slow, slow practice is a must for this piece, always listening to the different articulations.

Pieces from **Succeeding with the Masters®, Romantic Era, Volume Two.** *Choose from the following.*
The biographical information on Frédéric Chopin is found on p. 76.

Composer	Title, Page, and CD Track	Characteristics and Practice Strategies
Frédéric Chopin	Prelude in A major, Op. 28, No. 7, p. 82 / CD 23	p. 80-81 / CD 49
Frédéric Chopin	Prelude in C minor, Op. 28, No. 20, p. 83 / CD 24	p. 80-81 / CD 49
Frédéric Chopin	Prelude in B minor, Op. 28, No. 6, p. 84-85 / CD 25	p. 80-81 / CD 49

The Festival Collection®, Book 6

*Correlated with **Succeeding with the Masters®, Volume Two**
Baroque, Classical, and Romantic Eras*

*Pieces from The Festival Collection®, arranged in order of difficulty.
The section "About the Pieces and the Composers" beginning on p. 116 provides further valuable information.*

Era	Title, Page, and CD Track	Composer
Romantic	Fantasy Dance, Op. 124, No. 5, p. 76-77 / CD 28	Robert Schumann
Baroque	Divertimento, p. 28-29 / CD 10	Georg Christoph Wagenseil
20th/21st Cent.	Joc cu bâtă, p. 98-99 / CD 37	Béla Bartók
Classical	Sonatina in C major, Op. 88, No. 1 (1st Mvt.), p. 50-52 / CD 16	Friedrich Kuhlau

*Practice Strategies for The Festival Collection®, arranged in chronological order.
Refer to the corresponding era in **Succeeding with the Masters®, Volume Two** for a complete description of each Practice Strategy.*

Era	Title, Page, and CD Track	Practice Strategies from SWTM
Baroque	Divertimento, p. 28-29 / CD 10	• 8 times to perfection, p. 64 • Make every note count, p. 26
Classical	Sonatina in C major, Op. 88, No. 1 (1st Mvt.), p. 50-52 / CD 16	• Slow vs. fast practicing (3 x 1 rule), p. 36 / CD 31 • Impulse practicing, p. 47-48 / CD 34 for all scale passages and students should practice with the metronome.
Romantic	Fantasy Dance, Op. 124, No. 5, p. 76-77 / CD 28	• Strong sense of rhythm helping to define a piece, p. 41 / CD 39. Even though this piece is in a different time signature, the general information will still be valuable. • Playing with a supple wrist, p. 68 / CD 46
20th/21st Cent.	Joc cu bâtă, p. 98-99 / CD 37	• Baroque era, Volume Two: Practicing cadence points, p. 64 / CD 41. In the Bartók, there are definite cadence points where students need to feel that they have "arrived." Have students listen to the recording and mark in the score where these arrival points are in the music. When they play, they need to feel the forward direction of the line to these arrival points.

*Pieces from Succeeding with the Masters®, Baroque Era, Volume Two. Choose from the following.
The biographical information on Domenico Scarlatti is found on p. 74-75.*

Composer	Title, Page, and CD Track	Characteristics and Practice Strategies
Domenico Scarlatti	Sonata in E minor, p. 88-89 / CD 21	p. 86-87 / CD 46
Domenico Scarlatti	Sonata in A major, p. 92-95 / CD 22	p. 90-91 / CD 47

*Pieces from Succeeding with the Masters®, Classical Era, Volume Two. Choose from the following.
The biographical information on Wolfgang Amadeus Mozart is found on p. 40-41.*

Composer	Title, Page, and CD Track	Characteristics and Practice Strategies
Wolfgang Amadeus Mozart	Adagio in C for Glass Harmonica, p. 58-59 / CD 14	p. 57 / CD 37
Wolfgang Amadeus Mozart	Presto in B flat major, p. 62-63 / CD 15	p. 60-61 / CD 38

The Festival Collection®, Book 6

*Correlated with **Succeeding with the Masters®, Volume Two***
Baroque, Classical, and Romantic Eras

*Pieces from **The Festival Collection**®, arranged in order of difficulty.*
The section "About the Pieces and the Composers" beginning on p. 116 provides further valuable information.

Era	Title, Page, and CD Track	Composer
Romantic	Prelude, Op. 40, No. 3, p. 70-71 / CD 25	Anatol Liadov
Classical	Sonatina in C major, Op. 88, No. 1 (2nd Mvt.), p. 52-53 / CD 17	Friedrich Kuhlau
20th/21st Cent.	Run, Run!, p. 105-107 / CD 40	Octavio Pinto
Baroque	The Grape Pickers, p. 26-27 / CD 9	François Couperin

*Practice Strategies for **The Festival Collection**®, arranged in chronological order.*
*Refer to the corresponding era in **Succeeding with the Masters®, Volume Two** for a complete description of each Practice Strategy.*

Era	Title, Page, and CD Track	Practice Strategies from SWTM
Baroque	The Grape Pickers, p. 26-27 / CD 9	• Use the information about ornamentation on p. 8 and 9. • Practicing cadence points, p. 64 / CD 41
Classical	Sonatina in C major, Op. 88, No. 1 (2nd Mvt.), p. 52-53 / CD 17	• Slow vs. fast practicing (3 x 1 rule), p. 36 / CD 31 • Impulse practicing, p. 47-48 / CD 34 for all scale passages and students should practice with the metronome.
Romantic	Prelude, Op. 40, No. 3, p. 70-71 / CD 25	• Keen listening, p. 48 / CD 41
20th/21st Cent.	Run, Run!, p. 105-107 / CD 40	• Romantic era, Volume Two: How to play a piece faster, p. 68 / CD 46 • Playing rapid *staccato* notes, p. 60. This strategy will work for both hands in the Pinto.

*Pieces from **Succeeding with the Masters®, Romantic Era, Volume Two**. Choose from the following.*
The biographical information on Robert Schumann is found on p. 23.

Composer	Title, Page, and CD Track	Characteristics and Practice Strategies
Robert Schumann	St. Nicholas (Knecht Ruprecht), p. 36-39 / CD 12	p. 34 / CD 38
Robert Schumann	Little Hunting Song, p. 42-43 / CD 13	p. 41 / CD 39
Robert Schumann	The Horseman, p. 45-47 / CD 14	p. 44 / CD 40

The Festival Collection®, Book 6

Correlated with *Succeeding with the Masters®, Volume Two*
Baroque, Classical, and Romantic Eras

Pieces from The Festival Collection®, arranged in order of difficulty.
The section "About the Pieces and the Composers" beginning on p. 116 provides further valuable information.

Era	Title, Page, and CD Track	Composer
Classical	Sonatina in C major, Op. 88, No. 1 (3rd Mvt.), p. 53-56 / CD 18	Friedrich Kuhlau
Romantic	From Foreign Lands and People, Op. 15, No. 1, p. 69 / CD 24	Robert Schumann
20th/21st Cent.	No fundo do meu quintal, p. 94-95 / CD 35	Heitor Villa-Lobos
Baroque	Invention No. 1 in C major, p. 12-13 / CD 3	Johann Sebastian Bach

Practice Strategies for The Festival Collection®, arranged in chronological order.
Refer to the corresponding era in Succeeding with the Masters®, Volume Two for a complete description of each Practice Strategy.

Era	Title, Page, and CD Track	Practice Strategies from SWTM
Baroque	Invention No. 1 in C major, p. 12-13 / CD 3	• Practicing back to front, p. 22 / CD 29 • Establishing an inner pulse, p. 38 / CD 33
Classical	Sonatina in C major, Op. 88, No. 1 (3rd Mvt.), p. 53-56 / CD 18	• Slow vs. fast practicing (3 x 1 rule), p. 36 / CD 31 • Impulse practicing, p. 47-48 / CD 34 for all scale passages and students should practice with the metronome.
Romantic	From Foreign Lands and People, Op. 15, No. 1, p. 69 / CD 24	• Voicing the melody, p. 10 / CD 33 • Keeping a continuous flow, p. 20 / CD 35, very last paragraph underneath the music. • *Cantabile* playing, p. 24. The melody is clearly in the right hand of this piece in the A section, and then there is a countermelody in the bass in the B section.
20th/21st Cent.	No fundo do meu quintal, p. 94-95 / CD 35	• Romantic era, Volume Two: Playing dotted rhythms, p. 57 / CD 43 • Practicing "slightly under tempo" or "80% practice," p. 100 / CD 52

Pieces from Succeeding with the Masters®, Classical Era, Volume Two. Choose from the following.
The biographical information on Franz Joseph Haydn is found on p. 7 and 16.

Composer	Title, Page, and CD Track	Characteristics and Practice Strategies
Franz Joseph Haydn	Andante in G minor, p. 33-35 / CD 7	p. 32 / CD 30
Franz Joseph Haydn	Presto in C major, p. 38-39 / CD 8	p. 36-37 / CD 31

Pieces from Succeeding with the Masters®, Romantic Era, Volume Two. Choose from the following.
The biographical information on Frédéric Chopin is found on p. 76.

Composer	Title, Page, and CD Track	Characteristics and Practice Strategies
Frédéric Chopin	Cantabile in B flat major, p. 89 / CD 26	p. 86-87 / CD 50

The Festival Collection®, Book 6

Correlated with **Succeeding with the Masters®, Volume Two**
Baroque, Classical, and Romantic Eras

Pieces from The Festival Collection®, arranged in order of difficulty.
The section "About the Pieces and the Composers" beginning on p. 116 provides further valuable information.

Era	Title, Page, and CD Track	Composer
Romantic	Mazurka in B flat major, Op. 7, No. 1, p. 78-79 / CD 29	Frédéric Chopin
Classical	Sonata in C, K. 545 (2nd Mvt.), p. 57-61 / CD 19	Wolfgang Amadeus Mozart
20th/21st Cent.	To the Rising Sun, Op. 4, No. 1, p. 96-97 / CD 36	Trygve Torjussen
Baroque	Allegro, p. 20-22 / CD 7	Giovanni Battista Pergolesi

Practice Strategies for The Festival Collection®, arranged in chronological order.
Refer to the corresponding era in Succeeding with the Masters®, Volume Two for a complete description of each Practice Strategy.

Era	Title, Page, and CD Track	Practice Strategies from SWTM
Baroque	Allegro, p. 20-22 / CD 7	• Establishing an inner pulse, p. 38 / CD 33 • 8 times to perfection, p. 64
Classical	Sonata in C, K. 545 (2nd Mvt.), p. 57-61 / CD 19	• Communicating the piece to an audience, p. 44 / CD 33. This piece is similar to its counterpart in SWTM, so the various Practice Strategies can apply easily to this famous work.
Romantic	Mazurka in B flat major, Op. 7, No. 1, p. 78-79 / CD 29	• The importance of hands-alone practice, p. 77 / CD 48 • Trills as part of the melodic line, p. 90 / CD 51
20th/21st Cent.	To the Rising Sun, Op. 4, No. 1, p. 96-97 / CD 36	• Romantic era, Volume Two: The importance of hands-alone practice, p. 77 / CD 48. The left hand has such an interesting part that students should practice hands alone in order to hear all of the voices. • Baroque era, Volume Two: Establishing an inner pulse, p. 38 / CD 33

Pieces from Succeeding with the Masters®, Baroque Era, Volume Two. Choose from the following.
The biographical information on Johann Sebastian Bach is found on p. 10-11.

Composer	Title, Page, and CD Track	Characteristics and Practice Strategies
Johann Sebastian Bach	Prelude in D minor, p. 35-37 / CD 7	p. 34 / CD 32
Johann Sebastian Bach	Gavotte, p. 39-40 / CD 8	p. 38 / CD 33
Johann Sebastian Bach	Minuet in B minor, p. 42-43 / CD 9	p. 41 / CD 34

FJH2050

The Festival Collection®, Book 6

*Correlated with **Succeeding with the Masters®, Volume Two***
Baroque, Classical, and Romantic Eras

Pieces from The Festival Collection®, arranged in order of difficulty.
The section "About the Pieces and the Composers" beginning on p. 116 provides further valuable information.

Era	Title, Page, and CD Track	Composer
Classical	Sonata in C, K. 545 (3rd Mvt.), p. 61-63 / CD 20	Wolfgang Amadeus Mozart
Romantic	Little Troll, Op. 71, No. 3, p. 84-86 / CD 32	Edvard Grieg
Romantic	Valse in A minor, p. 87-89 / CD 33	Frédéric Chopin
20th/21st Cent.	Moment sérieux, p. 113 / CD 43	Alexandre Tansman

Practice Strategies for The Festival Collection®, arranged in chronological order.
*Refer to the corresponding era in **Succeeding with the Masters®, Volume Two** for a complete description of each Practice Strategy.*

Era	Title, Page, and CD Track	Practice Strategies from SWTM
Classical	Sonata in C, K. 545 (3rd Mvt.), p. 61-63 / CD 20	• Creating clear passagework, p. 52 / CD 36 • Articulating wedges and *staccatos*, p. 53 / CD 36
Romantic	Little Troll, Op. 71, No. 3, p. 84-86 / CD 32	• Practicing with forward direction, p. 20 / CD 35. Listening to the CD, can students hear this forward direction and other points in the Practice Strategy that are useful in this piece? • Practicing "slightly under tempo" or "80% practice," p. 100 / CD 52
Romantic	Valse in A minor, p. 87-89 / CD 33	• The importance of a singing *legato*, p. 86 / CD 50 • Applying Chopin's *rubato*, p. 91 / CD 51. Of course the idea of *rubato* can be used for his waltzes too, so students can listen to this recording as well as other recordings to get an idea of this special characteristic of romantic music.
20th/21st Cent.	Moment serieux, p. 113 / CD 43	• Classical era, Volume Two: Voicing the melody, p. 28 / CD 29. This piece can be thought of as having one long phrase, from the beginning to the end. If students can decide where the phrase goals are within the piece, the piece can be played with wonderfully undulating rhythmic and melodic feeling.

*Pieces from **Succeeding with the Masters®, Baroque Era, Volume Two**. Choose from the following.*
The biographical information on George Frideric Handel is found on p. 44.

Composer	Title, Page, and CD Track	Characteristics and Practice Strategies
George Frideric Handel	Allemande, p. 66-67 / CD 16	p. 64-65 / CD 41
George Frideric Handel	Sonata, p. 70-73 / CD 17	p. 69 / CD 42

*Pieces from **Succeeding with the Masters®, Romantic Era, Volume Two**. Choose from the following.*
The biographical information on Frédéric Chopin is found on p. 76.

Composer	Title, Page, and CD Track	Characteristics and Practice Strategies
Frédéric Chopin	Mazurka in F major, Op. 68, No. 3, p. 92-94 / CD 27	p. 90-91 / CD 51
Frédéric Chopin	Mazurka in G minor, Op. 67, No. 2, p. 95-97 / CD 28	p. 90-91 / CD 51
Frédéric Chopin	Mazurka in C major, Op. 67, No. 3, p. 98-99 / CD 29	p. 90-91 / CD 51

The Festival Collection®, Book 6

Correlated with **Succeeding with the Masters®, Volume Two**
Baroque, Classical, and Romantic Eras

Pieces from The Festival Collection®, arranged in order of difficulty.
The section "About the Pieces and the Composers" beginning on p. 116 provides further valuable information.

Era	Title, Page, and CD Track	Composer
Classical	Sonata No. 18 in A major, p. 30-32 / CD 11	Domenico Cimarosa
Romantic	Cradle Song, Op. 68, No. 5, p. 66-67 / CD 22	Edvard Grieg
Baroque	Solfeggietto, p. 6-7 / CD 1	Carl Philipp Emanuel Bach
20th/21st Cent.	Busy Toccata, p. 110-112 / CD 42	Emma Lou Diemer

Practice Strategies for The Festival Collection®, arranged in chronological order.
Refer to the corresponding era in **Succeeding with the Masters®, Volume Two** *for a complete description of each Practice Strategy.*

Era	Title, Page, and CD Track	Practice Strategies from SWTM
Baroque	Solfeggietto, p. 6-7 / CD 1	• Unit practicing, p. 58 / CD 39 • Slow vs. fast practice (3 x 1 rule), p. 76 / CD 43
Classical	Sonata No. 18 in A major, p. 30-32 / CD 11	• Voicing the melody, p. 28 / CD 29 • Improving muscle memory, pgs. 47-48 / CD 34
Romantic	Cradle Song, Op. 68, No. 5, p. 66-67 / CD 22	• Voicing the melody, p. 10 / CD 33 • Keen listening, p. 48 / CD 41
20th/21st Cent.	Busy Toccata, p. 110-112 / CD 42	• Romantic era, Volume Two: Playing rapid *staccato* notes, p. 60. This Practice Strategy will work for both hands in the Pinto. • Follow the leader, p. 60 / CD 44. The same general principle works in the Villa-Lobos.

Pieces from **Succeeding with the Masters®, Baroque Era, Volume Two.** *Choose from the following.*
The biographical information on Domenico Scarlatti is found on p. 74-75.

Composer	Title, Page, and CD Track	Characteristics and Practice Strategies
Domenico Scarlatti	Sonata in D minor, p. 97-99 / CD 23	p. 96 / CD 48
Domenico Scarlatti	Minuet in B flat major, p. 102-105 / CD 24	p. 101 / CD 49
Domenico Scarlatti	Gigue, p. 107-109 / CD 25	p. 106 / CD 50

Pieces from **Succeeding with the Masters®, Romantic Era, Volume Two.** *Choose from the following.*
The biographical information on Robert Schumann is found on p. 23.

Composer	Title, Page, and CD Track	Characteristics and Practice Strategies
Robert Schumann	Solitary Flowers, p. 49-51 / CD 15	p. 48 / CD 41
Robert Schumann	Evening Song, p. 54-55 / CD 16	p. 52 / CD 42

The Festival Collection®, Book 6

Correlated with **Succeeding with the Masters®, Volume Two**
Baroque, Classical, and Romantic Eras

Pieces from The Festival Collection®, arranged in order of difficulty.
The section "About the Pieces and the Composers" beginning on p. 116 provides further valuable information.

Era	Title, Page, and CD Track	Composer
Romantic	Chanson Triste, p. 74-75 / CD 27	Vasili Kalinnikov
Classical	Sonata in G major, Hob. XVI: 27 (3rd Mvt.), p. 33-37 / CD 12	Franz Joseph Haydn
Baroque	Toccata in F minor, p. 23-25 / CD 8	Carlos de Seixas
20th/21st Cent.	Golden Leaves, p. 100-101 / CD 38	Dimitar Ninov

Practice Strategies for The Festival Collection®, arranged in chronological order.
Refer to the corresponding era in **Succeeding with the Masters®, Volume Two** *for a complete description of each Practice Strategy.*

Era	Title, Page, and CD Track	Practice Strategies from SWTM
Baroque	Toccata in F minor, p. 23-25 / CD 8	• Unit practicing, p. 80 / CD 44 • Bringing a piece to life after it is learned, p. 69 / CD 42. Using the CD, students can mark directly in their score what they hear and then discuss interpretation with the teacher.
Classical	Sonata in G major, Hob. XVI: 27 (3rd Mvt.), p. 33-37 / CD 12	• Impulse practicing, p. 47 / CD 34 • Playing sixteenth notes evenly, p. 83 / CD 43 • Practicing *Alberti* basses, p. 66 / CD 39
Romantic	Chanson Triste, p. 74-75 / CD 27	• Applying *rubato*, p. 77 / CD 48 • The importance of a singing *legato*, p. 86 / CD 50
20th/21st Cent.	Golden Leaves, p. 100-101 / CD 38	• Baroque era, Volume Two: Inner listening, p. 54 / CD 38. The same general idea can be applied to this contemporary work. For point No. 4, students can think about the instruments in a jazz group—perhaps a piano, string bass, flute, and percussion. Once students have learned the notes, rhythms, and fingerings of this piece, then it is time to think about playing with emotion. Listening to the CD is a great way to help guide them in interpreting this piece. Almost every phrase begins with an upbeat, and students must feel that the upbeat always leads to the next downbeat.

Pieces from **Succeeding with the Masters®, Classical Era, Volume Two.** *Choose from the following.*
The biographical information on Ludwig van Beethoven is found on p. 64-65.

Composer	Title, Page, and CD Track	Characteristics and Practice Strategies
Ludwig van Beethoven	Minuet in D major, p. 94-95 / CD 22	p. 92-93 / CD 45
Ludwig van Beethoven	Six Variations on a Swiss Song, p. 98-101 / CD 23	p. 97 / CD 46

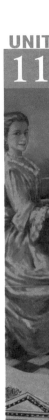

The Festival Collection®, Book 6

Correlated with *Succeeding with the Masters®, Volume Two*
Baroque, Classical, and Romantic Eras

Pieces from The Festival Collection®, arranged in order of difficulty.
The section "About the Pieces and the Composers" beginning on p. 116 provides further valuable information.

Era	Title, Page, and CD Track	Composer
Romantic	Sketch, p. 80-81 / CD 30	César Franck
Classical	Sonatina in E flat major, WoO 47, No. 1 (1st Mvt.), p. 38-41 / CD 13	Ludwig van Beethoven
20th/21st Cent.	A Blown-Away Leaf, p. 108-109 / CD 41	Leoš Janáček
Baroque	Invention No. 13 in A minor, p. 16-17 / CD 5	Johann Sebastian Bach

Practice Strategies for The Festival Collection®, arranged in chronological order.
Refer to the corresponding era in Succeeding with the Masters®, Volume Two for a complete description of each Practice Strategy.

Era	Title, Page, and CD Track	Practice Strategies from SWTM
Baroque	Invention No. 13 in A minor, p. 16-17 / CD 5	• Unit practicing, p. 58 / CD 39 • Playing contrapuntal pieces with success, p. 65
Classical	Sonatina in E flat major, WoO 47, No. 1 (1st Mvt.), p. 38-41 / CD 13	• Finding places to relax for better facility, p. 83 / CD 43. Even though this movement is light and *allegro*, students can find places in the music to release any tension in their muscles. • Finger pedaling, p. 44 / CD 33, for measures such as 5 and 6.
Romantic	Sketch, p. 80-81 / CD 30	• Follow the leader, p. 60 / CD 44 • Applying *rubato*, p. 29 / CD 48
20th/21st Cent.	A Blown-Away Leaf, p. 108-109 / CD 41	• Classical era, Volume Two: Bringing the piece to life, p. 32 / CD 30. The general idea for this Practice Strategy is that students listen to the recording and mark in their score what they hear. They need to pay special attention to the pedaling, how the sixteenth notes develop into trills (m. 24-30), and the repetitious main repeated motive. How does the overall piece sound like the title? And how do they bring out the melodic line when it is woven into other voices?

Pieces from Succeeding with the Masters®, Baroque Era, Volume Two. Choose from the following.
The biographical information on Frédéric Chopin is found on p. 76.

Composer	Title, Page, and CD Track	Characteristics and Practice Strategies
Frédéric Chopin	Polonaise in G minor, p. 102-103 / CD 30	p. 100 / CD 52
Frédéric Chopin	Largo in E flat major, p. 105 / CD 31	p. 104 / CD 53
Frédéric Chopin	Grand Valse Brillante in A minor, Op. 34, No. 2, p. 107-115 / CD 32	p. 106 / CD 54

FJH2050

PART III

*More ways to use **Succeeding with the Masters®** when **The Festival Collection®** is used as the core series for a completely well-rounded curriculum:*

1. A good way to motivate students how to be independent musicians is to have them work through a particular composer from a *Succeeding with the Masters®* era book on their own. The goal is to have students learn all of the pieces by a particular composer. When using the Practice Strategies for the pieces as well as listening to the Practice Strategy Workshop on the CD, students will be able to learn the pieces fluently and with ease. At a lesson that is designated as a performance day, the student can play all of the pieces they have learned and the teacher can discuss interpretation and style. Students who learn all of the pieces by each composer will certainly have achieved a great musical accomplishment! A sample of the *Succeeding with the Masters®* **Composer Certificate of Achievement*** is on page 156.

2. Use one *Succeeding with the Masters®* Era book for an extended period of time (up to a year) while the student works through an entire level of *The Festival Collection®*.
   • *The Festival Collection®*, *Book 1* at the same time as *On Your Way to Succeeding with the Masters®*.
   • *The Festival Collection®*, *Book 2* at the same time as *Succeeding with the Masters®*, *Classical Era, Volume One*.
   • *The Festival Collection®*, *Book 3* at the same time as *Succeeding with the Masters®*, *Baroque Era, Volume One*.
   • *The Festival Collection®*, *Book 4* (easier selections) at the same time as *Succeeding with the Masters®*, *Romantic Era, Volume One*.
   • *The Festival Collection®*, *Book 4* (more difficult selections) at the same time as *Succeeding with the Masters®*, *Classical Era, Volume Two*.
   • *The Festival Collection®*, *Book 5* at the same time as *Succeeding with the Masters®*, *Baroque Era, Volume Two*.
   • *The Festival Collection®*, *Book 6* at the same time as *Succeeding with the Masters®*, *Romantic Era, Volume Two*.

3. Use one *Succeeding with the Masters®* Era book for a period of time, such as 6 months. In this way, students will learn two eras per school year. This gives teachers as well as students the chance to explore the historical eras in depth. Since Volume One of *Succeeding with the Masters®* can be used for up to *three years of study*, students will have ample time to discover and work through each of the era books so that they truly understand the differences between each era.

4. Teachers can use *Succeeding with the Masters®*, *Volume One* with *The Festival Collection®*, *Books 2, 3*, and *4*. Then they can use *Succeeding with the Masters®*, *Volume Two* with *The Festival Collection®*, *Books 5, 6*, and *7*. In this way, teachers and students can freely choose which pieces from both series they would like to study and play.

5. Group lessons, or special summer sessions, can be spent with the *Succeeding with the Masters®*, *Student Activity Books*. These are an enjoyable and special way to learn about the master composers and the times they lived in. Since students learn about each era in a social as well as a historical perspective, they will be able to understand the differences in the eras more vividly when they use the *Student Activity Books*.

6. Use *Succeeding with the Masters®* with transfer students who might need to review fundamental master-composer repertoire, characteristics of each era, musical concepts, technique, and how to instill correct practice habits.

7. Use *Succeeding with the Masters®* with adult students who want to learn about the master composers. Adult students enjoy reading the text, listening to the Practice Strategy Workshop on the CD, working out of *The Student Activity Books*, and listening to the CD performances of the pieces.

8. Have students regularly listen to the Practice Strategy Workshop on each CD so that they learn how to practice correctly. The more they listen to the full performances as well as listen to the Practice Strategies, the easier it will be for them to learn all repertoire! Students will tend to gravitate to their favorite Practice Strategies. This is a great way to learn and remember for the rest of their lives.

* Permission is hereby given to photocopy the following certificate for the purpose of providing students with a Composer Certificate of Achievement.

CONGRATULATIONS!

on your terrific accomplishment
in completing the piano works of

_____

(Composer's Name)

in

Succeeding with the Masters®

_____ Era, Volume _____

_____   _____

(Teacher's Signature)   (Date)

Using 10 Essential Practice Strategies from Succeeding with the Masters® to Master All Repertoire

The following are the 10 essential Practice Strategies that can be used repeatedly in order to learn and master all repertoire. Students who understand these primary Practice Strategies, and how they relate to specific challenges in repertoire, will not have difficulty learning repertoire:

1. "Play-prepare" Practice Strategy.
   - Found in *SWTM, Baroque Era, Volume One*, p. 16-17.
   - Found in *SWTM, Classical Era, Volume Two*, p. 78.
   This Practice Strategy is essential for any section of music that requires the hands to move a distance.

2. "Blocking" Practice Strategy. This Practice Strategy is an essential way for students to see and feel the patterns of a piece more readily than if learning a piece note by note. Students also gain another perspective by hearing the piece harmonically.
   - Found in *SWTM, Classical Era, Volume One*, p. 20, 56-57.
   - Found in *SWTM, Romantic Era, Volume One*, p. 54.
   - Found in *SWTM, Baroque Era, Volume Two*, p. 16.
   - Found in *SWTM, Classical Era, Volume Two*, p. 60.

3. Practice Strategies that focus on rhythm.
   - Found in *SWTM, Baroque Era, Volume One*, p. 21, 24, 28, 55, 70, 74-75.
   - Found in *SWTM, Classical Era, Volume One*, p. 23 and 64.
   - Found in *SWTM, Romantic Era, Volume One*, p. 18, 29, 54, and 75.

4. Practice Strategies that focus on phrasing.
   - Found in *On Your Way to SWTM*, p. 33.
   - Found in *SWTM, Baroque Era, Volume One*, p. 11, 25, and 28-29.
   - Found in *SWTM, Classical Era, Volume One*, p. 38 and 42.
   - Found in *SWTM, Baroque Era, Volume Two*, p. 87.
   - Found in *SWTM, Classical Era, Volume Two*, p. 61.
   - Found in *SWTM, Romantic Era, Volume Two*, p. 14 and 20.

Muscle Memory –

Is a large concept that encompasses a variety of Practice Strategies. Used interchangeably and frequently, students have a way to learn all repertoire in the most efficient way possible. "Muscle memory" refers to how the muscles in the fingers, hands, wrists, and arms *remember* the feel of the keys as each note is played. The brain sends signals to the muscles in the body to tell them how to move. If one practices in the correct way, the muscles will learn much more quickly and the student will develop technique that is reliable even when they are nervous.

Improving muscle memory - Examples of topic:
   - Found in *SWTM, Baroque Era, Volume Two*, p. 30.
   - Found in *SWTM, Classical Era, Volume Two*, p. 47.
   - Found in *SWTM, Romantic Era, Volume Two*, p. 24.

Careful attention must be given to the importance of slow and thoughtful practice. When students spend time each day practicing slowly and attentively, the results are dramatic. Practice Strategies #5-9 that follow are other components of this main goal of gaining muscle memory.

5. "Unit practicing" is an important component to learning muscle memory. This Practice Strategy is found in *SWTM, Baroque Era, Volume Two*, p. 58 and 80. Unit practicing leads to section and then performance practice. This is clearly outlined in *SWTM, Romantic Era, Volume Two*, p. 24 and 25. Students first learn this Practice Strategy in "Learn and Practice" in *On Your Way to Succeeding with the Masters®*, p. 5; and then in *SWTM, Baroque Era, Volume One*, p. 74-75.

6. "Impulse" practicing." This Practice Strategy is used for any piece that has scales, broken triads, or arpeggios that are intended to be played quickly. It is also excellent for learning *Alberti* bass figures, cadenzas, and all sixteenth-note patterns.
   - Found in *SWTM, Classical Era, Volume One*, p. 51, 62, and 80.
   - Found in *SWTM, Romantic Era, Volume One*, p. 32-33.
   - Found in *SWTM, Baroque Era, Volume Two*, p. 41.
   - Found in *SWTM, Classical Era, Volume Two*, p. 47-48.

7. "8 times to perfection." This Practice Strategy focuses on the need for repetition in practicing.
   - Found in *SWTM, Baroque Era, Volume One*, p. 35.
   - Found in *SWTM, Romantic Era, Volume One*, p. 22.
   - Found in *SWTM, Baroque Era, Volume Two*, p. 64.

Continued on page 158

8. "Slow vs. fast practicing."
   - Found in *On Your Way to SWTM*, p. 41
   - Found in *SWTM, Baroque Era, Volume One*, p. 52.
   - Found in *SWTM, Classical Era, Volume One*, p. 70.
   - Found in *SWTM, Baroque Era, Volume Two*, p. 76.
   - Found in *SWTM, Classical Era, Volume Two*, p. 36-37.

9. "Practicing "slightly under tempo" or "80% practice."
   - Found in *SWTM, Romantic Era, Volume One*, p. 100.

10. Interpretation. After a piece is learned, this is the time when students must think about how to effectively communicate the piece to an audience. Many of these strategies guide students in their listening, using the CD for interpretive details.
   - Found in *SWTM, Baroque Era, Volume One*, p. 41, 59, and 65.
   - Found in *SWTM, Classical Era, Volume One*, p. 25, 54, and 66.
   - Found in *SWTM, Romantic Era, Volume One*, p. 19, 26, 36, 37, 40, 43, 51, and 59.
   - Found in *SWTM, Baroque Era, Volume Two*, p. 38, 54, 69, 84, and 86.
   - Found in *SWTM, Classical Era, Volume Two*, p. 25, 44, 50, 79, 92, 93, and 97.
   - Found in *SWTM, Romantic Era, Volume Two*, p. 81 and 104.

Practice Strategies to use for the Repertoire in The Festival Collection®, Book 7

It is extremely valuable for students to continue to apply the Practice Strategies they have learned from *Succeeding with the Masters®, Volumes One* and *Two* for their new repertoire. The goal is to make practicing more efficient. Students can easily apply the Practice Strategies from *Succeeding with the Masters®, Volume Two* to the pieces in *The Festival Collection®, Book 7*. Some general pedagogical ideas follow:

Baroque Era
For a general overview of Baroque performance practice, see page 7-9 of *SWTM, Baroque Era, Volume Two*.

Allemande in D minor, by J.S. Bach
- Use the Practice Strategy (P.S.) "Unit" practicing on p. 58, from *SWTM, Baroque Era, Volume Two*.
- Use the P.S. "8 times to perfection" on p. 64, from *SWTM, Baroque Era, Volume Two*.
- Use the P.S. "Playing contrapuntal pieces with success" on p. 65, from *SWTM, Baroque Era, Volume Two*.

Sarabande in D minor, by J.S. Bach
- Use the P.S. "Finger *legato*" on p. 20, from *SWTM, Baroque Era, Volume Two*.
- Use the P.S. "Finger independence" on p. 47, from *SWTM, Baroque Era, Volume Two*.
- Use the P.S. "Playing expressively" on p. 96, from *SWTM, Baroque Era, Volume Two*.

Allegro in G minor, by G.F. Handel
- Use the P.S. "Improving muscle memory" on p. 30, from *SWTM, Baroque Era, Volume Two*.
- Use the P.S. "Detached note" practicing on p. 41, from *SWTM, Baroque Era, Volume Two*.
- Use the P.S. "Learning to play faster" on p. 91, from *SWTM, Baroque Era, Volume Two*.

Allemande in E flat major, by J.S. Bach
- Use the P.S. "Detached note" practicing on p. 41, from *SWTM, Baroque Era, Volume Two*.
- Use the P.S. "Inner listening" on p. 54, from *SWTM, Baroque Era, Volume Two*.
- Use the P.S. "Practicing cadence points" and "Playing contrapuntal pieces with success" on p. 64 and 65, from *SWTM, Baroque Era, Volume Two*.

Giga, by Baldassare Galuppi
- Use the P.S. "Making every note count" on p. 26, from *SWTM, Baroque Era, Volume Two*.
- Use the P.S. "Establishing an 'inner pulse' " on p. 38, from *SWTM, Baroque Era, Volume Two*.
- Use the P.S. "Slow vs. fast practicing" on p. 76, from *SWTM, Baroque Era, Volume Two*.

Sinfonia No. 6 in E major, by J.S. Bach
- Use the P.S. "Smart" fingering on p. 13, from *SWTM, Baroque Era, Volume Two.*
- Use the P.S. "Practicing back to front" on p. 22, from *SWTM, Baroque Era, Volume Two.*
- Use the P.S. "Unit practicing" on p. 58, from *SWTM, Baroque Era, Volume Two.*

Prelude No. 4 in D major, by J.S. Bach
- Use the P.S. "Follow the leader" on p. 45, from *SWTM, Baroque Era, Volume Two.*
- Use the P.S. "Impulse practicing" on p. 41, from *SWTM, Baroque Era, Volume Two.*
- Use the P.S. "8 times to perfection" on p. 64, from *SWTM, Baroque Era, Volume Two.*

Sinfonia No. 15 in B major, by J.S. Bach
- Use the P.S. "Establishing an 'inner pulse' " on p. 38, from *SWTM, Baroque Era, Volume Two.*
- Use the P.S. "Playing contrapuntal pieces with success" on p. 65, from *SWTM, Baroque Era, Volume Two.*
- Use the P.S. "Regrouping" on p. 96, from *SWTM, Baroque Era, Volume Two.*

Sonata in C major, K. 159/L. 104, by D. Scarlatti
- Use the P.S. "Follow the leader" on p. 45, from *SWTM, Baroque Era, Volume Two.*
- Use the P.S. "Slow vs. fast practicing" on p. 76, from *SWTM, Baroque Era, Volume Two.*
- Use the P.S. "Bringing a piece to life after it is learned" on p. 69, from *SWTM, Baroque Era, Volume Two.*

Classical Era

For a general overview of ornamentation, see page 8, 9, and 20 of *SWTM, Classical Era, Volume Two.*

Fantasie in D minor, by W.A. Mozart
- For all of the cadenzas—measures 34, 44, and 87, use the P.S. "Impulse practicing" on p. 47 and 48, from *SWTM, Classical Era, Volume Two.*
- Use the P.S. "Creating long phrases" on p. 57, from *SWTM, Classical Era, Volume Two.*
- For measures such as 17, 29, 31, 45, 47, and 50, use the P.S. "Playing *portato*" on p. 97, from *SWTM, Classical Era, Volume Two.*

Sonata in G, K. 283 (1st Mvt.), by W.A. Mozart
- Use the P.S. "Practice with the metronome" on p. 78 and 79, from *SWTM, Classical Era, Volume Two.*
- For passages such as measures 31-35, 38-40, 45-50, and 51-53, use the P.S. "Voicing the melody" on p. 28 and 29, from *SWTM, Classical Era, Volume Two.*
- Use the P.S. "Thinking orchestrally to bring this piece to life" on p. 92, from *SWTM, Classical Era, Volume Two.*

Moonlight Sonata, Op. 27, No. 2, (1st Mvt.), by Ludwig van Beethoven
- Use the P.S. "Smart" fingering on p. 70, from *SWTM, Classical Era, Volume Two.*
- Use the P.S. "Using the *una corda* pedal" on p. 87, from *SWTM, Classical Era, Volume Two.*
- Use the P.S. "Bringing this piece to life" on p. 32, from *SWTM, Classical Era, Volume Two.*

Sonata in B flat major, by Muzio Clementi
- Use the P.S. "Balancing the melody with the accompaniment" on p. 9, from *SWTM, Classical Era, Volume Two.*
- Use the P.S. "Shaping the phrases" on p. 61, from *SWTM, Classical Era, Volume Two,* discussing with the student where the goals are for each phrase so that they truly listen for and play them.
- For Variation VII, use the P.S. "Practicing *Alberti* basses" on p. 66, from *SWTM, Classical Era, Volume Two.*

Sonata in E minor, Hob. XV: 34 (3rd Mvt.), by F. J. Haydn
- For the repeated notes in measures 127 and 129 of the piece, use the P.S. "Playing repeated notes quickly" on p. 29, from *SWTM, Classical Era, Volume Two.*
- Use the P.S. "Slow vs. fast practicing" on p. 36 and 37, from *SWTM, Classical Era, Volume Two.*
- Use the P.S. "Creating a dance-like accompaniment pattern" on p. 42, from *SWTM, Classical Era, Volume Two.*
- Use the P.S. "How to create clear passagework" and "articulating wedges and *staccatos*" on p. 52 and 53, from *SWTM, Classical Era, Volume Two.*
- Use the P.S. "Practicing *Alberti* basses" on p. 66, from *SWTM, Classical Era, Volume Two.*

Classical Era (continued)

Sonata in C major, K. 545, (1st Mvt.), by W. A. Mozart
- Use the P.S. "Practicing ornaments" on p. 20, from *SWTM, Classical Era, Volume Two*.
- For all sixteenth-note patterns in the piece, use the P.S. "Improving muscle memory" on p. 47 and 48, from *SWTM, Classical Era, Volume Two*.
- Use the P.S. "Creating long phrases" on p. 57, from *SWTM, Classical Era, Volume Two*.

Variations in G major, WoO 77, by Ludwig van Beethoven
- Use the P.S. "Voicing the melody" on p. 28 and 29, from *SWTM, Classical Era, Volume Two*.
- Use the P.S. "Communicating the piece to an audience" on p. 44, from *SWTM, Classical Era, Volume Two*.
- Use the P.S. "Bringing the piece to life after it is learned" on p. 25, from *SWTM, Classical Era, Volume Two*. Students can discuss different colors or moods for each variation.

Romantic Era

Moments musicaux, Op. 94, No. 3, D. 780, by Franz Schubert
- Use the P.S. "Strong sense of rhythm helping to define a piece" on p. 41, from *SWTM, Romantic Era, Volume Two*.
- Use the P.S. "Follow the leader" on p. 60, from *SWTM, Romantic Era, Volume Two*.

Waltz in G sharp minor Op. 39, No. 3, by Johannes Brahms
- Use the P.S. "Practicing with forward direction" on p. 20, from *SWTM, Romantic Era, Volume Two*.
- Use the P.S. "Keeping a continuous flow" on p. 28, from *SWTM, Romantic Era, Volume Two*.

Waltz in E minor Op. 39, No. 4, by Johannes Brahms
- Use the P.S. "Finding places to relax for better facility" on p. 44, from *SWTM, Romantic Era, Volume Two*. Students need to feel a sense of release in their arms after each phrase and after each rolled chord in the left hand from measure 19 to the end.
- Use the P.S. "Playing with a supple wrist" on p. 68, from *SWTM, Romantic Era, Volume Two*.

Waltz in A flat major Op. 70, No. 2, by Frédéric Chopin
- Use the P.S. "The importance of a singing *legato*" on p. 86, from *SWTM, Romantic Era, Volume Two*.
- Use the P.S. "Applying Chopin's *rubato*" on p. 91, from *SWTM, Romantic Era, Volume Two*. Students can review the entire section on Chopin in *SWTM, Romantic Era, Volume Two*, for their practice and interpretation.

Romanze in F sharp major Op. 28, No. 2, by Robert Schumann
- Use the P.S. "Balancing melody with accompaniment" on p. 64, from *SWTM, Romantic Era, Volume Two*. In *Romanze*, students will need to bring out the middle voices, using their thumbs in both hands. They can begin by playing only these voices, and then adding the harmonies in the treble and bass.
- Use the P.S. "Using imagery to create a successful performance" on p. 104, from *SWTM, Romantic Era, Volume Two*.

The Bamboula Op. 59, No. 8, by Samuel Coleridge-Taylor
- Use the P.S. "Practicing slightly under tempo" or "80% practice" on p. 100, from *SWTM, Romantic Era, Volume Two*.
- For the coda of the piece, measure 131 to the end, see the P.S. "play-prepare" on p. 78, from *SWTM, Classical Era, Volume Two*. Students should prepare each move carefully so as to play only the correct notes.

April, from *The Seasons, Op. 37b, No. 4*, by Pytor Ilyich Tchaikovsky
- Use the P.S. "Playing rapid *staccato* notes in the left hand" on p. 60, from *SWTM, Romantic Era, Volume Two*.
- Use the P.S. "Applying *rubato*" on p. 29, from *SWTM, Romantic Era, Volume Two*.

Notturno, Op. 54, No. 4, by Edvard Grieg
- Use the P.S. "Balancing melody with accompaniment" on p. 64, from *SWTM, Romantic Era, Volume Two*. In *Notturno*, students will work on bringing out the top voice in the right-hand part.
- For the sections where students play triplets with eighth-note duples in measures 5, 7, 9, 11, etc., see the P.S. "Playing 2 against 3" on p. 24, from *SWTM, Classical Era, Volume Two*.

Tarantella, by Albert Pieczonka
- For the middle section, use the P.S. "Voicing the melody" on p. 10, from *SWTM, Romantic Era, Volume Two*.
- Use the P.S. "Practicing slightly under tempo" or "80% practice" on p. 100, from *SWTM, Romantic Era, Volume Two*.

Romantic Era (continued)

Forest Birds, by Adolph Jensen
- Use the P.S. "Improving muscle memory" on p. 24 and 25, from *SWTM*, *Romantic Era*, *Volume Two*.
- Use the P.S. "Shaping phrases" on p. 52, from *SWTM*, *Romantic Era*, *Volume Two*.

Venetian Boat Song in F sharp minor Op. 30, No. 6, by Felix Mendelssohn
- Use the P.S. "Keen listening" on p. 48, from *SWTM*, *Romantic Era*, *Volume Two*.
- Use the P.S. "The importance of hands-alone practice" on p. 77, from *SWTM*, *Romantic Era*, *Volume Two*.

Study in D minor (Warrior's Song), Op. 45, No. 15, by Stephen Heller
- Use the P.S. "Playing dotted rhythms" on p. 57, from *SWTM*, *Romantic Era*, *Volume Two*.
- Use the P.S. "Voicing the melody" on p. 10, from *SWTM*, *Romantic Era*, *Volume Two*.

20th/21st Centuries

O Polichinello, by Heitor Villa-Lobos
- Use the P.S. "Slow vs. fast practicing" on p. 76, from *SWTM*, *Baroque Era*, *Volume Two*.
- Use the P.S. "8 times to perfection" on p. 64, from *SWTM*, *Baroque Era*, *Volume Two*.
- Use the P.S. "Slow vs. fast practicing" on p. 36 and 37, from *SWTM*, *Classical Era*, *Volume Two*.

Galop final, by Alfredo Casella
- Use the P.S. "Improving muscle memory" on p. 47 and 48, from *SWTM*, *Classical Era*, *Volume Two*.
- Use the P.S. "Finding places to relax for better facility" on p. 83, from *SWTM*, *Classical Era*, *Volume Two*.
- Use the P.S. "Slow vs. fast practicing" on p. 36 and 37, from *SWTM*, *Classical Era*, *Volume Two*.

Fantastic Dance No. 1, by Dmitri Shostakovich
- Use the P.S. "Impulse practicing" on p. 41, from *SWTM*, *Baroque Era*, *Volume Two*.
- Apply the P.S. "Practicing with forward direction" on p. 20, from *SWTM*, *Romantic Era*, *Volume Two* by listening to the CD and deciding where the phrase goal is in each phrase. Students should feel the forward momentum going towards each of these high points.
- Use the P.S. "Improving muscle memory" on p. 24, from *SWTM*, *Romantic Era*, *Volume Two*.

Playera, Op. 5, No. 5, by Enrique Granados
- Use the P.S. "Voicing the melody" on p. 28, from *SWTM*, *Classical Era*, *Volume Two*.
- Use the P.S. "Strong sense of rhythm helping to define a piece" on p. 41, from *SWTM*, *Romantic Era*, *Volume Two*.
- For the tranquil B section, use the P.S. "Keen listening" on p. 48, from *SWTM*, *Romantic Era*, *Volume Two*.

Cris dans la rue, by Federico Mompou
- Use the P.S. "Voicing the melody" on p. 28, from *SWTM*, *Classical Era*, *Volume Two*.
- Use the P.S. "Playing with a supple wrist" on p. 68, from *SWTM*, *Romantic Era*, *Volume Two*.
- Use the P.S. "How to play a piece faster" on p. 68, from *SWTM*, *Romantic Era*, *Volume Two*.

First Arabesque, by Claude Debussy
- Use the P.S. "Blocking" on p. 12, from *SWTM*, *Classical Era*, *Volume Two*.
- Use the P.S. "Practicing eighth notes against triplets" on p. 24 and 25, from *SWTM*, *Classical Era*, *Volume Two*.
- Use the P.S. "Applying *rubato*" on p. 29, from *SWTM*, Romantic Era, *Volume Two*.
- Use the P.S. "Creating your own interpretation through listening" on p. 81, from *SWTM*, *Romantic Era*, *Volume Two*.

Sonatina in C major for Piano, (1st Mvt.), by Aram Khachaturian
- Use the P.S. "Creating a dance-like accompaniment pattern" on p. 42, from *SWTM*, *Classical Era*, *Volume Two*.
- Use the P.S. "Impulse practicing" on p. 47 and 48, from *SWTM*, *Classical Era*, *Volume Two*.
- Use the P.S. "Shaping the phrases" on p. 61, from *SWTM*, *Classical Era*, *Volume Two*.

Succeeding with the Masters® & The Festival Collection® correlated with The FJH Contemporary Keyboard Editions

On Your Way to Succeeding with the Masters® / The Festival Collection®, Book 1
Contemporary Collage, Volume 1, Book 1 • Echoes, Pictures, Riddles, and Tales for Piano Solo

Succeeding with the Masters®, Volume One / The Festival Collection®, Book 2
Echoes, Pictures, Riddles, and Tales for Piano Solo • Contemporary Collage, Volume 1, Book 2 •
Modern Miniatures for Piano Solo, Volume 1

Succeeding with the Masters®, Volume One / The Festival Collection®, Book 3
Echoes, Pictures, Riddles, and Tales for Piano Solo • Contemporary Collage, Volume 1, Book 2 •
Modern Miniatures for Piano Solo, Volume 1 • Reaching Out, for Solo Piano • Sound/World, Volume 1 •
Preludes, Volume 1

Succeeding with the Masters®, Volume One / The Festival Collection®, Book 4 (easier selections)
Echoes, Pictures, Riddles, and Tales for Piano Solo • Contemporary Collage, Volume 1, Book 2 •
Modern Miniatures for Piano Solo, Volume 1

Succeeding with the Masters®, Volume Two / The Festival Collection®, Book 4 (more difficult selections)
Reaching Out, for Solo Piano • Sound/World, Volume 1 • Preludes, Volume 1 • Musical Treasures, Volume 1 •
Contemporary Collage, Volume 1, Book 2 • Sound/World, Volume 2 • Watercolors for Ten Fingers •
Modern Miniatures for Piano Solo, Volume 2 • Concertino No. 1

Succeeding with the Masters®, Volume Two / The Festival Collection®, Book 5
Sound/World, Volume 2 • Watercolors for Ten Fingers • Modern Miniatures for Piano Solo, Volume 2 •
Concertino No. 1 • Preludes, Volumes 1 and 2 • Outside the Box • Piano Album • Intuitive Journeys •
Contemporary Collage, Volume 1, Book 2

Succeeding with the Masters®, Volume Two / The Festival Collection®, Book 6
Sound/World, Volume 2 • Watercolors for Ten Fingers • Modern Miniatures for Piano Solo, Volume 2 •
Preludes, Volumes 1 and 2 • Outside the Box • Piano Album • Intuitive Journeys

Succeeding with the Masters®, Volume Two / The Festival Collection®, Book 7
Sound/World, Volume 2 • Watercolors for Ten Fingers • Modern Miniatures for Piano Solo, Volume 2 •
Piano Album • Intuitive Journeys • Preludes, Volume 2

Succeeding with the Masters®, Volume Two / The Festival Collection®, Book 8
Intuitive Journeys • Preludes, Volume 2 • Phantasie Variations, Op. 12 • Piano Sonata No. 1, Op. 25 •
Piano Sonata No. 2, Op. 31 • Piano Sonata No. 3, "Odyssey," Op. 83 • Piano Sonata No. 4, Op. 128 •
Dance Preludes for Piano Duet

Index of all the pieces within Succeeding with the Masters® and The Festival Collection® by Composer.

* SWTM stands for Succeeding with the Masters®
** FC stands for The Festival Collection®

FJH2050